JEWELLERY IN ISRAEL

MULTICULTURAL DIVERSITY
1948 TO THE PRESENT

To Richard

Iris Fishof

JEWELLERY IN ISRAEL

MULTICULTURAL DIVERSITY 1948 TO THE PRESENT

ARNOLDSCHE Art Publishers

Author
Dr Iris Fishof, Jerusalem

Hebrew to English translation and text editing
Einat Adi, Tel Aviv

ARNOLDSCHE project coordination
Dirk Allgaier, Wiebke Ullmann, Anke Sommer

Offset reproductions
Repromayer, Reutlingen

Printed by
Gorenjski tisk storitve, Kranj, Slovenia

Paper
Core Silk, 170 gsm

Bibliographic information published by the Deutsche Nationalbibliothek
The Deutsche Nationalbibliothek lists this publication in the Deutsche Nationalbibliografie; detailed bibliographic data are available on the Internet at www.dnb.de.

ISBN 978-3-89790-396-8

Made in Europe, 2013

Front cover
Gregory Larin, *Penetration*, neckpiece from the series "Fragmentation", 2009 (see page 211)

Back cover
Top left: David H. Gumbel, necklace, early 1950s (see page 21)
Top centre: Bridal jewellery, Sana'a, Yemen, 1930s–1940s (see page 32)
Top right: Leon Israel, comb, 1971 (see page 73)
Bottom left: Zahara Schatz, bracelet, 1953–54 (see page 67)
Bottom centre: Esther Knobel, *Requiem*, box pendants, 1994 (see page 139)
Bottom right: Attai Chen, *Free Radicals (Part 3)*, brooch from the series "Compounding Fractions", 2013 (see page 183)

Back inside flap
Author's photo by Reuven Milon

This publication has been made possible by the kind support of an anonymous donor.

Photograph credits
Igal Amar: figs. 3.24, 3.25; Ron Amir: figs. 5.67–5.69; Oded Antman: fig. 4.42; Edgar Asher: fig. 4.8; Sean Axelrod: figs. 5.41, 5.42, 5.43; Ilit Azoulay: figs. 4.79, 5.1, 5.7, 5.54, 5.63; Vered Babai: figs. 5.14–5.16; Ariel Balak: figs. 2.50, 2.52, 5.4; Michal Bar-On Shaish: fig. 5.50; Josef Bercovich: figs. 5.57–5.59; Etienne Boisrond: figs. 5.8–5.10; Claus Bury: figs. 3.56 a–g, 3.57 a–d; Boris Carmi: figs. 2.5–2.8; Attai Chen: figs. 5.17 a–d, 5.19–5.22, 5.70; Malka Cohavi: fig. 5.31; Thomas R. Du Brock: fig. 4.69; Pierre-Alain Ferrazzini: fig. 2.3; Iris Fishof: figs. 2.16, 2.28, 2.35, 2.44–2.47, 3.29–3.32, 3.35, 4.2–4.6; Sasha Flit: fig. 5.62; Shaya Gamil: fig. 2.51; Uri Gershuni: figs. 4.1, 4.7, 4.9–4.11, 4.16–4.19, 4.43, 4.46 a, b, 4.53, 4.55, 4.57–4.61, 5.36; Leon Goldsmith: figs. 5.38–5.40; William Gross: figs. 1.1 a, b–1.6, 2.13, 2.17–2.21; Uri Grun: figs. 4.62 a, b–4.65, 4.75 a, b, 4.77, 4.78, 4.80–4.82, 5.44, 5.45, 5.47; David Harris: figs. 2.2, 2.39; Leon Israel: figs. 3.15, 3.16 a, 3.17, 3.18; Oleg Kalashnikov: fig. 2.9; Vered Kaminski: figs. 4.20–4.23, 4.25, 4.26, 4.29–4.37, 4.41; Amitai Kav: figs. 3.44–3.50; Ephraim Kidron: fig. 3.38; Zoltan Kluger: figs. 2.1, 2.4; Studio Shuki Kook: figs. 3.19, 3.20; Ben Lam: fig. 2.27; Einat Leader: figs. 5.55, 5.56 a, b; Tehila Levy Hyndman: fig. 5.5; Oded Löbel: figs. 1.7, 2.10, 2.11; Mauro Magliani: fig. 2.12; Reuven Milon: figs. 3.1, 3.11, 3.43 a, b; Mula & Haramaty: fig. 3.37; Rigmor Mydtskov: fig. 3.13; Tamir Niv: fig. 4.56; Boaz Nobelman: figs. 5.2, 5.3, 5.24, 5.25, 5.64 a, b–5.66; Ido Noy: figs. 5.26–5.28; Michal Oren: figs. 5.52 a, b–5.54; Leonid Padrul: figs. 2.48, 2.49, 4.28, 5.11 a, b, 5.12, 5.51 a, b; Micha Pariser: figs. 3.39, 3.40, 3.42; Ran Plotnizky: figs. 5.6, 5.32; Elie Posner: figs. 1.9, 1.11, 1.13, 1.15, 1.17, 1.18, 3.3, 3.4, 3.6; Moshe Pridan: fig. 2.22; Jack Ramsdale: figs. 4.73, 4.74; Yoav Reinshtein: figs. 5.60, 5.61; Menachem Reiss: fig. 5.35; Baruch Rimon: figs. 2.40, 2.42, 2.43; Andrew Roth: figs. 4.44, 4.45, 4.47 a–e–4.49, 4.51, 4.52, 4.54; Kobi Roth: figs. 5.48, 5.49 a–d; Yakov Rozenblatt: figs. 3.7, 3.8 a–c; Gideon Sella: fig. 5.34; Ofer Shafir: fig. 5.13; Miki Sivan Ben David: figs. 2.24, 2.34; Nat Suffrin: figs. 3.33 a, b, 3.34; Mirei Takeuchi: figs. 5.18, 5.23, 5.71; Piotr Topperzer: figs. 3.9, 3.10, 3.14; Michael Topyol: figs. 4.27, 4.38–4.40 a, b, 5.29; Michael Tropea: figs. 4.50, 4.67, 4.68, 4.72, 4.76; Edda Vardimon Gudnason: fig. 5.46; Batia Wang: fig. 5.33; Aya Wind: fig. 5.30; Ken Yanoviak: figs. 4.12 a, b; Margie Yemini: figs. 2.36–2.38 a–c.

Every effort has been made to trace copyright holders and photographers of images reproduced in this book. Omissions brought to our attention will be remedied in future editions.

Acknowledgments
I would like to convey my deep gratitude to Iris Fishof, the author; Einat Adi, the translator and editor; and all the artists presented in this publication for their confidence in our publishing house and for a fruitful collaboration.
Dirk Allgaier, Publisher
Arnoldsche Art Publishers, Stuttgart

Contents

Foreword

Soon after I left the Israel Museum, Jerusalem in 2003 after having served there as chief curator of Judaica and Jewish ethnography and in various other capacities, I directed my energy towards my former love – contemporary jewellery. It was natural for me to turn my passion into a profession and I have since delved deeply into the field. Shortly thereafter, I also began teaching modern and contemporary jewellery at the Shenkar College of Engineering and Design.

I began writing this book with a sense of mission. Although there are several publications about Israeli jewellery, they each focus on a specific aspect, artist or period. What I felt was sorely missing was a comprehensive study of jewellery in this country. I therefore undertook the task of researching and documenting its rich history. From that stage on, I felt as if the jewellery itself was telling a story and revealing its secrets. A piece of jewellery is not merely an ornament. It is an indication of the wearer's social status and identity and may be seen as communicating the ideology and concerns of its artist and wearer alike. It was fascinating to learn how a piece of jewellery can reflect the history of the society of which it is part. The entire history of the state of Israel is reflected in the jewellery created during its sixty five years of existence.

Israel is a country of immigrants where East and West meet. It is a place whose inhabitants have started life anew, attempting to forge a new, collective identity while still maintaining diversity. Eastern and Western traditions continue to this day to coexist in Israel as part of a pluralistic society. This has greatly affected Israeli culture in general and Israeli jewellery in particular. As a meeting point for different jewellery-making traditions, Israel has been a fertile ground for innovative creation. It is perhaps the multicultural diversity of Israeli society which is responsible for the exceptional quality of its art jewellery and its unique aesthetic and thematic characteristics.

Jewellery in Israel: Multicultural Diversity, 1948 to the Present is an overview of jewellery in Israel from its early pre-state years when immigrants from Europe brought the modernist spirit of the Bauhaus with them and met local Oriental traditions of craftsmanship. It follows the development of jewellery in Israel right up to contemporary artistic production, focusing at each stage on key figures in the field.

My research involved considerable fieldwork. A great deal of information was gathered through numerous conversations I held with artists, collectors and leading personalities in the field. It is impossible to mention by name all the many persons in charge of collections and institutions, and especially all the artists who responded promptly to my requests, answered my e-mails and calls and were exceptionally positive and encouraging in their assistance. Nevertheless, I am extremely grateful to all of them. I am immensely grateful to all the jewellery artists whose creative output is at the heart of this book. Unfortunately I am unable to include all of the gifted jewellery artists that are presently active in Israel and whose work I admire.

Special thanks go to Ruth Dayan, Moshe Ben David, Hannah Libon, Amos Slor and others, who helped me study the story of Maskit. I am grateful to Thomas Leitersdorf, Rina Meir, Michal Dalva and David Tartakover, who helped me in tracing the jewellery designed by Finy Leitersdorf. It was a pleasure to meet Arje Griegst in Copenhagen and to have fascinating conversations with him about the time he spent as a teacher at the Bezalel Academy of Arts and Design in Jerusalem. Thanks to Arie Ofir for providing me with information about the time he headed the gold- and silversmithing department at Bezalel. I am indebted to Esther Knobel for the invaluable information she provided about the Bezalel silversmithing department under the directorship of her late husband, Alex Ward. My conversations with collector Yossi Benyaminoff were very informative. Unfortunately, due to his untimely death he was unable to view the completed book. William Gross has been very helpful in allowing me to study his collection and in providing photos of particular pieces. Thanks to Sharon Weiser-Ferguson of the Israel Museum, Jerusalem for her collegial collaboration. I am indebted to Margie Yemini for providing me with images and information concerning the Yemini family. Thanks to Vivian Mann for her interest and assistance. Special thanks are extended to Dalia and Werner Renberg of New York, who were extremely helpful in acquiring images of the Zahara Schatz jewellery. Thanks to Helen W. Drutt English of Philadelphia, Pennsylvania, for her continuous encouragement to publish this book. I am grateful to Daniel Kruger for advising me extensively about his experience at Bezalel. Special thanks go to Claus Bury and to Fritz Falk, who supplied me with photographs and texts respectively related to their experiences at Bezalel.

I am deeply grateful to Dirk Allgaier of Arnoldsche Art Publishers for believing in my vision for this project and for his good advice throughout. I am grateful to Einat Adi, who translated and edited my text so discerningly. Thanks are extended to Wiebke Ullmann and other members of staff at Arnoldsche Art Publishers for their help in producing the book. I would like to convey my appreciation and gratitude to Silke Nalbach for the book's beautiful design.

My personal gratitude goes to my partner, Richard Oestermann, for his endless support and encouragement in making this book come true. Many thanks to Ohad and Dani Fishof, to Noa Zuk and to my beloved Kima. Last, but not least, *Jewellery in Israel: Multicultural Diversity, 1948 to the Present* could not have come to fruition without the support of an anonymous donor, whom I would like to thank profusely.

Iris Fishof, Jerusalem

1 Prelude

Jewellery in Pre-State Israel

1 Prelude

Jewellery in Pre-State Israel

Folk artists of the nineteenth century

Local folk artists developed their crafts in a poor, deserted, provincial region in the Southern Levant under the rule of the Ottoman Empire. This was the Holy Land, where years later the State of Israel would be established.[1] These artists, who were mostly Muslim, mainly produced souvenirs for pilgrims heading for the Holy Land. Jewellery items made of olive wood and mother of pearl, often produced in Bethlehem, were popular among the Christian pilgrims. There is evidence that in the 1870s Jews, too, took an active part in the souvenir industry in Jerusalem which produced such objects (figs. 1.1 a, b). However, Jewish pilgrims preferred printed maps of holy places, embroideries, vessels made of bitumen (a black stone found near the Dead Sea), and silver amulets worn for protection (fig. 1.2) (Fischer 1979; Fishof and Bar'am-Ben Yossef 1996). In Hebron, an industry of glass beads and bracelets developed and this industry continues to this day. Glass jewellery was especially popular among the Bedouins. Arab silver jewellery, where coins were often used as an ornamental component, was to become a source of inspiration in later periods.[2]

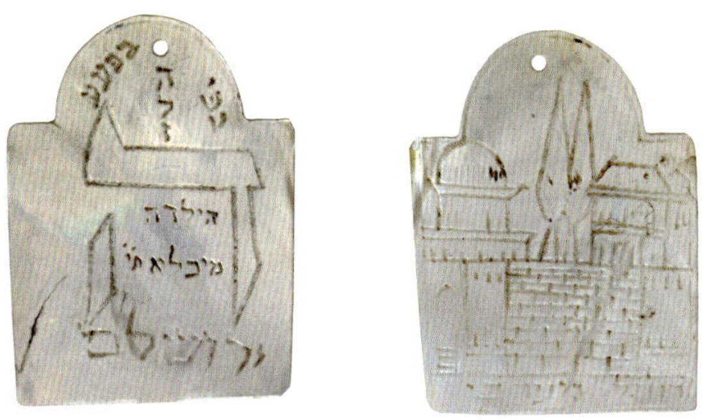

1.1 a, b Amulet pendant with a traditional depiction of the Western Wall, Jerusalem, *c.* 1925, mother of pearl, 4.7 × 3.3 cm (front and back), Gross Family Collection Trust

1.2 Amulet pendant, Jerusalem, *c.* 1930, silver, 7.2 × 5.0 cm, Gross Family Collection Trust

1_ The total population in the Holy Land prior to World War I numbered some 800,000 inhabitants.

2_ The vast diversity of ethnic groups in the Holy Land during the nineteenth and early twentieth centuries, comprising Muslims, Christians, Jews and others, is reflected in a variety of objects, materials and techniques. Within the scope of the present book, however, which focuses on jewellery produced in Israel, only a brief mention of these diverse cultures is possible.

The production of souvenirs (fig. 1.3) and especially of jewellery amulets continued as a form of folk art in the early twentieth century, after the Bezalel School of Arts and Crafts[3] was established in 1906 (see this chapter below). Silver and lead amulets (fig. 1.4), cast or stamped, were often inscribed with the word *Jerusalem* in Hebrew letters. They included symbolic magic elements for protection and continued to be produced in the twentieth century (fig. 1.5). They also took the form of pendants, rings and at times chains (fig. 1.6). Most of these amulets were produced by Jewish newcomers from Islamic countries who had arrived as individuals or in small groups during the nineteenth century from countries such as Kurdistan, Uzbekistan (Bukhara), Morocco and Georgia. Since the 1880s, several waves of immigration gradually increased the size of the Jewish population in Palestine.[4] Of special significance to the field of jewellery was the first immigration wave of 1882–1903, as it included Jews from Yemen. Among the Yemeni newcomers were many silversmiths who would leave their mark on the jewellery scene in the country.

In the late nineteenth century, Zionism – a national revival movement that endeavoured to establish a

1.3 Snuff box with a depiction of the Western Wall, the Holy Land, *c.* 1920, silver, 1.8 × 6.1 × 3.8 cm, Gross Family Collection Trust

1.4 Amulet pendant with a depiction of Rachel's Tomb, Jerusalem, *c.* 1920, cast lead, 4.1 × 3.0 cm, Gross Family Collection Trust

1.5 *Khamsa* amulet in Persian style, Jerusalem, *c.* 1930, silver, 8.0 × 5.4 cm, Gross Family Collection Trust

3_ The name of the school changed several times over the years: 1906, the Bezalel School of Arts and Crafts; 1935, the New Bezalel School of Arts and Crafts; 1955, the Bezalel Academy of Art; 1969, the Bezalel Academy of Arts and Design. Henceforth, the school will be called by the name relevant to the period of time discussed.

4_ In 1914, on the eve of the First World War, 45,000 out of a total of 85,000 Jewish people in the country lived in Jerusalem (Ben-Arieh 1979, pp. 9–12).

Jewish State in the Land of Israel – emerged in central and eastern Europe. Its leader and visionary was Theodor Herzl. In 1903, the artist Boris Schatz presented Herzl with a proposal to establish an arts and crafts school in the Land of Israel. In 1905, the Seventh Zionist Congress in Basel passed a resolution to establish the Bezalel School of Arts and Crafts in Jerusalem.

The Bezalel School of Arts and Crafts

Jewellery production in Israel received a special boost with the establishment of the Bezalel School of Arts and Crafts founded by Boris Schatz in 1906. Named after the biblical artist Bezalel Ben Uri, who was instrumental in the decoration of the Tabernacle, the Bezalel School was part of the Zionist enterprise. For ideological reasons it endeavoured to create a new, local "Hebrew" style. The motifs it promoted included the Hebrew alphabet, Jewish symbols, biblical scenes, archaeological artefacts, the flora and fauna of the Holy Land, views of the holy sites of the land and portraiture of its exotic inhabitants. The Bezalel style was a combination of various influences from East and West. These included oriental arabesques mixed with Art Nouveau or Jugendstil elements. Echoing the Arts & Crafts movement, which had developed in England in the late nineteenth century, Bezalel decorative objects often combined different techniques (Zalmona and Shilo-Cohen 1983, pp. 213–245). Schatz's vision for Bezalel was that of a spiritual centre which would combine a fine arts academy and craft workshops and would supply objects for sale to tourists and to the local Jewish population (Zalmona 2010, p. 27). As part of this approach, the silver-filigree department[5] was established in 1908, where Yemeni silversmiths produced objects designed by European artists who ignored their expert traditions (Guilat 2009, pp. 90–153).

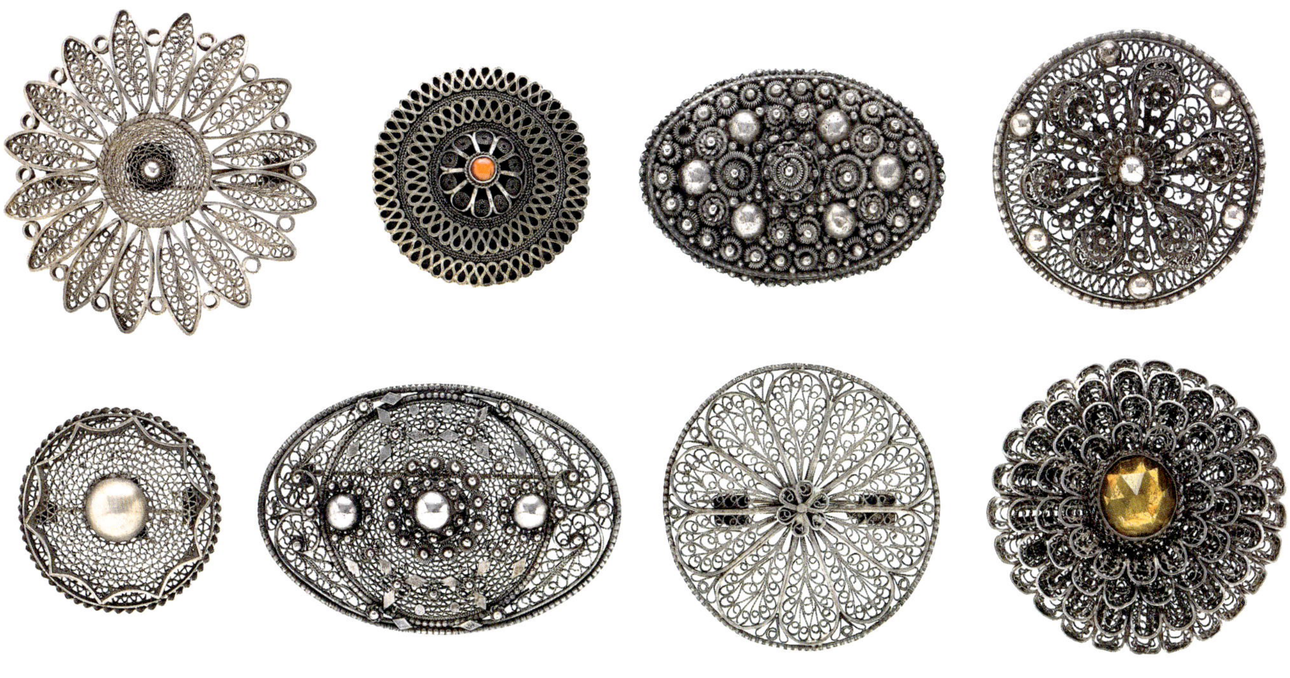

1.6 Opposite page: Chain with amuletic charms, Jerusalem, *c.* 1900, silver, glass, paper, carnelian, l. 64.0 cm, Gross Family Collection Trust

1.7 Brooches, Bezalel School, Jerusalem, 1908–29, silver, filigree, granulation, inlaid with coral and glass, diam. 3.6–5.6 cm (round); 3.9 × 5.5 and 4.4 × 6.5 cm (oval), the Israel Museum, Jerusalem, from the Alan B. Slifka collection

5_ The name of the department changed several times over the years, in accordance with its changing foci of interest: 1908, the Silver-Filigree Department; 1935, the Metalwork Department; 1972, the Gold- and Silversmithing Department; 1999, the Department of Silversmithing, Accessories and Objects; 2003, the Jewellery and Accessories Department; 2006, the Jewellery and Fashion Design Department. Henceforth, the department will be called by the name relevant to the period of time discussed.

1.8 The silver-filigree department at the Bezalel School of Arts and Crafts, 1909 (standing in the middle: Yehieh Yemini), the Israel Museum, Jerusalem

The jewellery produced in Bezalel was a mixture of European forms such as round brooches shaped like rosettes of stylised flowers and Yemeni filigree, occasionally set with a stone, or carved ivory and mother-of-pearl cameos (fig. 1.7) (Benjamin 2008). Although produced by Yemeni silversmiths, these pieces were quite distanced from the tradition of Yemeni jewellery. While jewellery was not central to Bezalel production, it played a significant role in the institution's endeavour to create an "original" style, evident not only in the metal filigree jewellery but also in jewellery and decorative pieces which included figural motifs featuring biblical figures of ethnic types (fig. 1.9).

One of the talented employees at the metal workshops was a young man by the name of Yehieh Yemini, born in 1896, who, as a young boy, immigrated to Palestine from Sana'a with his parents. He came from a family of several generations of silversmiths in Yemen and started working as an apprentice in the Bezalel silver-filigree workshop when he was about fourteen years old (fig. 1.8). He would become one of the key figures in the field of jewellery in the young State of Israel (see "Individual silversmiths" in Chapter 2 below).

The New Bezalel School of Arts and Crafts

The original Bezalel School closed down in 1929, mainly because of severe financial difficulties. In 1935, it reopened under the name The New Bezalel School of Arts and Crafts. Its teachers were newly arrived immigrants who had fled from Nazi Germany following Hitler's rise to power in 1933. Many of the highly cultured immigrants who arrived from Germany to Palestine, which was then under the rule of the British Mandate, settled in Jerusalem. Some of them who had studied in the Bauhaus School or were associated with it brought the fresh spirit of modernism with them.[6] In the New Bezalel they established what art historian Gideon Ofrat calls a "Zionist Bauhaus" – that is, a style that encompasses an inherent contradiction between

6_ German immigrants played an important role in the development of the arts and architecture of the country. Hedwig Grossman and Rudi Lehman, for example, who arrived from Berlin in 1933, were pioneers in the field of ceramics, and the ideas of modern architecture in the International Style were widely adopted around the country. In 2003, UNESCO proclaimed Tel Aviv a World Heritage site for its International Style architecture.

1.9 Mirror with a depiction of Jacob and Rachel, Bezalel School, Jerusalem, 1908–29, silver, semi-precious stones, 22.0 × 13.5 cm, the Israel Museum, Jerusalem

the International Style of the Bauhaus and the nationalist movement of Zionism.

The New Bezalel was established out of contempt for the Arts & Crafts style of what came to be known as the Old Bezalel and advocated a sharp change from it. In fact, however, it created a bridge between the Eastern European Romanticism of the Old Bezalel and the Western modernism of the New Bezalel (Ofrat 1984, pp. 80–102; Ofrat 1987; Ofrat 2006). From the mid-1930s to the mid-1950s the metalwork department was co-headed by Ludwig Yehudah Wolpert (1935 to 1956) and David Heinz Gumbel (1936 to 1955), both of whom encouraged their students to create functional objects devoid of any kind of ornamentation.[7] The designs were geometrical, minimalistic and clean. Under the first director of the New Bezalel, Joseph Budko (1935 to 1940), a lathe was introduced into the metalwork department. Under the directorship of his successor, Mordecai Ardon-Bronstein (1940 to 1952), who was a graduate of the Bauhaus School, the new trend received further encouragement. He emphasised the need for training in the use of machinery, so that students would be able to take part in industrial production. Gumbel and Wolpert took a rather complex view of the use of machinery.[8] On the one hand, Gumbel, in the spirit of Bauhaus, hailed the machine in a 1941 article for its precision in creating pure forms (Gumbel 1941, p. 12). On the other hand, as a master craftsman who was strict about hammering techniques and a perfect finish, he emphasised the special nature of the craft, which allowed the artist to create an object from beginning to end with his own hands (Ardon-Bronstein, early 1940s). Wolpert, in support of mechanical progress, stressed the benefits of the machine in saving time and guaranteeing high quality.

7_ In 2012 the Israel Museum held an exhibition devoted to Wolpert and Gumbel (Weiser-Ferguson 2012).

8_ For the handcraft vs. industry argument in the field of metalwork in Israel, see Leader's article "Hi-Craft: Academic Metalwork – From Handicraft to Valued Craft" (2010).

Wolpert and Gumbel: Heading the metalwork department at the New Bezalel

Ludwig Yehudah Wolpert was born in Germany in 1900 (fig. 1.10). He studied art in Frankfurt and worked as a sculptor. He then continued his silver-smithing studies at the Frankfurt Art School, under Christian Dell (who had been a designer at the Bauhaus school) and specialised in designing Jewish ritual objects. In 1933 he immigrated to Palestine and in 1935, with the establishment of the New Bezalel, became co-director of the metalwork department with Gumbel. In 1956 he moved to New York, where he headed the Tobe Pascher Workshop at the Jewish Museum until his death in 1981.

1.10 Ludwig Y. Wolpert, Frankfurt am Main, late 1920s or early 1930s, courtesy Chava Wolpert Richard

Wolpert was famous for incorporating cut-out Hebrew letters in novel fonts in his designs (fig. 1.11), using them as the key design element – for instance, in decorating ceremonial objects with biblical verses – and refraining from any other kind of ornamentation, a practice that became his "trade mark". In a brief article, Wolpert (1941, p. 10) commented on the mystical attitude towards the written letter that had developed among the Jewish people. He focused on designing Judaica (Jewish ceremonial objects) (figs. 1.11, 1.13) and produced very few pieces of jewellery – mainly in the form of lapel pins, which were given as gifts to persons who made donations to the Torah Fund of Women's League for Conservative Judaism. In these pins, too, which he designed when he was already living in New York, the Hebrew alphabet was the main decorative component (fig. 1.12).

1.11 Ludwig Y. Wolpert, Mezuzah case, 1950s, silver, 11.3 × 4.1 × 1.2 cm, the Israel Museum, Jerusalem © Chava Wolpert Richard

1.12 Ludwig Y. Wolpert, Torah Fund donor pin, 1978, silver, courtesy of the Women's League for Conservative Judaism © Chava Wolpert Richard

1.13 Ludwig Y. Wolpert, Hanukkah lamp, 1958, brass, 29.5 × 30.5 × 12.0 cm, the Israel Museum, Jerusalem
© Chava Wolpert Richard

1.14 David H. Gumbel, Jerusalem, 1960s, courtesy of Malka Cohavi

David Heinz Gumbel was born in 1906 in Sinsheim near Heidelberg, Germany (fig. 1.14). Several years later his family, who were the owners of a silverware factory, moved to Heilbronn and established a factory there. In Heilbronn Gumbel worked at Bruckmann and Sons, and became a certified steel engraver. He then left Heilbronn to study silversmithing at the School of Arts and Crafts in Charlottenburg, Berlin (Weiser-Ferguson 2012, pp. 191–192). He immigrated to Palestine in 1936 and soon joined the New Bezalel, where he taught design of Jewish ceremonial objects and jewellery and co-headed the metalwork department with Wolpert. In his Jerusalem studio he had a large circle of clients who commissioned special items (fig. 1.15). He was often commissioned to design and create official gifts for the Israeli Ministry of Foreign Affairs, among them a bible with a silver cover presented around 1950 by the first president of Israel, Chaim Weizmann, to Argentina's president Juan Perón. Gumbel gained world fame for his Judaica, but his jewellery is less well known and not many of these pieces have survived (figs. 1.17, 1.18). His hugely prolific work in the field of jewellery is evidenced by the many jewellery design sketches he has left behind (figs. 1.16, 1.19 a, b).[9]

1.15 David H. Gumbel, coffee set, 1970s, silver, private collection, Jerusalem © Malka Cohavi

1.16 David H. Gumbel, sketches for jewellery, *c.* 1940s, pencil and watercolours on paper © Malka Cohavi

9_ David H. Gumbel has bequeathed his lifework and designs to Malka Cohavi and Studio Gumbel. Cohavi is the sole owner of their copyright.

1.17 David H. Gumbel, necklace, early 1950s, gold, 41.5 × 2.0 cm, collection of Miriam Adler, Hod Hasharon © Malka Cohavi

1.18 David H. Gumbel, necklace with pendant, 1950s, silver, crystal, 40.0 × 5.5 cm, collection of Miriam Avrahami, Jerusalem © Malka Cohavi

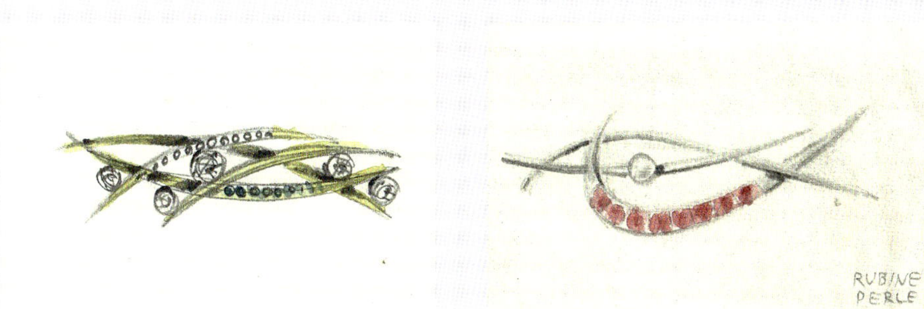

1.19 a, b David H. Gumbel, sketches for jewellery, *c.* 1940s, pencil and watercolours on paper © Malka Cohavi

2 The Melting Pot

1950s to 1970s

2 The Melting Pot

1950s to 1970s

Influx of ethnic jewellery from Muslim lands, 1950s to 1960s

Rich Islamic craftsmanship traditions

Jewellery was certainly not high on the agenda of the young State of Israel declared in 1948. The country was recovering from the War of Independence while trying to come to grips with the trauma of the Holocaust. The following years were marked by large waves of immigration, which doubled the country's population within three years to about 1.3 million inhabitants. The newly arrived immigrants were Holocaust survivors from Europe and Jews fleeing from Arab lands in North Africa, the Middle East and Central Asia. Newcomers were housed in transit camps of tents or tin huts, and the main concern was to provide them with some employment for their livelihood. From 1949 to 1959 austerity set in, and food rationing was enforced to ensure equal distribution for all citizens. The immigrants themselves experienced a cultural shock. For those who had come from Europe it was a challenge to adjust to the bareness and heat of their new country, which was covered by sand and thorns (fig. 2.1). The transition was also difficult for immigrants from Islamic lands, who, despite the fact that some of them were highly professional craftsmen, could no longer practice their skills in their new country. As a result, they had to make a living from random jobs – often in agriculture, which was foreign to them.

This is where jewellery comes into the picture. In Islamic lands, jewellery making was a Jewish profession. Muslims often refrained from dealing with precious metals, following a religious restriction stated in the Koran against their accumulation. The righteous in Paradise, on the other hand, are described in the Koran as wearing jewels (Koran 3 : 14, 9 : 34, 18 : 31; Brosh 1987, p. 70). Muslim women were allowed to wear jewellery, and in Muslim countries it was often the Jews who provided silver and gold jewellery for Muslims and Jews alike. Many of the immigrants to Israel from Islamic lands were Jewish jewellers, some of whom have left their mark on the Israeli jewellery scene.

2.1 Zoltan Kluger, an immigrant couple from Czechoslovakia arriving at their new home in Ein Ayala (a moshav south of Haifa), 1951, Central Zionist Archive

With the influx of immigrants from Islamic lands came a flow of ethnic jewellery which was often the only property of value that these immigrants were able to carry with them: earrings, bracelets, anklets, necklaces, headgear decorations and amulets. This great variety was an expression of the rich craftsmanship traditions of many generations among the Jewish communities in Yemen, Morocco, Uzbekistan (fig. 2.3) and Kurdistan, to mention but a few.

In **Yemen**, silversmithing was a Jewish craft of the highest level. After the majority of the Jews left for Israel from 1949 to 1950, jewellery of good quality

2.2 Festive necklace (*labbeh*), Sana'a, Yemen, early 20th century, gilt silver, filigree, semi-precious stones, 30.0 × 15.0 cm, the Israel Museum, Jerusalem

2.3 Forehead ornament (*parkhane*), Bukhara, Uzbekistan, early–mid 20th century, gold, tourmalines, pearls, 7.5 × 10.0 × 0.8 cm, the Israel Museum, Jerusalem

handicraft, such as embroidery, weaving and knitting, also employed male silversmiths from the Hadhramaut region. In 1954 Dayan founded Maskit, Israel Village Craft Ltd., an enterprise that began by promoting immigrants' village crafts and turned into a successful fashion house (see this chapter below), and for a while these silversmiths worked for Maskit, too. In her book *And Perhaps …*, Dayan describes her first encounter with the immigrants in the early 1950s: "The men of Hadhramaut had a long tradition as silversmiths. When one of their brides married, she wore forty-five pounds

became scarce in Yemen. Yemeni silversmiths excelled in the techniques of filigree (delicate metalwork made with twisted wire) and granulation (the application of small spheres of metal on a metal surface). These required great precision and patience. A typical example of fine filigree work is found in the festive necklace (*labbeh*) worn by Jewish brides in Sana'a on their wedding day and on other festive occasions (fig. 2.2) (Mucawsky-Schnapper 1999, p. 129).

There was a great difference between the jewellery made in the capital of Sana'a and that which was made in other regions of Yemen. A group of people from a remote Jewish tribe immigrated to Israel from Habban, in the region of Hadhramaut in south-east Yemen.[1] They made their new home in a settlement by the name of Bareket, not far from the present-day Ben Gurion Airport. Ruth Dayan, a social activist (married at the time to Israel Defence Forces General Moshe Dayan), volunteered to help the newcomers. She founded the Eshet Chayil (Woman of Valour) project – active from 1943 to 1953 – on behalf of the Jewish Agency. The project, which endeavoured to integrate women immigrants into the Israeli economy through traditional

2.4 Zoltan Kluger, *Portrait of a Yemenite Habbani Man*, 1940s, Israeli National Photo Collection, Government Press Office

1_ Most of the Jewish community in the Hadhramaut region lived in the town of Habban. For a study of the garments of Habban Jews, see Abdar (2008, pp. 271–287).

2.5 Boris Carmi, woman from Habban in the region of Hadhramaut, south-east Yemen, wearing her traditional dress and jewellery in her new home in Bareket, Israel, 1963

of silver jewelry, and for an ordinary workday a belt of ten pounds" (Dayan and Dudman 1973, p. 131). She comments on the similarity between Jewish immigrants from remote lands and other inhabitants of those countries. The men, in their striking robes and long hair (fig. 2.4), looked to her exactly like Arabs from that area. "To add to the mix-up," she writes, "I learned that the silversmiths from Hadhramaut needed the silver in the Maria Theresa thaler for their work,[2] not sterling, but the softer mixture in this old European coin, long preferred as currency in the region" (Dayan and Dudman 1973, p. 131). One day, Dayan came across an elderly, one-legged silversmith from Hadhramaut in a little hovel in the new settlement, hammering away on his small supply of Maria Theresa thalers. She asked him to make items for Maskit. In 1963, Herbert Pundik (Nahum Pundak), a Danish journalist living in Israel, visited the same one-legged silversmith of the Hillel family from Hadhramaut in Bareket (Pundik 1964, pp. 7–15; Pundik 1966, pp. 21–26). He was accompanied by photographer Boris Carmi, who took photos of the silversmith (fig. 2.6), and of other inhabitants in traditional dress and jewellery (figs. 2.5, 2.7, 2.8).

2_ The Maria Theresa thaler is a silver coin named after Empress Maria Theresa of Austria, Hungary and Bohemia, with a silver content of 0.833. It was first minted in 1751 and has been in use in world trade and throughout the Arab world, especially in Saudi Arabia and Yemen.

2.6 Top: Boris Carmi, silversmith from Habban in the region of Hadhramaut, south-east Yemen, working in his new home in Bareket, Israel, 1963 © Meitar Collection Ltd., Israel

2.7 Bottom left: Boris Carmi, necklace (*lazem*), early 20th century, brought to Israel in 1949 by immigrants from the region of Hadhramaut, Yemen, 1963 © Meitar Collection Ltd., Israel. A plastic button was added to the necklace, perhaps to increase its amuletic power.

2.8 Bottom right: Boris Carmi, Danish silversmith Amos Slor with a Yemeni silversmith during a visit to an immigrant village in Israel, 1963 © Meitar Collection Ltd., Israel

2.9 Left: Earring pendant, Tahala, Morocco, early 20th century, diam. 10.0 cm, the Israel Museum, Jerusalem. Cloisonné enamel was a local Jewish craft.

2.10 Right: Bridal earrings (detail), Tetuan, Morocco, late 19th century, gold, emeralds, rubies, pearls, the Israel Museum, Jerusalem. This type of earring shows Spanish influence, and its craftsmanship is highly esteemed.

2.11 Opposite page: Necklace, Djerba, Tunisia, early 20th century, moulded spice-mix beads, brass, gilt silver, enamel, glass beads, 85.0 cm, the Israel Museum, Jerusalem, from the Zeyde Schulmann Collection

Morocco was home to one of the oldest and largest Jewish communities. There, too, goldsmithing and silversmithing were exclusively Jewish crafts. As every region in Morocco had its own traditional costume and jewellery, the variety in styles was considerable (figs. 2.9, 2.10). Moroccan Jews started immigrating to Israel right after the establishment of the state, but a major wave of immigration from Morocco only began in 1954–1955 and continued until 1964. All in all, close to a quarter of a million Jews came to Israel from Morocco.

During the period of mass immigration from Morocco, an ardent collector by the name of Zeyde Schulmann acquired an important collection of Jewish ceremonial objects and jewellery in Morocco, Algeria and Tunisia (fig. 2.11) (Benjamin 2003, pp. 12–25). Travelling to remote Jewish communities just before they ceased to exist, he managed to save and document their traditional artefacts. In 1963, Schulmann brought his collection of 1,500 items to Jerusalem and donated it to the Bezalel National Museum, which was later to become part of the Israel Museum, Jerusalem. The collection was first exhibited at the newly opened Israel Museum in 1965.

Unfortunately, most newcomers did not continue to practice their craft in Israel. One such silversmith, who came to Israel from Morocco and settled in the southern town of Dimona, was Joseph Castiel. After his immigration to Israel, he could no longer work as a silversmith and had to work as a janitor for the municipality. When Aviva Muller-Lancet (former curator of Jewish ethnography at the Israel Museum) and Alyah Ben Ami (of the Israel Museum's department of ethnography) came to see him in 1970, he showed them an old suitcase full of his silversmith's tools and moulds for making jewellery, which he had stored away in a courtyard shed. These are now on view at the Israel Museum next to jewellery made from the very same moulds.

The melting pot ideology

The jewellery of the newcomers to Israel had been part of their tradition and culture. Pieces of jewellery, in addition to their decorative function, were charged with symbolic meanings. In Yemen, for example, the jewellery worn by the Jewish bride in Sana'a – such as the heavy silver necklaces whose decoration represented

2.12 Bridal jewellery, Sana'a, Yemen, 1930s–1940s, silver and gilt-silver filigree and granulation, corals, coins, the Israel Museum, Jerusalem

2.13 Bracelet with tomb motif, Yemen, *c.* 1880, silver, diam. 7.1 cm, Gross Family Collection Trust

grains of barley and lentils (fig. 2.12) – was meant to bring her a good life, abundance and fertility. The shape of the bracelets worn by women after birth recalls house-like tombstones, a reminder of life and death (fig. 2.13). Different kinds of amulets were meant to protect newly born infants against evil forces, especially against the female demon, Lilith. A silver amulet made in Persia (present-day Iran), for example, shows the figure of Lilith bound in chains, with an inscription in Hebrew which explains the engraved image, and other Kabalistic incantations (fig. 2.14) (Shachar 1971).

All those folk beliefs were soon to disappear as a result of the Zionist melting-pot doctrine. Throughout the early years of the State of Israel, the hegemonic ideology encouraged the absorption of immigrants by urging them to give up their culture of origin and forego their traditional dress, language and way of life, even to adopt new, Hebrew family names. Immigrants coming from Islamic lands and Europe alike were forced to give up their culture of origin. They were made to feel ashamed of their heritage and consequently hastened to part with decorative objects that had been part of their material culture. These found their way to the shops or flea markets (Chinski 2002), as well as to a few discerning collectors.

2.14 Amulet for a woman in childbirth and her infant, Persia, 19th century, silver, 11.2 × 7.1 cm, the Israel Museum, Jerusalem. In the centre: the female demon Lilith bound in chains.

Individual collectors of ethnic jewellery

Yossi Benyaminoff In Islamic countries, jewellery made in a variety of techniques and styles was given to a woman by her father or future husband. It was part of her dowry, solely her own possession, and she could sell it in times of need. Yossi Benyaminoff (1942–2011), an avid collector of folk jewellery from Islamic countries, was based in New York and Tel Aviv. His father, Nissan Benyaminoff, had owned a jewellery shop in Jerusalem and was a jeweller in his own right (see this chapter below). The son vividly recalls women who would walk into his father's shop, take off a pair of earrings and put them on the scales. Sometimes his father, noting a woman's agony at parting with a beautiful piece of jewellery, would convince her not to sell it but rather keep it in the family.[3] However, many jewellery pieces were in fact sold through dealers, who would arrive at the big city with a bag full of immigrants' jewellery and offer them to jewellery merchants. Soon the souvenir shops of Jaffa, Tel Aviv and mainly Jerusalem had an abundance of ethnic jewellery.

As Jerusalem-born Benyaminoff describes it, "In the 1950s one could buy jewellery from immigrants in kerosene containers." His own passion for folk jewellery from Islamic countries started at a very early age. As a young man he saw an exhibition of prints by Abel Pann at the Doron bookstore in Jerusalem and was thrilled by it. Pann's depictions of biblical female figures (modelled on young Yemeni and Bedouin girls) wearing fabulous gold jewellery on their foreheads under their head covers (fig. 2.15) left a deep impression on him. "I was fascinated by those grandiose pieces of jewellery which no modern woman would dare to wear," he says. His passion for Islamic and Jewish ethnic jewellery continued to develop after he moved to New York in 1966. He gradually built up a unique collection, parts of

2.15 Abel Pann, *Rebekah*, 1950s, pastel on cardboard, 42.0 × 38.5 cm, collection of Yael Gahnassia, Mayanot Gallery, Jerusalem, courtesy of the artist's family

2.16 Bridal earring (fragment), Morocco, 19th century, gold, precious stones (emerald, rubies, pearls, amethyst), Yossi Benyaminoff Collection

3_ Yossi Benyaminoff in a series of interviews with the author, Tel Aviv, Israel, 2009.

4_ So named to commemorate Muhammad's daughter Fatima Zahra.

which are exhibited at the Islamic Museum in Jerusalem and at the Israel Museum, Jerusalem. A compulsive collector, he tirelessly hunted for beautiful and rare pieces all over the world (fig. 2.16).

William Gross was born in Minneapolis, USA, immigrated to Israel in 1969 and lives in Tel Aviv. He is known as the owner of a comprehensive private collection of Judaica. Within this varied collection of Jewish ceremonial objects, books and manuscripts, there is a collection of Jewish ethnic jewellery. Gross is primarily attracted to jewellery of talismanic nature, such as amulets worn by Jews in Islamic countries for protection against the evil eye and demons (figs. 2.17, 2.18) and for good fortune. He is fascinated by the *khamsa* (in Arabic, "five"), the palm-shaped amulet also known in Islamic countries as the Hand of Fatimah,[4] because it was popular among Jews and Muslims alike (figs. 2.19, 2.20). In 2002, his collection of *khamsas* was exhibited at the Eretz-Israel Museum in Tel Aviv (Behroozi 2002).

Gross has acquired jewellery from collectors, from dealers, on expeditions abroad and through auction houses. Like all fervent collectors, he is thrilled by

2.17 Amuletic necklace, Baghdad, Iraq, *c.* 1892–93, gold, turquoise, wood, wolf's tooth, l. 66.0 cm, Gross Family Collection Trust

2.18 Amulet, Iraq, *c.* 1900, silver, overall l. 102.0 cm, plate 9.5 × 7.6 cm, Gross Family Collection Trust. In addition to the inscription on the central plate of this extremely heavy amulet, the tubes contain four paper amulet scrolls. These were prepared at different times for the same woman.

2.19 *Khamsa* amulet, Persia, c. 1925, silver, 6.1 × 3.1 cm, Gross Family Collection Trust. The inscriptions provide protection against the evil eye.

2.20 *Khamsa* amulet, Algeria, c. 1900, gold, sapphire, rubies, pearls, 7.5 × 4.5 cm, Gross Family Collection Trust

some of the stories behind his acquisitions. Such is the tale of a pair of gold earrings from Djerba, Tunisia, with a Hebrew amuletic inscription. This pair of earrings somehow got separated. One earring is in the Stieglitz collection at the Israel Museum, Jerusalem while the other found its way to a minor auction house in Tel Aviv and was bought by Gross (fig. 2.21).[5]

Gross's jewellery collection includes a rich variety of jewellery from Kurdistan. Brought to Israel by immigrants, a large number of these original pieces were sold to silversmiths to be melted down for the value of the silver. Unfortunately, quite a few newcomers, wishing to assimilate in the new country and hide any evidence of their origins, felt especially ashamed of their so-called primitive amulets and sold their jewellery. Gross bought his Kurdish silver collection from a Tel Aviv collector who had had an agreement with a silversmith to buy whatever jewellery he had bought from immigrants, for an additional ten per cent of its silver value.

5_ William Gross in an interview with the author, Tel Aviv, Israel, 2011.

2.21 Earring, Djerba, Tunisia, 1905–17, gilt silver, gold, semi-precious stones, 22.0 × 8.0 cm, Gross Family Collection Trust. The companion piece is in the Stieglitz Collection at the Israel Museum, Jerusalem.

Preserving traditional crafts, 1950s to 1970s: The jewellery of Maskit

"If it were not for the water shortage and rat plague in the Judean Mountain *moshavim* (cooperative villages), I would have probably continued teaching those *moshav* women how to cook and how to grow vegetables, like all the other agricultural instructors" (Donner 2003, p. 4). With these words, Ruth Dayan (fig. 2.22) sums up the story of the establishment of Maskit in 1954. She volunteered together with other Israeli women to help the newly arrived immigrants – who were scattered in remote villages – to adjust to a new way of life in their new country. "Rats ate the vegetable seeds," Dayan continues with her story, "and thus I decided to harness the knowledge and skills of the inhabitants... to improve their living conditions" (Donner 2003, p. 4). Dayan started by setting up embroidery and weaving projects, to which she later added jewellery. Gradually, she established Maskit, a state-owned company, the goal of which was to provide a source of income to the immigrants, supplying them with raw materials and marketing the products in Israel and abroad. At the same time, Maskit took on the role of preserving the traditional crafts of immigrants from Muslim countries. The biblical word *Maskit*, which means "a beautiful ornament", became a household name for fine taste and elegant design which combined traditional Jewish crafts and Western modernism. This style represented the young state's new national identity.

2.22 Ruth Dayan, founder and managing director of Maskit, Israel Village Craft Ltd., 1955, Israeli National Photo Collection, Government Press Office

In the field of jewellery, Ruth Dayan first "discovered" the aforementioned Yemeni silversmiths who came from the town of Habban in the region of Hadhramaut and worked for Maskit for a short while. But the company's top craftsmen in silver were the Jewish silversmiths who had immigrated to Israel from the city of Beihan in south-east Yemen. Dayan encountered them in a transit camp for immigrants near Jerusalem, where they were living in tents under terrible conditions (Dayan and Dudman 1973, pp. 142–143). These highly accomplished men, who came from families of several generations of silversmiths, resorted to all kinds of jobs and ended up working in an orange grove near the town of Rehovot. "I have no words to describe what Ruth Dayan did for all these frustrated immigrants. She practically saved many of us," says Moshe Ben David (figs. 2.23, 2.24), who worked for Maskit from 1954 until its sale in 1978.[6]

The Beihan silversmiths started to work in Maskit in 1955, under Hannah Libon. Libon, a 1944 graduate of the metalwork department in Bezalel and a disciple of the German teachers Gumbel and Wolpert, faced a new challenge in working with the Yemeni silversmiths of Maskit. She wanted to preserve as much as possible of their traditional designs yet make them wearable for

6_ All quotations from Moshe Ben David are from a series of interviews with the author, Ness Ziona, Israel, 2009–11.

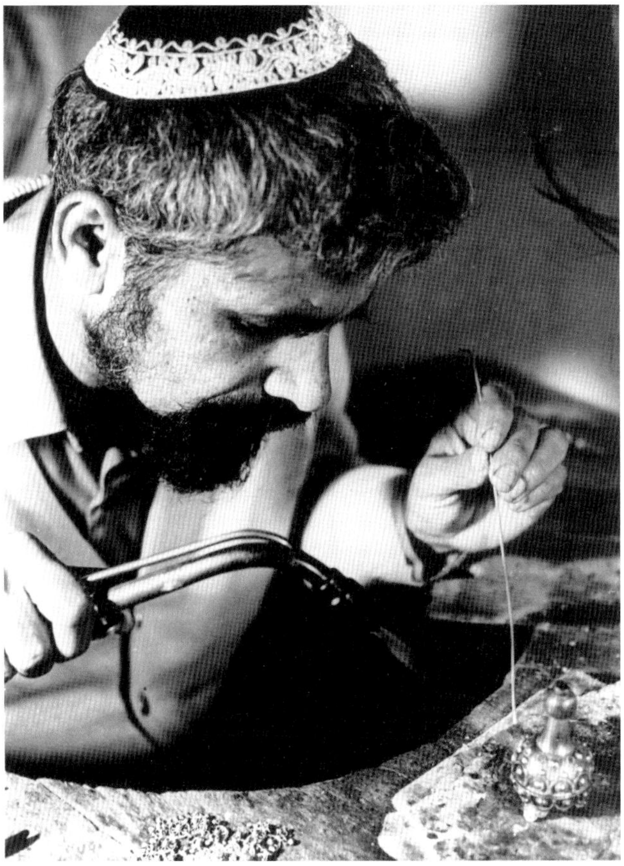

2.23 Moshe Ben David, head of the Maskit silversmithing department, at work, 1970s, courtesy of Moshe Ben David

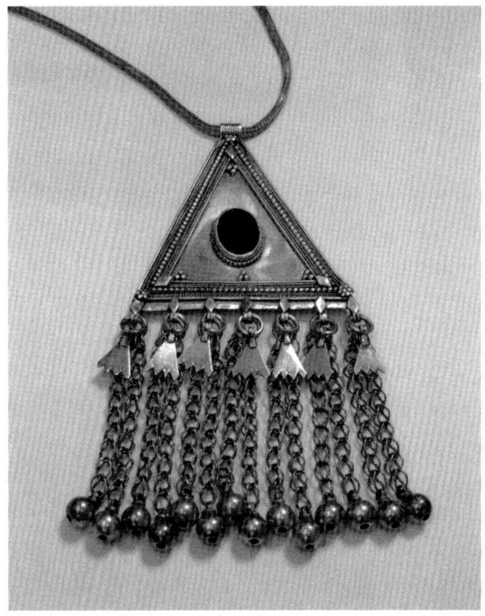

2.24 Reconstruction of a typical Maskit piece of jewellery from the 1950s by Moshe Ben David, 2011, silver, carnelian, 14.0 × 11.0 cm, courtesy of Moshe Ben David

her contemporaries in Israel by making slight adaptations, such as introducing modern locking devices. She provided them with raw materials and working tools and oversaw their payment.[7] At the very beginning, Haim David and Moshe Ben David worked at Libon's Tel Aviv home on Rothschild Boulevard for a short time. Soon afterwards, in 1955, they were given a workshop in a basement on 106 Hayarkon Street in Tel Aviv, opposite the Dan Hotel, which they shared with the weaving and needlework departments. Later, a shop was opened on the floor above. Some silversmiths worked from their homes where they were visited by Libon, who delivered the raw material and collected the ready pieces to be given a final touch at the main workshop. Such was the case of the jewellers from Habban who worked at their homes in Bareket. The pieces produced by silversmiths who worked at home were bought by Maskit, whereas the silversmiths who worked in the workshop were employed on a salary basis. This was the system over the years. Soon Haim David, an outstanding craftsman who had been the private jeweller of the ruler of Beihan before he came to Israel, ran the silversmithing department together with Hannah Libon. Later, from 1964 on, it was run by Moshe Ben David.

In 1963, the Maskit flagship store was opened in the new El Al Building on Ben Yehuda Street, Tel Aviv. Jewellery and decorative artefacts were sold on the

7_ Hannah Libon in an interview with the author, Tel Aviv, Israel, 2012.

2.25 a, b Model wearing Maskit jewellery from the "Village Craft" exhibition, Tel Aviv Museum, 1955, courtesy of Hannah Libon

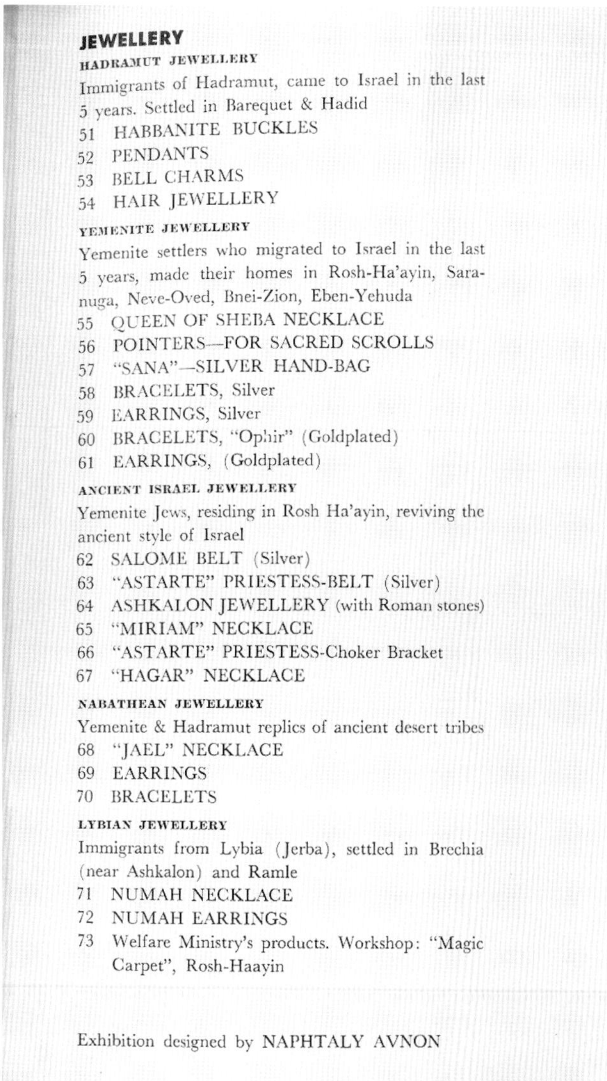

JEWELLERY

HADRAMUT JEWELLERY

Immigrants of Hadramut, came to Israel in the last 5 years. Settled in Barequet & Hadid

51 HABBANITE BUCKLES
52 PENDANTS
53 BELL CHARMS
54 HAIR JEWELLERY

YEMENITE JEWELLERY

Yemenite settlers who migrated to Israel in the last 5 years, made their homes in Rosh-Ha'ayin, Saranuga, Neve-Oved, Bnei-Zion, Eben-Yehuda

55 QUEEN OF SHEBA NECKLACE
56 POINTERS—FOR SACRED SCROLLS
57 "SANA"—SILVER HAND-BAG
58 BRACELETS, Silver
59 EARRINGS, Silver
60 BRACELETS, "Ophir" (Goldplated)
61 EARRINGS, (Goldplated)

ANCIENT ISRAEL JEWELLERY

Yemenite Jews, residing in Rosh Ha'ayin, reviving the ancient style of Israel

62 SALOME BELT (Silver)
63 "ASTARTE" PRIESTESS-BELT (Silver)
64 ASHKALON JEWELLERY (with Roman stones)
65 "MIRIAM" NECKLACE
66 "ASTARTE" PRIESTESS-Choker Bracket
67 "HAGAR" NECKLACE

NABATHEAN JEWELLERY

Yemenite & Hadramut replics of ancient desert tribes

68 "JAEL" NECKLACE
69 EARRINGS
70 BRACELETS

LYBIAN JEWELLERY

Immigrants from Lybia (Jerba), settled in Brechia (near Ashkalon) and Ramle

71 NUMAH NECKLACE
72 NUMAH EARRINGS
73 Welfare Ministry's products. Workshop: "Magic Carpet", Rosh-Haayin

Exhibition designed by NAPHTALY AVNON

2.26 Page from the catalogue of the exhibition "Village Craft" held at the Tel Aviv Museum, 1955, listing the jewellery pieces in the exhibition (Kolb 1955)

ground floor, and fashion, rugs, curtains and furniture were sold in the basement. The state-owned company developed quickly. By 1960, there were Maskit stores in Jerusalem, Haifa and other towns in Israel, and by 1961 there were approximately a thousand employees in the company's various manufacturing branches. Fashion shows and exhibitions were organised both locally and abroad, and Maskit products were sold not only in Israel but also in the United States, Britain, Italy and Switzerland.

The Yemeni silversmiths in Maskit were allowed a great deal of freedom. They were asked to make the traditional pieces of jewellery which they were familiar with, and subsequently, these pieces were adjusted to the demands and tastes of modern women by other craftsmen (figs. 2.25 a, b). Large necklaces were divided into several pieces, and in this way, a necklace could end up as earrings, brooches or buttons. At the same time, in the spirit of the melting pot, elements from various ethnic traditions were combined into a single piece.

As early as 1955, Maskit held its first exhibition, showing its first comprehensive collection of fabrics, carpets and jewellery (fig. 2.26), and also some fashion designs. During the show held at the Tel Aviv Museum (which was then under the directorship of Eugene Kolb), some of the craftsmen worked in the museum's galleries, demonstrating their traditional craft (Kolb 1955).

The most important designer for Maskit was Finy Leitersdorf, who won world fame for her *Desert Coat* (fig. 2.27) and other fashion designs.[8] Born in Komarom, Hungary, in 1906, she immigrated to Palestine and settled in Tel Aviv in 1939. From 1955 she worked for Maskit together with Ruth Dayan and continued to work on her fashion designs until her death in 1986. In addition to fashion design, Leitersdorf also designed jewellery for Maskit. She was one of the first to use ancient Roman glass in Israeli jewellery. She used to collect the pieces of broken ancient glass which were washed up by the sea on the beach in Caesarea and use them instead of precious stones, which were not affordable in the young, poor country. Her silver jewellery incorporating the Roman glass was first exhibited as a collection in Expo 1967 in Montreal. Her jewellery designs (figs. 2.28 – 2.33), executed by Moshe Ben David, were quite original in style yet sometimes reflected the ethnic traditions that she had got to know in Israel. There may be an echo of the Yemeni *labbeh* festive neckpiece, for instance, in her design for a necklace which comprises many layers of pieces of glass inlaid in

8_ In 1958 Leitersdorf also designed costumes for the Inbal Dance Troupe (Tartakover 1983).

2.27 Finy Leitersdorf (right) and Batia Disenchik modelling the *Desert Coat* designed by Finy Leitersdorf for Maskit, 1970, courtesy of the designer's family

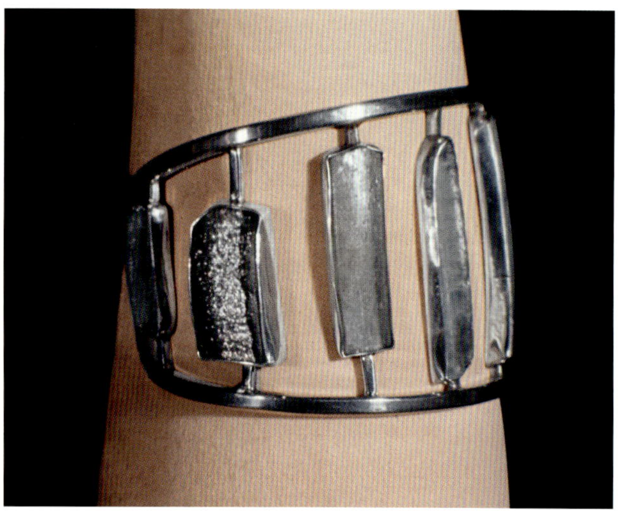

2.28 Top left: Finy Leitersdorf (design), Moshe Ben David (execution) for Maskit, necklace, mid-1970s, silver, Roman glass, 30.0 cm, collection of the designer's family

2.29 Top right: Finy Leitersdorf (design), Moshe Ben David (execution) for Maskit, necklace, 1976, silver, Roman glass, courtesy of the designer's family

2.30 Bottom: Finy Leitersdorf (design), Moshe Ben David (execution) for Maskit, bracelet, mid-1970s, silver, Roman glass, courtesy of the designer's family

2.31 Opposite page: Finy Leitersdorf (design), Moshe Ben David (execution) for Maskit, necklace, 1976, silver, Roman glass, courtesy of the designer's family

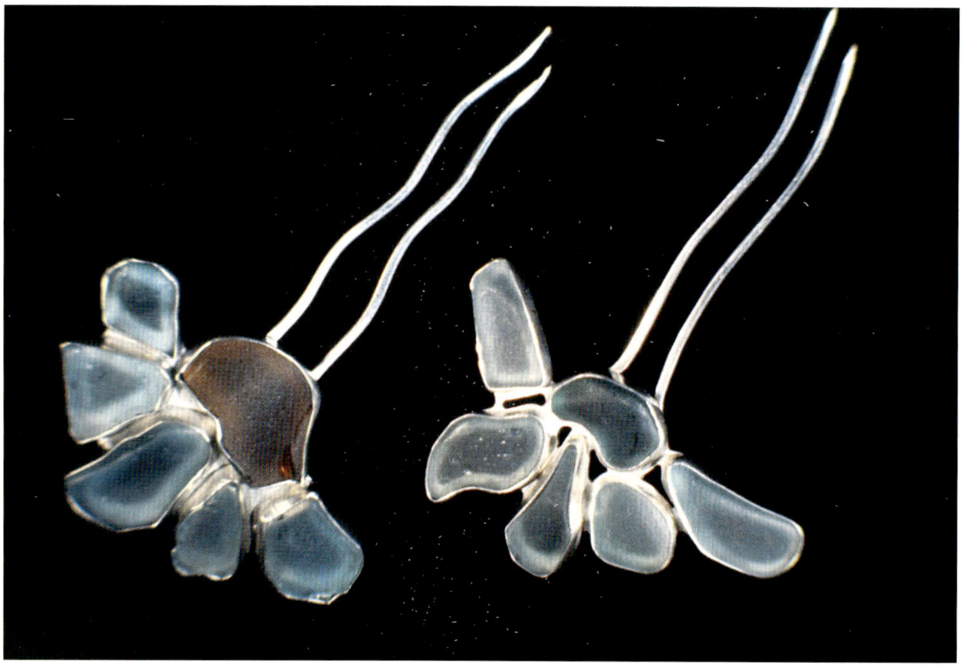

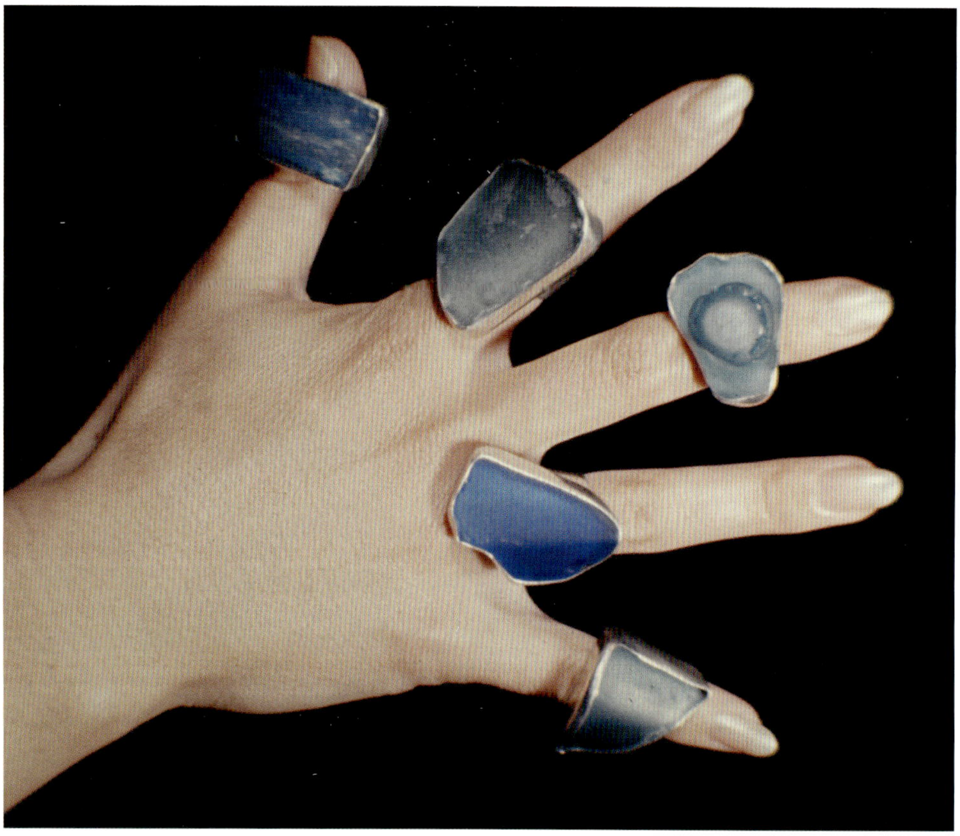

2.32 Top: Finy Leitersdorf (design), Moshe Ben David (execution) for Maskit, hair pins, 1970s, silver, Roman glass, courtesy of the designer's family

2.33 Bottom: Finy Leitersdorf (design), Moshe Ben David (execution) for Maskit, rings, 1970s, silver, Roman glass, courtesy of the designer's family

2.34 Reconstruction of a Maskit necklace from the 1970s by Moshe Ben David, 2011, silver, 35.0 × 4.0 cm, courtesy of Moshe Ben David. Model inspired by ancient jar-shaped earrings from the period of the Bar Kokhba revolt, CE 2nd century, found in the Caves of Letters south of Ein Gedi, Israel.

silver and hanging down from the neck (fig. 2.31) (Tartakover 1983).

Roman glass jewellery was part of an "archaeology craze" in the Israeli society of the 1960s. Archaeology (mainly biblical archaeology) was a means of creating a collective memory and national narrative based on a shared heritage. It became the "national hobby", and this was reflected in some of the garments and jewellery designed for Maskit. A pair of earrings from the period of the Bar Kokhba revolt (CE 2nd century) found in the Cave of Letters south of Ein Gedi, for instance, inspired the creation of a silver necklace for Maskit (fig. 2.34) (Dayan and Feinberg, 1974, p. 35, figs. 44–45; Raz 1996, p. 188). Nevertheless, the jewellery of Maskit was varied. In addition to the folk jewellery made by immigrant silversmiths and original jewellery pieces designed by Finy Leitersdorf, Maskit started cooperating with individual jewellery artists. In 1970, Bianca Eshel Gershuni, who would become one of Israel's leading jewellers (see below, Chapter 4), created a collection of gold jewellery for Maskit which was exported to the United States. Other independent art jewellers started to work with Maskit in the 1970s. Among them were Rachel Gera, Maury Golan, Hannah Bahar-Paneth,[9] Rachel Pariser, Miriam Libraider-Tzafrir and others (Donner 2003, p. 110).

In 1963, Amos Slor, a Danish silversmith, was invited by Ruth Dayan to come to Israel for six months in order to instruct the Yemeni silversmiths of Maskit. Slor worked with Haim David and Moshe Ben David at the Tel Aviv workshop and visited some of the immigrant silversmiths in their villages (fig. 2.8). When recently interviewed, Slor expressed his admiration for the technical skill of the Yemeni craftsmen, claiming modestly that the only thing he could teach them was how to improve the finish of their pieces and how to make the work process easier.[10] He made a plan for an improved silversmith's workshop with modern tools and machines, but his plan never came to fruition for lack of budget. Slor was accompanied by his wife Susanne, also a silversmith. Their visit attracted a lot of attention in the local press. "It is amazing to see the understanding between Amos and Haim, the Yemeni silversmith who is in charge of our workers," a newspaper article quotes jeweller Meira Gera of Maskit (Weinstock 1963, p. 13). And another paper states: "Representatives of Two Worlds Work Together in Maskit" (*LaMerhav* 1963, p. 3).

Maskit was a leading enterprise geared towards elitist customers. It marketed high-quality and original designs for relatively high prices. However, after many years, it began to decline. In 1970, it was bought by a private company, Israel Investors Corporation, with Ruth Dayan staying on as director. That same year, a gold jewellery department was opened under the leadership of Maury Golan, who joined Maskit upon his return to Israel after a period of studying and teaching in the United States (see below, Chapter 3). In the field of jewellery, the company's emphasis moved to individual artists, mainly Bezalel graduates, and there were some attempts to turn to industrial production. In 1978, the company was sold to businessman Shimon Horn, and Ruth Dayan retired from Maskit. Subsequently, Finy Leitersdorf and Moshe Ben David also retired. The company continued to function until its final closure in 1994.

9_ Hannah Bahar-Paneth's name is variously spelled in different publications; this is how she herself spells it.

10_ Amos Slor in an interview with the author, Copenhagen, Denmark, 2010. Slor had lost his ability to hear at an early age, and the conversation with him took place with the assistance of his sister, Naomi Rubinstein.

Individual silversmiths

In addition to the state-owned Maskit and other publicly organised enterprises such as WIZO,[11] there were several notable individual silversmiths who opened their own shops in Jerusalem and Tel Aviv at the time. Following, are three examples.

The Yemini family silversmiths, 1920s to the present

This Jerusalem-based dynasty of silversmiths started with Yehieh Yemini (1896–1983), who came from a family with a long tradition of silversmithing in Sana'a, Yemen (fig. 2.35). He immigrated to Jerusalem with his parents at the age of three. In 1908, when the silver-filigree department in Bezalel was opened, the young Yemini, an outstanding craftsman, was one of its workers (see fig. 1.8 in Chapter 1 above). In 1914, after he and others were dismissed from Bezalel due to financial difficulties, Yemini joined other Jerusalem silversmiths who continued to work in the Bezalel style (Ofrat 1989, n.p.).[12] From 1927 he worked from his home at 6 Hirshenberg Street in a picturesque old quarter of Jerusalem. There he was later joined by his son Yaacov and his grandson Boaz (fig. 2.36). Boaz Yemini continues to work in this place, which has come to be known as the Yemini Studio, to this day (Ofrat 1989; *Yemini* 1999).

2.35 Traditional jewellery that was brought to Jerusalem from Sana'a, Yemen, by the parents of Yehieh Yemini, in 1899, courtesy of Yemini Silversmiths. This bridal jewellery is still in the possession of the family members, who recall that their grandmother wore it at her wedding.

2.36 Four generations of the Yemini family, 1981 (right to left: Yehieh, Yaacov, Boaz, and baby Nadav), courtesy of Yemini Silversmiths

Yehieh Yemini worked closely with leading Bezalel artist Ze'ev Raban, who designed Jewish ceremonial objects and some jewellery for him. One of the most splendid series of jewellery Raban designed for him in the late 1930s and early 1940s was a series of round and oval brooches portraying biblical female figures, such as Rachel, Ruth and Miriam. The elegantly clad women, depicted in vivid postures, are completely Western in style (figs. 2.37 a–c, 2.38 a–c).

Yehieh Yemini's bracelets (fig. 2.39), on the other hand, in spite of the fact that their general form is composed of rectangular units connected by chain hinges, show greater affinity to his Yemeni roots. They are decorated with filigree ornaments and various traditional motifs. Some bracelets are inlaid with semi-precious stones, and their general appearance is reminiscent of Art Deco bracelets.

A blend of traditional Yemeni ornamentation on the one hand and the new ideas of modernism on the other is also apparent in the work of Yehieh's son Yaacov Yemini (1929–2010). Yaacov studied in the metalwork department at the New Bezalel. He started his studies in 1947, when the director was Bauhaus graduate,

11_ WIZO (Women's International Zionist Organization) encouraged home industries and in the 1950s opened shops selling immigrants' crafts.

12_ Yemini joined three such groups: Keter, Kav Lavan, and Sharar (Ofrat 1989, n.p.).

2.37 a–c Left: Ze'ev Raban, designs for a series of brooches portraying biblical female figures (top to bottom: Judith, Miriam and the Song of Songs Shulamite), to be executed by Yehieh Yemini, 1937–46, pencil on paper, courtesy of Yemini Silversmiths

2.38 a–c Right: Yehieh Yemini, brooches portraying biblical female figures after designs by Ze'ev Raban (on left), 1937–46, silver, h. 4.0–4.5 cm, courtesy of Yemini Silversmiths

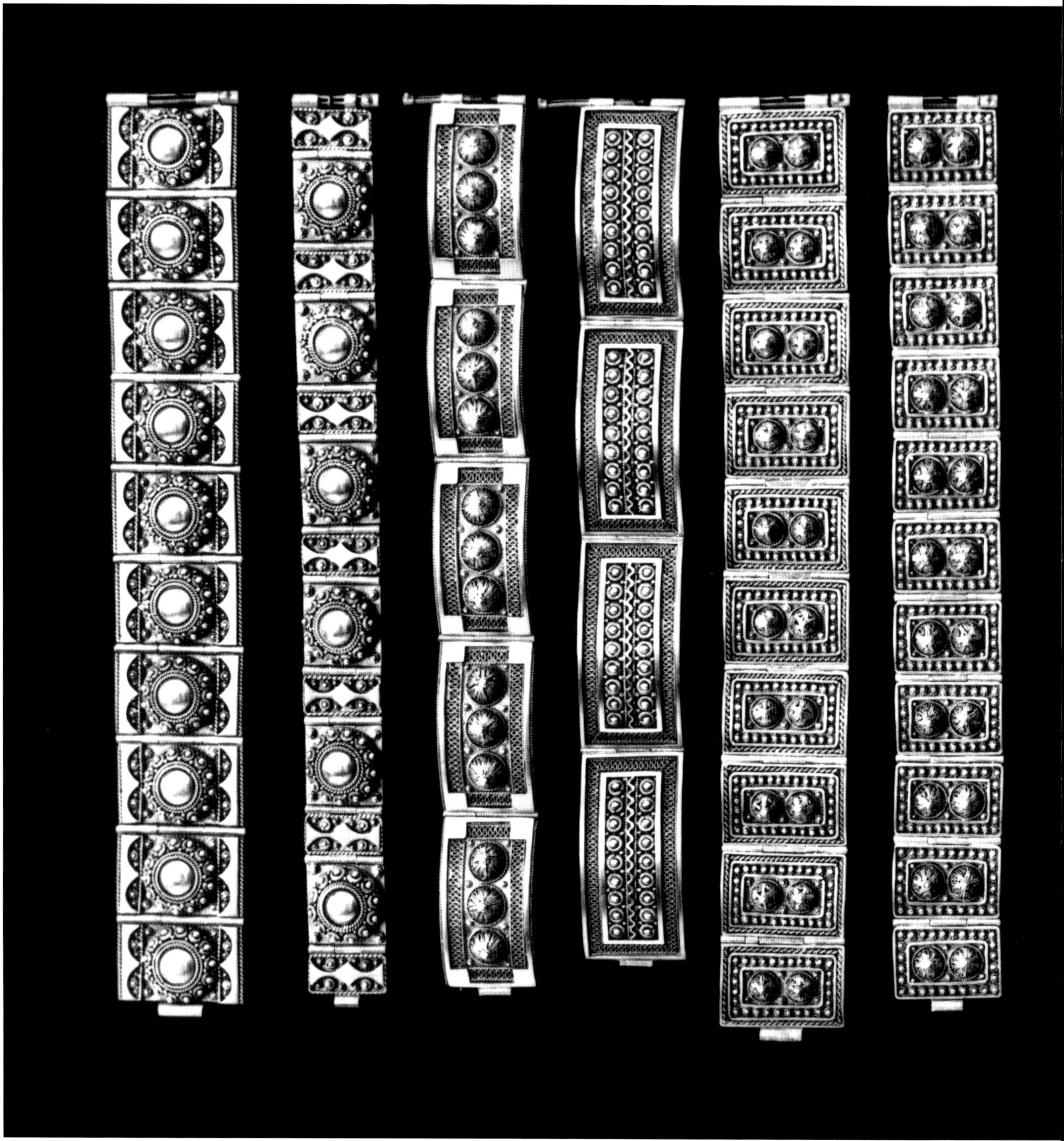

2.39 Yehieh Yemini, bracelets and brooches, 1930–50, silver, semi-precious stones, 18.0 × 1.5 cm to 18.0 × 4.0 cm, courtesy of Yemini Silversmiths

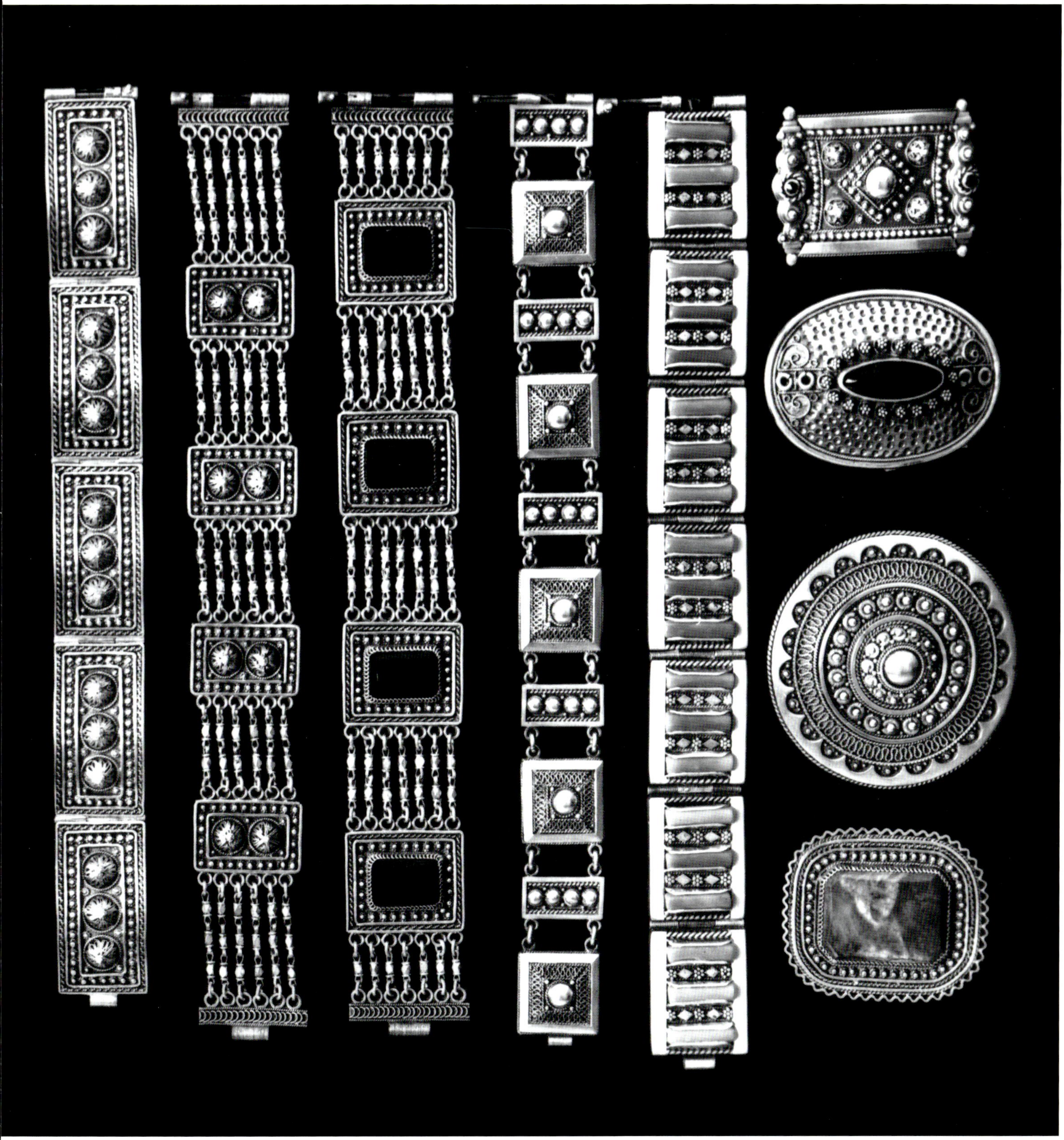

2.40 Yaacov Yemini, necklace presented to Queen Margrethe II of Denmark, 1987, silver, rubies, 10.0 × 7.0 cm, courtesy of Yemini Silversmiths

2.41 Israel's President Chaim Herzog and Mrs Ora Herzog present a piece of jewellery by Yaacov Yemini to Queen Margrethe II of Denmark, 1987, courtesy of Yemini Silversmiths

2.42 Bottom left: Boaz Yemini, brooch, 1995, 18-ct gold, garnets, moonstone, lapis, aventurine, 1.5 × 6.0 cm, courtesy of Yemini Silversmiths

2.43 Bottom right: Boaz Yemini, brooch, 1995, 18-ct gold, turquoise, 2.5 × 5.0 cm, courtesy of Yemini Silversmiths

painter Mordecai Ardon. His teachers were Ludwig Yehudah Wolpert and David Heinz Gumbel, who had also brought the spirit of modernism with them from Germany. Yaacov designed and produced mainly ceremonial objects but made some jewellery as well. His works were often purchased by the Israeli diplomatic corps as official gifts of the state. Two of his necklaces were presented by President Chaim Herzog to Queen Margrethe II of Denmark (figs. 2.40, 2.41) and to the wife of President Ronald Reagan, Nancy Reagan.

Today, Yaacov's son Boaz Yemini (born 1956), the third generation of this family of silversmiths, continues to work in the Yemini Studio. Boaz studied at Bezalel in the 1970s under Arie Ofir. It was an exciting period of openness to international innovations and change (see below, Chapter 3). Boaz Yemini remembers the great impact left by Claus Bury of Germany, one of the visiting teachers from abroad.[13] This was the period in which the New Jewellery movement was adopted in Israel. After his graduation, Boaz Yemini designed Judaica (Jewish ceremonial objects) in a geometric, minimalistic style which was quite different from the traditional family line. In the 1990s, however, he turned back to the old traditions of his father and his grandfather, adding some inscriptions as well as stones and ornamental elements to his work. At the same time, he made a series of gem-set gold jewellery featuring floral motifs (figs. 2.42, 2.43).

13_ Boaz Yemini in an interview with the author, Jerusalem, Israel, 2011.

Nissan Benyaminoff, 1930s to 1980s

Nissan Benyaminoff (1912–1991) was a Zionist. According to his son, jewellery collector Yossi Benyaminoff (see box on page 34), Nissan Benyaminoff walked all the way to Jerusalem from his native town of Urmia in Persian Azerbaijan. A young entrepreneur, he opened a workshop in downtown Jerusalem (opposite the Rex Cinema) shortly after immigrating, where he employed several workers (fig. 2.46). He made both Jewish ceremonial objects and jewellery pieces (fig. 2.44). The jewellery was made in a modest, simple, local style in keeping with the ideology and living conditions of his new country and incorporated some traditional eastern elements. These were very colourful necklaces and brooches which combined semi-precious stones and at times also small pearls, while using the filigree technique (fig. 2.45).

After the establishment of the State of Israel in 1948, Nissan Benyaminoff specialised in round or oval three-tiered brooches holding a big stone (fig. 2.47). These modest, light pieces of jewellery were popular among Israel's leading female politicians, such as Golda Meir and Beba Idelson and visiting members of Hadassah, the Women's Zionist Organization of America. In the 1970s, Benyaminoff moved his Jerusalem studio and shop to King David Street. By that time, he was an old-timer in the country and employed newly arrived immigrants from Iraq, Iran and Morocco in the spirit of the melting-pot ethos.

2.44 Nissan Benyaminoff, engagement belt, 1950s, gold, filigree, private collection, Tel Aviv

2.45 Top right: Nissan Benyaminoff, necklace, 1950s, silver, semi-precious stones, pearls, private collection, Tel Aviv

2.46 Bottom left: Nissan Benyaminoff's maker's mark on the back of a silver necklace, 1950s, private collection, Tel Aviv

2.47 Bottom right: Nissan Benyaminoff, three-tiered brooch, 1950s, silver, turquoise, private collection, Tel Aviv

2.48 Jacobi Jewelry, net-like necklace, Jaffa, 1950s–1960s, gilt silver, turquoise © Eretz-Israel Museum, Tel Aviv

Jacobi Jewelry, 1949 to the present

Jacobi Jewelry is the only early Israeli enterprise which has been thoroughly studied. In 2008, Professor Nurith Kenaan-Kedar curated an exhibition of Jacobi Jewelry at the Eretz-Israel Museum in Tel Aviv, accompanied by a book. The founder of this family business was Shimon Jacobi (year of birth unknown, died 1982), born in the city of Urmia in Persian Azerbaijan. As Kenaan-Kedar (2008, pp. 21–22) recounts, "Shimon, a goldsmith and scion to generations of goldsmiths," immigrated to Palestine in 1935 and settled in Jerusalem close to his brother, also a goldsmith, who had immigrated before him. The two started working together. After losing his son Ephraim in the 1948 War of Independence, Jacobi moved his family to the centre of the country, finally settling in Tel Aviv. Since 1949, the Jacobi workshop and shop has been located on 8 Raziel Street (formerly Bustrus Street) in Jaffa, which is now part of the Tel Aviv-Jaffa municipality. It is presently run by Shimon's son Jacob.

Unlike other individual entrepreneurs discussed above, who also produced Jewish ritual objects, the Jacobi workshop focused only on jewellery. It produced a great variety of pieces in diverse styles, including brooches, necklaces, bracelets, earrings, rings and amulets. These products reflect the multiculturalism of Israeli society. They vary from ethnically inspired pieces, at times echoing Bedouin jewellery, to modern pieces in Western style. As Kenaan-Kedar (2008, p. 22) points out, Shimon Jacobi took many trips abroad and was familiar with European goldsmithing.

The widespread wish of jewellers in the early years of Israel to adapt traditional styles and techniques to a new style befitting their new, modern surroundings is also evident in the Jacobi jewellery. An immigrant himself, Jacobi employed jewellers who had immigrated to Israel from various Muslim countries such as Iraq, Yemen, Morocco, Persia and Libya. They all brought their expertise and contributed to the workshop's creative production and eclectic style. Original Islamic folk jewellery and Bedouin pieces were taken apart and adapted to more subdued designs. Diverse techniques and materials, mainly silver and stones, were used, but also some base metals. A typical product of the Jacobi workshop is a mesh-like necklace which consists of several rows of intertwined ornamental elements. The repeated elements, which look like stylised flowers, are inlaid with tiny stones, such as turquoise or coral (fig. 2.48). Also typical of the Jacobi jewellery are brooches set with green Eilat stones which are sometimes referred to as Israel's national stone (fig. 2.49).[14] The stones are of geometrical shape, at times angular and asymmetrical, and are framed by filigree work.

2.49 Jacobi Jewelry, brooches, Jaffa, 1950s, partly gilt silver filigree, Eilat stones © Eretz-Israel Museum, Tel Aviv

14_ Eilat stone, found when copper mining started in Timna near the city of Eilat, Israel's southernmost city, became popular in the 1950s. From 1983, copper mining was stopped and the stones are no longer easily available.

Multiculturalism and the return of tradition

The melting-pot ideology promoted in Israel's early years was later challenged by trends advocating multiculturalism and cultural diversity. Over the last decades, the revival of traditional customs, music, dress and food has become widespread in Israel. Brides of Yemeni origin, for example, choose to wear traditional Sana'a costume and jewellery for their *henna* ceremony, which has also found revival. During this ceremony, held about a week before the wedding, the hands and feet of the bride are decorated with a red dye made from henna leaves. The *henna* is one of several fertility rituals, preparing the bride for her wedding. It also signifies the chasing away of demons and conveys good blessings (Polak-Sahm 2009, pp. 166–169). The stained marks on the skin are like a piece of jewellery serving as an amulet with magic powers. Unfortunately, the jewellery worn on these ceremonies is often of local production, a pale imitation of the original Yemeni jewellery.

Recently, however, some silversmiths of Yemeni extraction have taken it upon themselves to reconstruct the traditional jewellery of their country of origin in all its glory. One such outstanding jeweller, who immigrated to Israel in 1949, is Moshe Ben David (born *c.* 1927), who was the leading jeweller of Maskit for many years (see this chapter above). He reconstructed all the silver ornaments worn by brides in his native city of Beihan. "Unfortunately, we were told not to bring any jewellery with us when we immigrated," Ben David explains, "so I decided to reconstruct the bridal set from memory" (fig. 2.51). The reconstructed jewellery is a source of pride for the entire Beihan descendants' community in the town of Ness Ziona in central Israel.

Moshe David (Moshe Ben David's nephew) is another jeweller of the same family who belongs to a younger generation. He has spent years researching the history of his elders and studying Beihan traditions and customs. In an article he published about the dress and jewellery of Jewish women from Beihan, David (2008, pp. 247–269) describes how his father, jeweller Zadok David (1924–2011), dedicated himself after his retirement in 1990, some forty years after his immigration, to a reconstruction of the jewellery worn by Jewish women in Beihan (fig. 2.50). He undertook this task so that his own granddaughter could wear this jewellery when she married. The entire set was completed in 1994. During the process of making the jewellery, Moshe David worked together with his father Zadok, proudly describing himself as his father's apprentice.[15] Today, having learnt some of the special techniques developed by his father, such as the twisted knitted wire (fig. 2.52), he passes them on to his daughter, Aviya David-Shoham, a jeweller in her own right (see below, Chapter 5).

2.50 Zadok David and his son Moshe David, reconstruction of a silver knitted belt set with carnelian, part of an outfit traditionally worn by brides in Beihan, Yemen, 1990, courtesy of Moshe David

15_ Moshe David in an interview with the author, Ness Ziona, Israel, 2009.

2.51 Top: Moshe Ben David, reconstruction of jewellery traditionally worn by brides in his native city of Beihan, Yemen, 1989, courtesy of Moshe Ben David

2.52 Bottom: The twisted, knitted wire technique passed on from generation to generation of descendants of jewellers from Beihan, Yemen, courtesy of Aviya David-Shoham

3 From Isolation to Exposure

International Contacts and New Beginnings

3 From Isolation to Exposure

International Contacts and New Beginnings

Isolation, 1950s

For the young State of Israel, the 1950s were years of relative isolation from the world. For ideological reasons that had to do with both the nascent state's search for national identity and its meagre financial means, people rarely travelled overseas. Therefore, Israelis were hardly exposed to international art. At the New Bezalel metalwork department, the Bauhaus spirit continued to set the tone. David Heinz Gumbel and Ludwig Yehudah Wolpert continued teaching at the Bezalel metalwork department until 1955 and 1956, respectively (fig. 3.1). They taught on alternating weeks, so that each was free to work in his own studio while the other was teaching. Gumbel went on working in his Jerusalem studio after he left Bezalel, making both Judaica and jewellery (figs. 3.3–3.6). Two of their students eventually

3.1 David H. Gumbel (front row, third from right) and students in front of the New Bezalel entrance, 1952. Among the students are Hannah Bahar (top row, left), Miriam Libraider (top row, right), Menahem Berman (second row from top, third from right), Zelig Segal (fourth row from top, first on left).

replaced them as department heads – Menahem Berman in 1955, followed by Zelig Segal in 1964 – and they too continued to expound the unornamented, functional Bauhaus style, placing an emphasis on the pieces' meticulous finish.

The first person to expose Israeli jewellers to a different kind of jewellery was **Zahara Schatz**, daughter of Bezalel's founder, Boris Schatz. Born in Jerusalem in 1916, she left for Paris with her mother and her brother, Bezalel ("Lilik"), after her father's death. She studied art in Paris at the Académie de la Grande Chaumière and industrial design at the École nationale supérieure des Arts Décoratifs (Ofrat 2006a, pp. 4–7). In 1938 she joined her brother in California and lived and worked in the United States until her return to Israel in 1951. While living in San Francisco and then in New York, Schatz developed a unique assemblage technique. She combined metal items (nets and wires), leaves and ferns and affixed them between Perspex panels (figs. 3.7–3.8a–c). She used this technique to create both abstract works (in an airy style somewhat recalling Paul Klee) and decorative objects, such as bowls, trays and jewellery.

In 1948 Zahara Schatz participated in a group show of modern jewellery, "Modern Jewelry under Fifty Dollars", at the Walker Art Centre, Minneapolis (Schon 2001). She showed a bracelet, a choker and a brooch, all of which were assemblages of Perspex, wire, sequins and painted materials. Among the participants were key figures in the American Studio Jewelry movement, such as Margaret De Patta, Art Smith, Sam Kramer and Harry Bertoia. Schatz's works were in keeping with the spirit of this movement, which promoted unconventional, alternative designs. They combined free craftwork and unorthodox use of materials (such as plastic and readymade objects), which blurred the boundaries between art and jewellery.

On her return to Israel, Schatz's innovative jewellery drew a lot of attention. "I still recall the excitement we all felt at Bezalel when Zahara showed us a bracelet she had made of Perspex and diverse materials," recounts jeweller Rachel Pariser.[1] In 1954 Schatz won the Gold Medal at the Tenth Milan Triennale of Industrial Design and Decorative Arts (fig. 3.2). In addition to her work, the Israeli Pavilion at the exhibition featured pieces by Gumbel, Wolpert and Segal. *Domus* magazine (299, October 1954, pp. 13–16) devoted an extensive article to the Israeli Pavilion, which featured several photos of Schatz's works, including her jewellery.[2] In 1955 Schatz was awarded the prestigious Israel Prize for Art. She continued travelling between Israel and the United States (where she lived from 1960 to 1978) until she passed away in Jerusalem in 1999. However, it is unclear to what extent Schatz facilitated other Israeli jewellers' exposure to contemporary overseas trends.

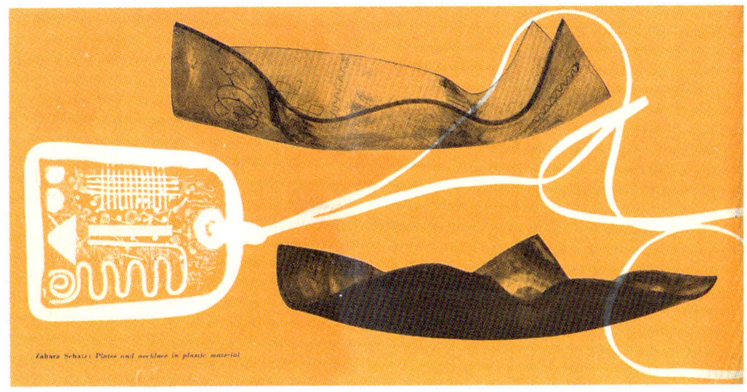

3.2 Page from the catalogue of the Israeli Pavilion at the Tenth Triennale of Milan, 1954, showing Perspex plates and necklace by Zahara Schatz

Winds of change from abroad, 1960s: Arje Griegst's influence

The isolation of the Israeli art and jewellery scene continued well into the 1960s. Yona Fischer, then a young, influential curator of contemporary Israeli art at the Bezalel National Museum (which was to become the Israel Museum, Jerusalem in 1965), recalls, "As to influences of international art, one must point out that in the early 1960s there was very little awareness in Israel regarding what was happening around the world. No modern or contemporary art magazine arrived here regularly; there was no TV prior to 1968; art books were

1_ All quotations from Rachel Pariser are from an interview with the author, Jerusalem, Israel, 2012.

2_ *Domus* had already published photos of Schatz's works – some plastic jewellery – while she was still living in the USA (*Domus*, 241, December 1949).

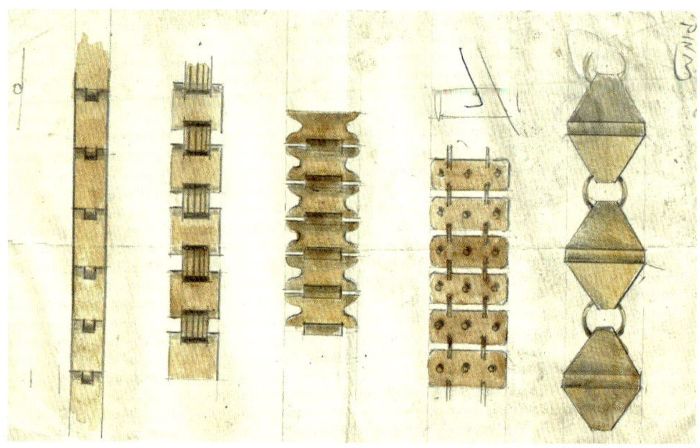

3.3 Top left: David H. Gumbel, choker, 1960s, silver, crystal, 2.3 × 36.0 cm, private collection, Australia © Malka Cohavi

3.4 Top right: David H. Gumbel, bracelet, 1960s, gold, private collection, Australia © Malka Cohavi

3.5 Bottom: David H. Gumbel, sketch for bracelets, pencil and watercolours on paper © Malka Cohavi

3.6 Opposite page: David H. Gumbel, bracelet, 1960s, silver, 4.0 × 18.6 cm, private collection, Australia © Malka Cohavi

3.7 Top: Zahara Zahara Schatz, brooch, 1953–54, Perspex combined with various items, nets and wires, collection of Dalia Hardof Renberg, Chappaqua, New York

3.8 a–c Zahara Schatz, set of pendant (bottom left), earrings (bottom right) and bracelet (opposite page), 1953–54, Perspex combined with metal items, nets and wires, collection of Dalia Hardof Renberg, Chappaqua, New York

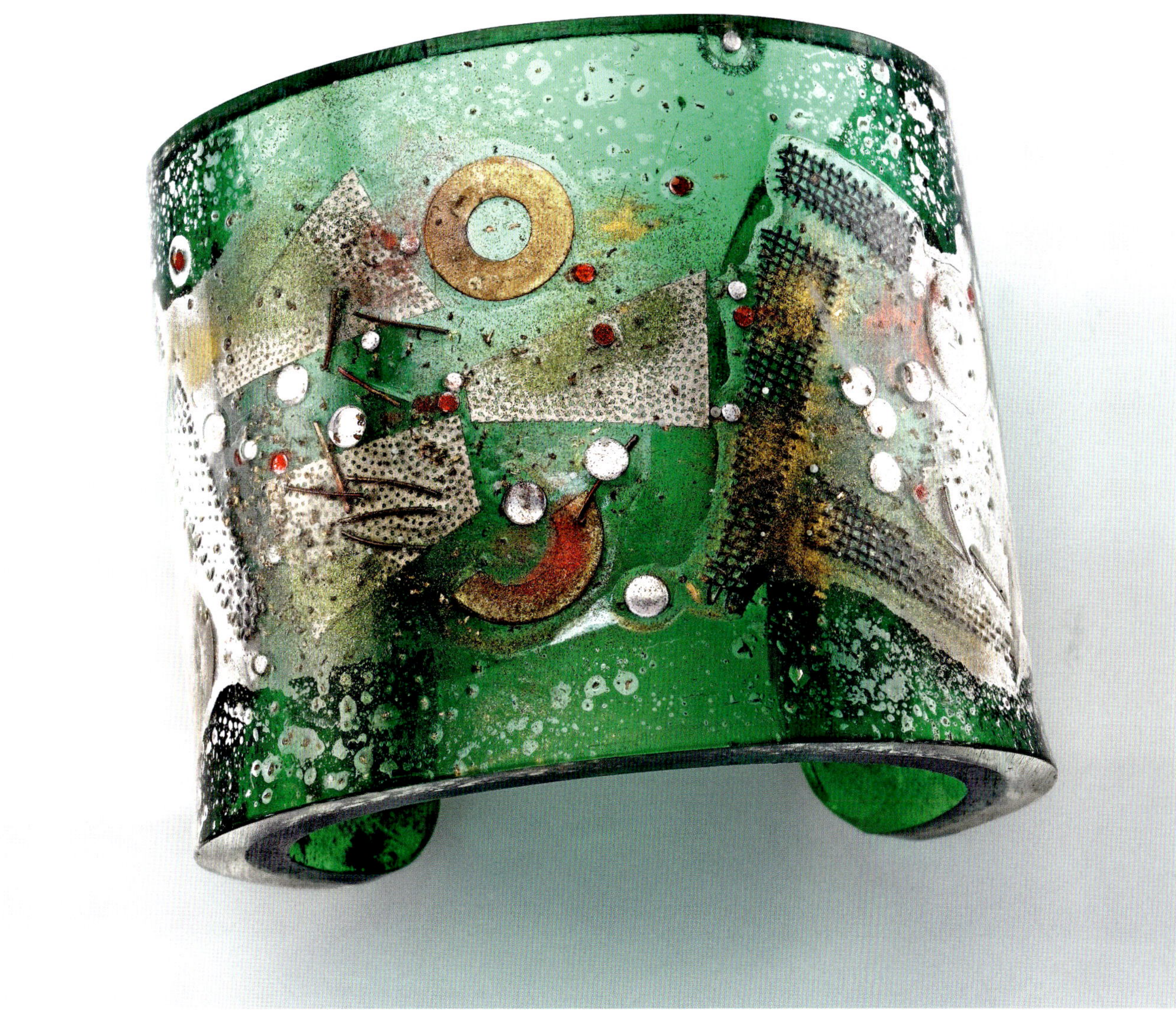

at the mercy of individual importers; and Bezalel had not yet become an art academy with all that this implies in relation to curriculum and teachers – not yet professors – who taught there" (Fischer and Manor-Friedman 2008, p. 10).

Against this backdrop, Danish jeweller **Arje Griegst's** arrival in Jerusalem was highly significant. Born in Copenhagen in 1938, Griegst too had a family connection to Boris Schatz's Bezalel. In 1914, his father Baruch Griegst (1889–1958), a silversmith and an ardent Zionist, was supposed to teach at Bezalel. He corresponded to that effect with Boris Schatz, but for some reason, the plan did not come to fruition.[3] Arje Griegst visited Israel several times. In 1963 he started teaching at the Bezalel metalwork department while travelling between Copenhagen and Jerusalem for several years, before heading the department from 1968 to 1972.

The Jerusalem jewellery scene of the 1960s was still ruled by the uncompromising modernist line of Gumbel and Wolpert. Griegst, a master goldsmith of the first degree, brought winds of change with him. Griegst created fantastic, at times surreal works whose soft, winding, organic forms are reminiscent of Art Nouveau or Baroque art. His pieces were usually made of gold or gilt silver and inlaid with precious stones and pearls, and he often used the lost-wax technique and techniques preserved by ancient cultures (figs. 3.9, 3.10, 3.14). He made pieces such as jewellery for the back of the hand (fig. 3.12) or a facial ornament shaped like tear drops, which he called *Paribanou's Tears* (1962) in reference to "The Story of Prince Ahmed and the Fairy Paribanou" from the famous collection of stories *1001 Arabian Nights* (fig. 3.13). In Jerusalem he met Ernst Fuchs, an Austrian painter who was one of the founders of Fantastic Realism. Fuchs influenced Griegst greatly, both in his attraction to symbolism and mysticism and in his use of classic techniques. Griegst's style left a significant mark on the local jewellery scene. This is evident, for example, in a piece of jewellery for the back of the hand, made by a Bezalel student in 1971 (fig. 3.11). "In retrospect, my contribution to the work of my students in Israel was to animate their designs," Griegst says in our conversation.

In 1963, Yona Fischer curated a group exhibition, "Today's Form", at the Bezalel National Museum and invited Griegst to participate. The exhibition featured works by ten young Israeli artists: five painters and five artists in different media, such as sculpture, ceramics, jewellery and architecture. Griegst showed thirteen pieces of jewellery and a pair of Torah Rimonim[4] executed by the Bezalel metalwork department students. In the introduction to the exhibition catalogue, Fischer (1963, n.p.) writes: "Between formal severity and functionalism and their opposite pole – a longing for Baroque and naturalist Romanticism – there is an intermediate route. This is where one may find the common thread between our ten artists". Indeed, Griegst was one of the first artists to open up a window – for the Israeli public and for jewellers alike – onto jewellery informed by imagination and expressive sensibilities. In 1964 art critic Meir Ronnen (1964, p. VI), reviewing a modest exhibition featuring works by Bezalel students and graduates, notes Griegst's impact: "While Griegst's influence can be felt in the sweeping lines of pendants and bracelets, and in the grouping of the elements of some of the earrings, the clean design and technical handling of the silver is a tribute to the standards of Mr Berman, who himself studied at Bezalel under Messrs. Wolpert and Gumpel [*sic*]. This tradition has developed a feeling for cunning simplicity that puts accent on form and on contrast with the stones or enamel used in the rings and other jewellery."

Griegst's impact reached far beyond Bezalel. Groundbreaking jewellery designs inspired by his work were on view in an exhibition co-organised by Maskit and the Bat-Sheva Craftwork Company in Tel Aviv in 1964. The exhibition featured pieces by eight young jewellers. Among them were Bianca Eshel Gershuni, who would become one of the leading jewellery artists in Israel (see below, Chapter 4), and Bezalel graduates, such as Hannah Bahar-Paneth, Miriam Libraider-Tzafrir and Rachel Pariser (*Haaretz* 1964, p. 14; Nevo 1964, p. 6).

A jeweller particularly influenced by Griegst's work was **Leon Israel**. Born in Tangier, Morocco, in 1943, he immigrated to Israel at the age of twelve. He started

3_ Arje Griegst in an interview with the author, Copenhagen, Denmark, 2008. All quotations from Griegst are from this interview.

4_ Torah Rimonim are finials that adorn the top of the rollers (or staves) of Torah scrolls.

3.9 Arje Griegst, Queen Margrethe II's tiara in the shape of "a summer meadow", 1976, 18-ct and 21-ct gold, amber, diamonds, moonstone, pearls, opal, emerald

3.10 Top left: Arje Griegst, *Oriental Night*, from a series of rings made in Paris for the Georg Jensen company, Copenhagen, 1964, 20-ct gold, diamonds, moonstone, sapphires, brilliants, blue opal, oriental pearls

3.11 Bottom left: Unknown Bezalel student, hand jewellery showing the influence of Arje Griegst, 1970

3.12 Top right: Arje Griegst, hand jewellery designed to be worn around the wrist and fingers, 1962, 21-ct gold and fine-gold sheet, emerald, rubies, almandines, oriental pearls

3.13 Bottom right: Arje Griegst, *Paribanou's Tears*, face jewellery worn by Royal Danish Ballet prima ballerina Anna Lærkesen, 1962, emeralds, star sapphires, oriental pearls, rubies, hung on a twisted chain in 20-ct gold

3.14 Opposite page: Arje Griegst, *Face of the Night*, pendant, 1966–67, 20-ct gold, coloured oriental pearls, diamonds, lost wax technique

3.15 Left: Leon Israel, drawing of a comb submitted to De Beers International Diamond Jewellery Design Competition, 1971, courtesy of Leon Israel

3.16 a, b Right: Leon Israel, comb, 1971, gold, diamonds, emeralds, pearls. Winner of the Diamond International Award at the De Beers International Diamond Jewellery Design Competition, 1971. Opposite page: Model showing Leon Israel's award-winning comb.

3.17 Left: Leon Israel for Leon Israel Designs Ltd., pendant, 1990s, 18-ct gold, diamonds, Tahitian pearl, 3.0 × 6.0 cm

3.18 Right: Leon Israel for Leon Israel Designs Ltd., pendant, 1990s, 18-ct gold, diamonds, Tahitian pearl, 4.0 × 5.0 cm

carving in wood and sculpting as a child and from 1966 to 1969 studied at the metalwork department in Bezalel under Zelig Segal, Arie Ofir, Arje Griegst and Shaul Seri, among others. Israel was attracted to wax work and to the Art Nouveau style, and Griegst soon became his mentor.

In 1971 Leon Israel was awarded the Diamond International Award by the De Beers Corporation, for a gold comb inlaid with diamonds, emeralds and pearls. With its flowing organic branches, the comb clearly reflects the influence of Griegst (figs. 3.15, 3.16 a, b). The news that an Israeli jeweller had won this prestigious international award received great media attention both in Israel and internationally. The Jewish press abroad dubbed the award the "'Oscar' for jewellery design" (*The Jerusalem Post* 1971, p. 17; *Zionist Record* 1971, p. 7; Levine 1971, p. 24). The award-winning comb was shown with twenty-nine other award-winning works in a travelling exhibition in Italy, Japan and Australia. It was then returned to Israel and exhibited at the Harry Oppenheimer Diamond Museum in the Diamond Center of Ramat Gan. Production of the comb was sponsored by Mr Yona Hatzor of Hennig Company (Ami 2008, pp. 159–161).

Under Griegst's guidance, Leon Israel chose the professional path that he has followed to this day: mass production, as opposed to one-of-a-kind pieces. He designs his pieces by sculpting them in wax, prepares rubber moulds and then casts the finished products, which are mostly gold pieces set with diamonds, pearls and semi-precious stones. Leon Israel Designs has been located at the same studio in the Old City of Jaffa since 1978, and his jewellery is marketed worldwide (figs. 3.17, 3.18).

Another of Griegst's students in Jerusalem who was greatly influenced by him was **Israel Meshi**, born in Israel in 1948. He, too, started carving in wood at a young age. From 1969 to 1973 he studied in the metalwork department at Bezalel (which changed its name to the gold- and silversmithing department in 1972), where Griegst became his mentor and role model. Like Leon Israel, it was his penchant for sculpting that drew Meshi to Griegst, since the latter sculpted his pieces in wax and then cast them in metal. Shortly after graduation, Meshi became a "born-again" Jew and eschewed jewellery making in favour of Yeshiva studies. Eventually, after ten years, he returned to his old craft and made a few pieces of jewellery inspired by Jewish mysticism. Among his early works was his *Novloth Hokhmah* pendant (titled after a book on metaphysics published in 1631 by Rabbi Yoseph Shlomo Delmedigo), which according to Meshi signifies the perpetual circular

3.19 Left: Israel Meshi, *Novloth Hokhmah*, pendant, 1975, 18-ct and 20-ct gold, pearls, lapis lazuli, 6.3 × 4.2 cm

3.20 Right: Israel Meshi, *Dove Hiding in the Clefts of the Rock*, brooch, 1980, 20-ct gold, silver, lapis lazuli, emerald, 4.0 × 3.5 cm

movement of Divine Wisdom that spreads downwards and then moves upwards again (fig. 3.19).[5] He also made a brooch which refers to the dove described in the Song of Songs (2:14) as hiding in the clefts of the rock and not showing its face (fig. 3.20). However, Meshi has since focused on Jewish ceremonial objects, which he fashions from carved wood, silver, gold and precious or semi-precious stones. Griegst's influence is still evident in Meshi's sculptural work and in the continuous spiral movement of his pieces.

5_ Israel Meshi in an e-mail exchange with the author, July 2013.

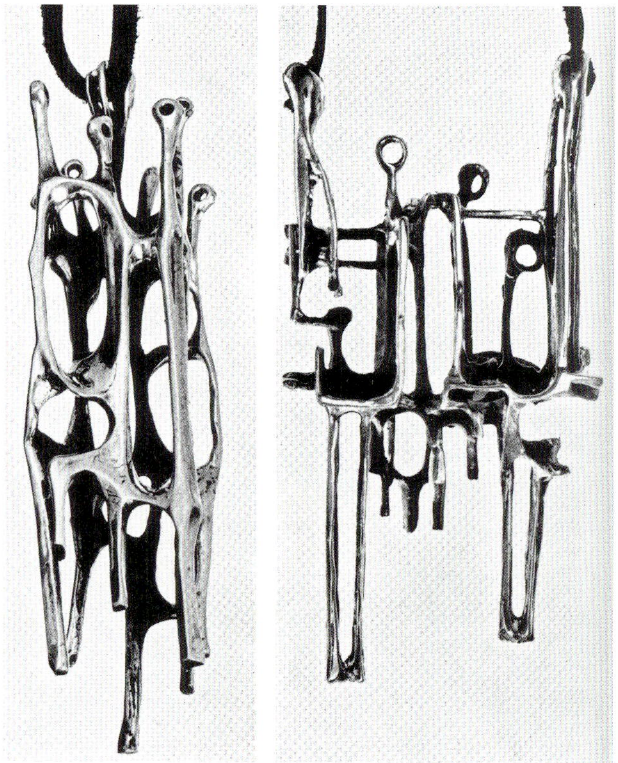

3.21 Aharon Bezalel (manufactured by J. Bier Ltd, Jerusalem), two pendants, late 1960s, cast silver

Exposure of Israeli jewellery abroad, 1960s

Around the same time that international influences began making their way into Israel, Israeli products were becoming exposed to international venues. A key agent in promoting this exposure was the Arts and Crafts Center (later known as the Jewelry Center) at the Israel Export Institute. The Arts and Crafts Center was established in 1958 in cooperation with the Israeli Ministry of Commerce and Industry. Although the main idea behind this enterprise was to encourage mass production of jewellery to be exported abroad, initially it also exported one-off designs. In the early years even authentic handmade ethnic jewellery pieces were exported and featured in the Export Institute catalogues. Gradually, however, industrially mass-produced items became the main export.

Particularly instrumental in the exposure of Israeli jewellery abroad was **Menahem Berman**. Born in Jerusalem in 1929, Berman studied at Bezalel under Gumbel and Wolpert and graduated in 1950. When Wolpert left the metalwork department, Berman took on its directorship, a post he would hold intermittently for ten years. He himself mainly made Jewish ceremonial objects, although he also taught jewellery making at Bezalel. By his own account, however, his main contribution to the Israeli jewellery scene was through his activity on behalf of the Israel Export Institute from 1965 to 1970.[6] Until then, the Export Institute had focused on fashion. In addition, it operated the Arts and Crafts Center, which helped people present and market their products abroad. The centre was originally headed by Malka Vardi, who was later replaced by Esther Ben-Yosef – assisted by Berman as a professional consultant. Berman set himself the challenge of fostering

6_ Menahem Berman in an interview with the author, Jerusalem, Israel, 2012.

3.22 Left: Hannah Bahar-Paneth (manufactured by Chaim Paz, Jerusalem), rings, late 1960s, cast silver

3.23 Right: Mimi Rabinovitch (manufactured by Chaim Paz, Jerusalem), rings, late 1960s, cast silver

collaborations between jewellery designers and the jewellery industry. To that end, he initiated the Modelling Programme, where he acted as a middleman between the industry and designers, commissioning models which could serve as prototypes to be industrially mass-produced. This resulted in fruitful collaborations. For instance, models by sculptor and jewellery designer Aharon Bezalel (1926–2012) were cast in Jizchak Bier's workshop (Bier Enterprises Ltd.) (fig. 3.21).[7]

One of the participants in Berman's Modelling Programme was **Chaim Paz**, who had a workshop in Jerusalem. Paz was born in Germany in 1930 and immigrated to Palestine with his parents at the age of four. When he graduated from Bezalel in 1955, he set up a small studio near the Old City of Jerusalem. Around the same time, he met Ruth Dayan and for a while worked for Maskit.[8] In 1959, Paz opened a shop called Idit on Ben Yehuda Street in Jerusalem. He also set up a workshop with state-of-the-art mechanical equipment, where some twenty employees produced his own jewellery as well as the designs of others. Thanks to Berman's programme, the workshop was able to produce cast jewellery designed by leading designers. Notable among them were Hannah Bahar-Paneth (fig. 3.22), Mimi Rabinovitch (fig. 3.23), Aharon Bezalel and others. The workshop prospered until 1976, when Paz decided to shut it down after it was burgled. The shop and the adjoining workshop are still open, but at a different Jerusalem location (figs. 3.24, 3.25). Nowadays, after years in the industry, Paz has returned to manual craftsmanship and is working at home on a new collection, inspired by Henri Matisse's paper cut-outs.

Menahem Berman also made a connection with the important Internationale Handwerksmesse (International Trade Fair for Crafts) in Munich. At first, three jewellery pieces of Berman's own design (fig. 3.26) were

7_ Their work was exhibited, together with other examples of jewellery from Israel, at the Frankfurt Fair of 1968 (*Kunst+Handwerk* 1968, pp. 25–29).
8_ Chaim Paz in an interview with the author, Jerusalem, Israel, 2012.

3.24 Top: Chaim Paz (design and manufacture), pendant from the "Squares and Triangles" line in the "Book" collection, 1990s, sterling silver, 18-ct gold, 2.0 × 2.1 cm

3.25 Bottom: Chaim Paz (design and manufacture), pin and pendant from the "Towers" line, late 1960s, 18-ct gold, ruby, 3.6 × 4.5 cm

exhibited in the fair's Sonderschau (Special Show), and the next year additional Israeli designers were invited to participate in the show.

To encourage jewellers to take part in the Export Institute programme, Berman established a jewellery design competition. This soon became a significant creative catalyst stimulating creativity on the local jewellery scene. The extent to which the annual jewellery competition boosted the jewellery scene in Israel is evidenced by the media attention it received. In 1967, a year after the first competition, newspaper headlines announced: "42 Objet d'Art Artists Compete for Prizes" (*Ma'ariv* 1967, p. 8) and "Brooch and Earrings Set Is the Subject of Jewellery Competition" (*Haaretz* 1967, p. 11).

New beginnings, late 1960s

Looking at the jewellers who won the first Export Institute awards in the late 1960s, one notes a change in style – from the modernist rigidity expounded by Gumbel and Wolpert, to ethnic influences, organic forms and an eclectic use of materials, as well as to a more extensive use of inlaid stones.

In the first jewellery competition, in 1966,[9] the First Prize was awarded to **Miriam Libraider-Tzafrir**. She received it for a gold necklace inlaid with rubies, topaz, amethyst and pearls (fig. 3.27), which presented a modernist take on oriental ethnic jewellery. The piece was purchased by a foreign national who told her that he intended to frame and hang it on a wall.[10] Libraider-Tzafrir was born in Israel in 1934 and was raised in a small agricultural village in the south of the country. After graduating from Bezalel in 1958, she was awarded a three-year scholarship from Bezalel. During those years, she engaged in designing Jewish ceremonial objects together with two other Bezalel alumni, Hannah Bahar-Paneth and Rachel Pariser. In 1967, she once again won a prize in the Israel Export Institute competition. This time it was Second Prize, for a brooch and earrings (figs. 3.28 a, b). Already then, the somewhat harsh geometric style of her school years (fig. 3.31) was giving way to organic forms, curlicues and inlaid

3.26 Menahem Berman, bracelet with pendant jewels, 1960s, gold, pearls, tourmalines, single ruby

9_ The Israel Export Institute jewellery competition was preceded by a smoking paraphernalia competition.

10_ All remarks by Miriam Libraider-Tzafrir are from an interview with the author, Jerusalem, Israel, 2012.

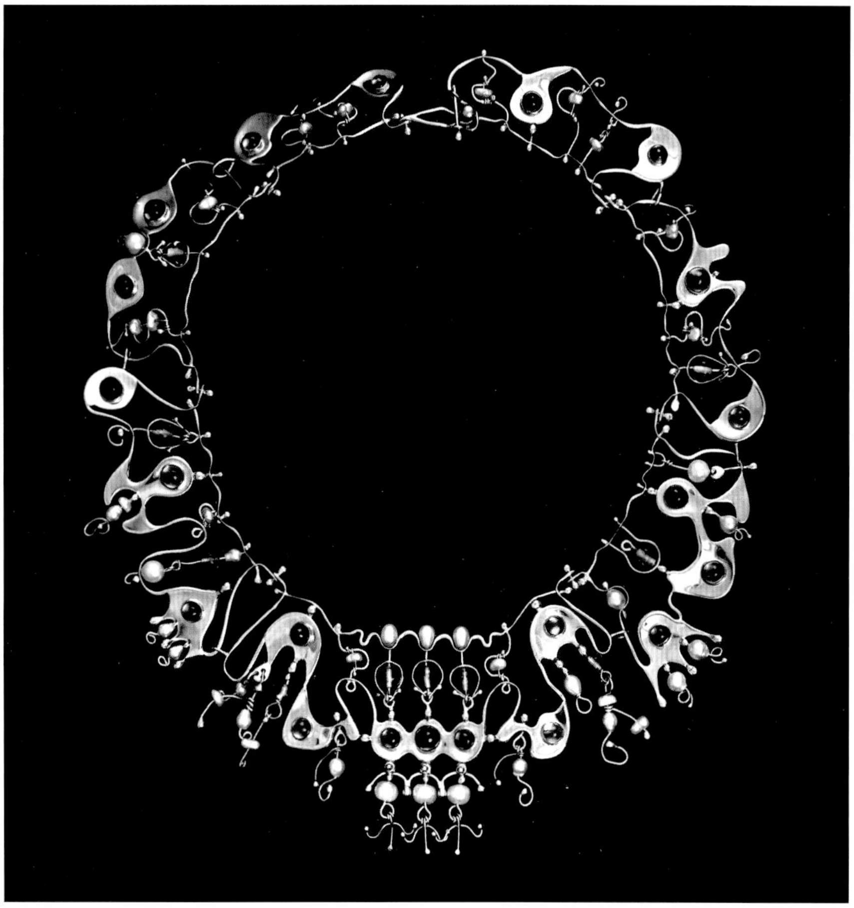

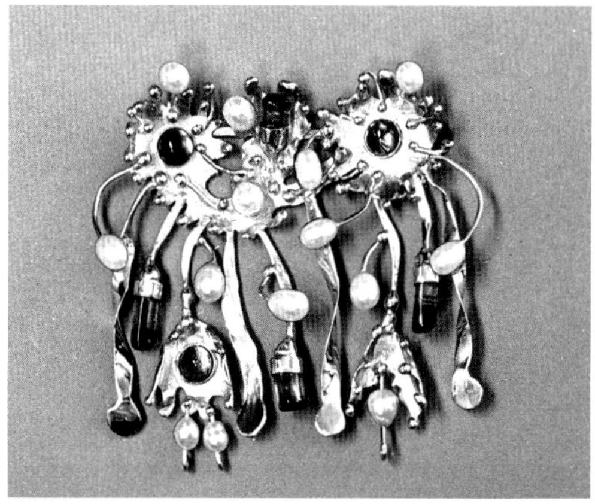

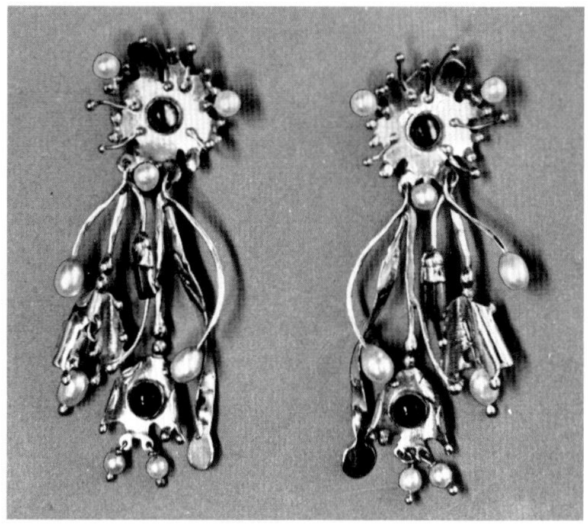

stones. She attributes this new style to her strong connection as a village child to nature, as well as to ethnic inspiration. The latter is most evident in her palette and in the forms of her pendants, which at times resemble the palm-shaped *khamsa* amulet popular throughout the Middle East and North Africa (figs. 3.29, 3.30, 3.32).

Hannah Bahar-Paneth, a descendent of an old Jerusalemite family, graduated from Bezalel in 1957. She had also studied under Gumbel and Wolpert. Her studio is located in the vicinity of Libraider-Tzafrir's studio, both of which are at the Jerusalem House of Quality in Jerusalem. In 1967 Bahar-Paneth was awarded First Prize in the Export Institute competition, for a brooch-and-earrings set of her design (fig. 3.33 a, b),

3.27 Left: Miriam Libraider-Tzafrir, necklace, 1966, gold, pearls, topaz, amethyst, rubies. First Prize winner at the Israel Export Institute Competition, 1966.

3.28 a, b Right top and bottom: Miriam Libraider-Tzafrir, brooch-and-earrings set, 1967, gold, semi-precious stones. Second Prize winner at the Israel Export Institute Competition, 1967.

3.29 Top left: Miriam Libraider-Tzafrir, *He and She*, pendant, 1970s, 18-ct gold, sapphire, tourmaline, ruby, opal

3.30 Bottom left: Miriam Libraider-Tzafrir, *Mask*, pendant, 1960s, silver, semi-precious stone, 10.0 × 5.5 cm

3.31 Top right: Miriam Libraider-Tzafrir, necklace, late 1950s, 18-ct gold, tourmalines, 23.0 × 15.0 cm

3.32 Bottom right: Miriam Libraider-Tzafrir, *The Tree of Knowledge*, brooch/pendant, 1970, 18-ct gold, tourmalines, 7.0 × 7.0 cm

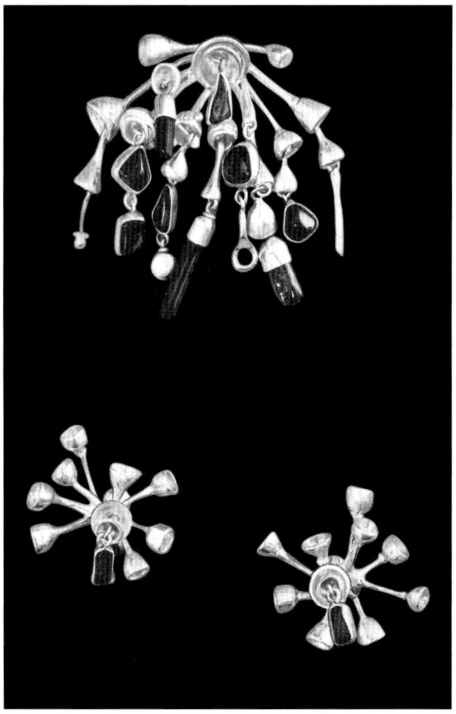

3.33 a, b Left top and bottom: Hannah Bahar-Paneth, brooch-and-earrings set, 1967, silver, tourmalines, garnets. First Prize winner at the Israel Export Institute Competition, 1967.

3.34 Right: Hannah Bahar-Paneth, *Leaves*, necklace, 1966, silver, 27.0 × 13.0 cm; 12.0 × 6.0 cm (leaves). Third Prize winner at the Israel Export Institute Competition, 1966.

having won Third Prize for a necklace in the previous year (fig. 3.34). The award-winning brooch was inspired by a brooch from Bukhara, Uzbekistan, which she had seen at the Israel Museum.[11] In addition to ethnic jewellery, her works are inspired by natural forms, mainly fruit and seeds (figs. 3.36 – 3.38). She uses a variety of materials and techniques. For instance, she mixes silver with leather and fabric[12] and combines hammering with various casting techniques. This was common practice among international art jewellers at the time. Four of her pieces (e.g. fig. 3.35) appear in Oppi Untracht's renowned book on jewellery-making techniques, *Jewelry: Concepts and Technology* (Untracht 1982, p. 5, fig. 1–17; p. 269, fig. 7–27; p. 489, fig. 11–8; p. 693, fig. 16–12). In June 1976 a feature article about her was published in the *Schweizerische Uhrmacher und Goldschmiede Zeitung* (Swiss Watchmaker and Goldsmith Magazine), emphasising the element of movement in her works (L.D. 1976, pp. 70–71). A year later, the Austrian magazine *Die Vitrine* (The Showcase) published an overview of the jewellery scene in Israel, devoting an illustrated article to Bahar-Paneth's work (Sorger 1977, pp. 24–25).

When the Natif Arts and Crafts Gallery was opened in the Old City of Jaffa in 1970, the first exhibition held there featured a hundred pieces of jewellery by Hannah Bahar-Paneth, Miriam Libraider-Tzafrir and Mimi Rabinovitch. **Mimi Rabinovitch**, a 1947 Bezalel graduate, lives in Moshav HaYogev in the Jezreel Valley. She was associated with Maskit and trained immigrant jewellery craftsmen (Halpert 1970, p. 20).

Leaving behind the Bauhaus spirit in favour of Oriental, ethnic influences also meant a more extensive use of colour. Some jewellers, such as Hannah Bahar-Paneth and Miriam Libraider-Tzafrir, enriched their palette through the use of coloured stones. **Rachel Pariser** added colour to her jewellery by applying enamel, a technique she mastered and taught at Bezalel for several years. In the 1967 Export Institute competition, she received honourable mention for a brooch

11_ Hannah Bahar-Paneth in an interview with the author, Jerusalem, Israel, 2012.

12_ Cases in point are her neckpieces shown during the 1979 Fashion Week in the USA, which were also on view in Bloomingdales (Bat-Ya'ar 1979, pp. 32–33).

Clockwise from top left:

3.35 Hannah Bahar-Paneth, *Two Olive Trees*, pendant, 1970s, cast gold, 6.0 × 5.5 cm. Cuttlebone served as a mould for the casting of this piece.

3.36 Hannah Bahar-Paneth, pendant, early 1960s, silver, semi-precious stones, exhibited in a 1964 Bezalel exhibition

3.37 Hannah Bahar-Paneth, *Bells*, necklace, 1970, gold

3.38 Hannah Bahar-Paneth, necklace made for Maskit's gold department, *c.* 1970, 18-ct gold, pearls

Clockwise from top left:

3.39 Rachel Pariser, brooch, 1980s, cast silver, silver-wire macramé knotting

3.40 Rachel Pariser, pendant, 1980, gilt silver, pearl, silver-wire macramé knotting, 5.5 × 4.0 cm

3.41 Rachel Pariser, brooch (part of a brooch-and-earrings set), 1967, gold with transparent enamel, 6.0 × 8.0 cm. Received honourable mention at the Israel Export Institute Competition, 1967.

sporting round enamel discs in lieu of stones (fig. 3.41). Born in Haifa in 1937 to parents of German extraction, she graduated from Bezalel in 1962 and, as mentioned above, designed Jewish ceremonial objects for a few years on a Bezalel scholarship. Pariser then developed a unique technique for making jewellery. She used textile techniques like macramé – a form of textile making through knotting rather than weaving or knitting – to knot thin silver and gold wires. Using this technique she made chokers, brooches, pendants (figs. 3.39, 3.40) and even a skullcap, for which she received honourable mention at the 1978 Export Institute competition

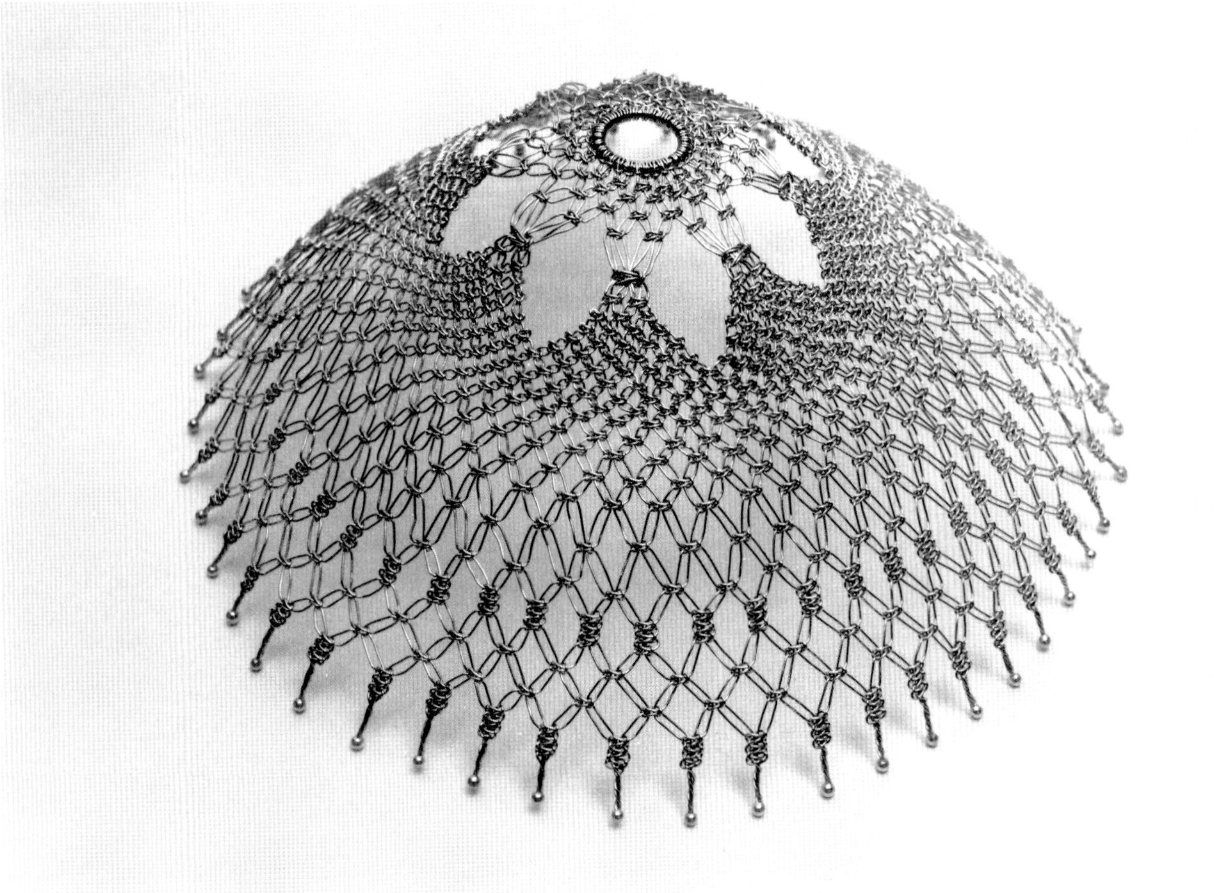

3.42 Rachel Pariser, skullcap, 1978, silver-wire macramé knotting, diam. 19.0 cm. Received honourable mention at the Israel Export Institute Competition, 1978.

(fig. 3.42). In 1978 she held a solo exhibition at Maskit in Jerusalem titled "Jewellery: Entwined in Silver and Gold" (Pariser 1993, p. 32). She developed the use of this textile technique in metal long before she would become acquainted with the work of Arline Fisch, an American jeweller famous for her use of textile techniques such as weaving and knitting. Pariser recalls her surprise when Fisch's book *Textile Techniques in Metal for Jewelers, Textile Artists & Sculptors* (1975) arrived in Israel and she realised that her invention was nothing new. "But I was happy to note," Pariser says, "that Fisch doesn't do macramé."

The awakening jewellery scene, encouraged by the Export Institute activities, drew leading artists who had specialised in other media to experiment with jewellery making. One such artist is **Zelig Segal**, a world-renowned designer of Jewish ceremonial objects. Segal, a multidisciplinary artist born in Jerusalem in 1933, engages, in addition to his Judaica designs, in drawing, painting and sculpting. He studied under Gumbel and Wolpert in Bezalel and graduated in 1954. That same year, he won the Bronze Medal at the Tenth Milan Triennale of Industrial Design and Decorative Arts for a copper candlestick. From 1964 to 1968 he headed the

3.43 a, b Zelig Segal, choker, early 1970s, silver. This award-winning "caterpillar" choker has great flexibility thanks to its design of half spheres strung together.

metalwork department in Bezalel (Fishof and Zalmona 1992). He was awarded Third Prize at the 1967 Export Institute competition, in which participants were asked to design a brooch-and-earrings set. In an Export Institute catalogue, his brooch is described as a "gold brooch with natural tourmaline crystals springing out of their gold sockets as if they were growing out of the natural rock" (The Israel Export Institute n.d., p. 8). Searching for the logic inherent in materials and for simplicity in designs has been the hallmark of Segal's entire creative output. Every now and then he would return to jewellery making. The catalogue published by the Export Institute in the early 1970s shows an award-winning choker of Segal's design (figs. 3.43 a, b). It is made of silver half-spheres strung together, similar to a caterpillar, in a way that allows the piece great flexibility and enables the wearer to play with it (The Israel Export Institute n.d., p. 32).

Another artist who started out with different artistic pursuits and then arrived at jewellery making was **Amitai Kav**. Having studied painting at the Avni Institute in Tel Aviv and dance at the Academy of Music and Dance in Jerusalem, he took up jewellery in 1968, at first in silver and then in gold. Being a self-taught jewellery maker may have contributed to the originality of his style. After a bracelet he designed won an award at the Export Institute competition in 1968, he decided to make jewellery his main pursuit. In 1970 he was invited to hold a solo show at Maskit, Tel Aviv (which had just opened a high-end gold-jewellery department), and in 1972 he held another solo show at the Natif Gallery in the Old City of Jaffa. Arie Ofir, who headed the Bezalel gold- and silversmithing department at the time, invited him to join the department as a faculty member, a post he would hold for twelve years. From 1978 to 1980, Kav taught at the Tyler School of Art in Philadelphia, and in 1979 he also taught at the Parsons School of Design in New York. In Philadelphia he met renowned jewellery artist Albert Paley. During the early years of his career, Paley (born 1944) made jewellery using a forging technique. Although he stopped making jewellery in 1978, his ornamental style

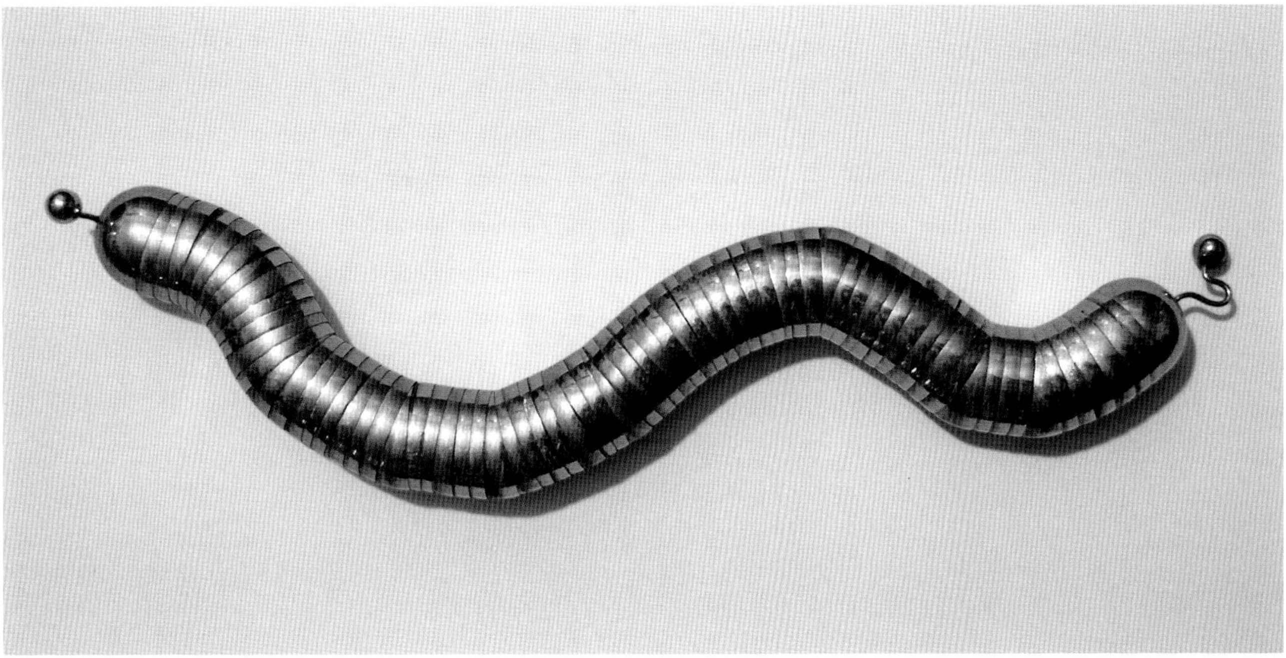

left an enormous impact on a number of artists, Amitai Kav among them. Kav was influenced not only by Paley's technique and flowing, curving style but also by his interest in the form of the Greco-Roman fibula (figs. 3.44, 3.45).[13] Kav also formed a connection with Paley's teacher Stanley Lechtzin. As head of the Metals/Jewellery Programme at the Tyler School of Art, Lechtzin (born 1936) was instrumental in making Philadelphia a centre of American jewellery. He was a pioneer in applying the technique of electroforming to produce lightweight jewellery in organic forms, incorporating stones and other materials. In 1977 Lechtzin was invited by Arie Ofir to teach at the Bezalel gold- and silversmithing department. Together, they established a teacher and student exchange programme. It was as part of this programme that Kav was invited to teach at the Tyler School of Art.

Kav's jewellery is complex and heavy and is characterised by sensuously convoluted, organic forms. First, he makes a pencil sketch and then sculpts the gold directly. He never uses casting, and each piece is one of a kind. His inspiration sources are varied. They include the anatomy books of his father, who was a biology teacher (he is fascinated with the bones and skeleton of the human body) (figs. 3.46, 3.47); the dance scene of his early years; and mechanical elements, such as parts of machinery and antique guns. The mechanical aspects of jewellery are of paramount importance to him and an essential part of the design. At times, the clasp *is* the piece (fig. 3.50). Lately, he has taken inspiration from Bedouin and African jewellery, designing necklaces and bracelets composed of coils, spheres and protuberances of his own making, whose movement produces sound (fig. 3.48). Kav's jewellery is usually made of fine yellow, white or red gold, at times combined with blackened silver. A peace-dove silver brooch he designed in 1994 was presented by the State of Israel to the wives of the participants in the Israel–Jordan peace-treaty ceremony and was worn by the then American First Lady, Hillary Clinton; Queen Noor of Jordan; and the Israeli Prime Minister's wife, the late Mrs Lea Rabin (fig. 3.49).

13_ Amitai Kav in an interview with the author, Jerusalem, Israel, 2012.

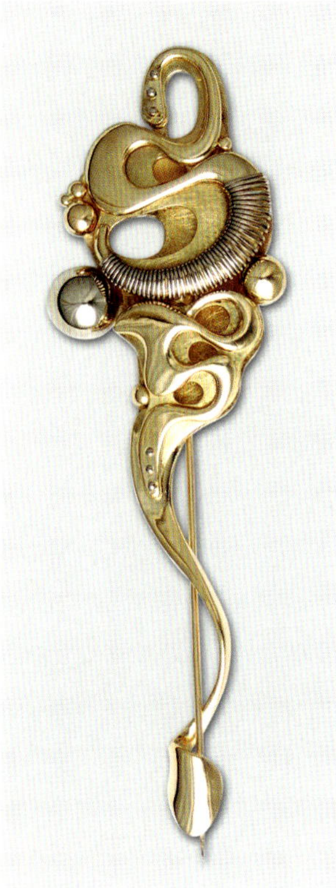

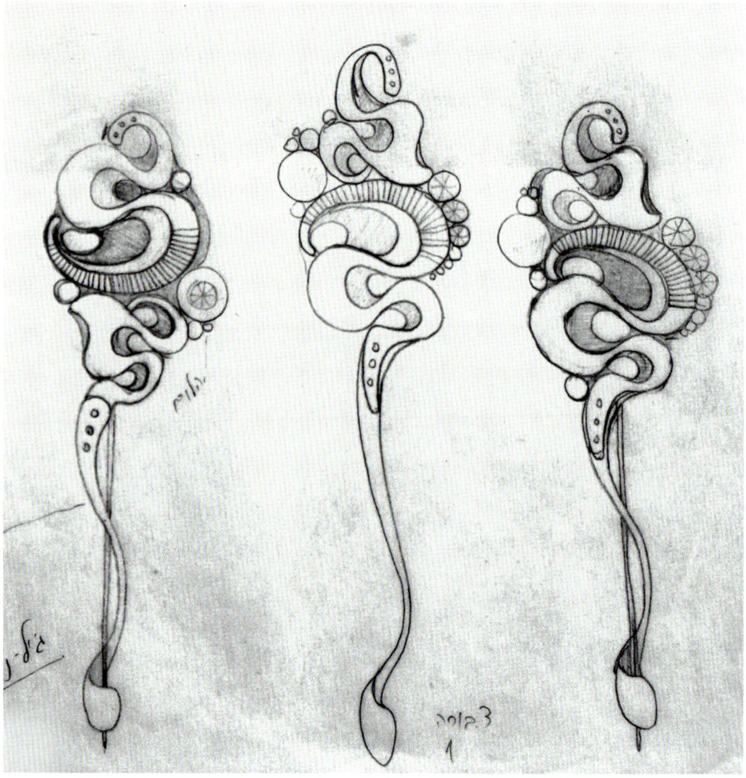

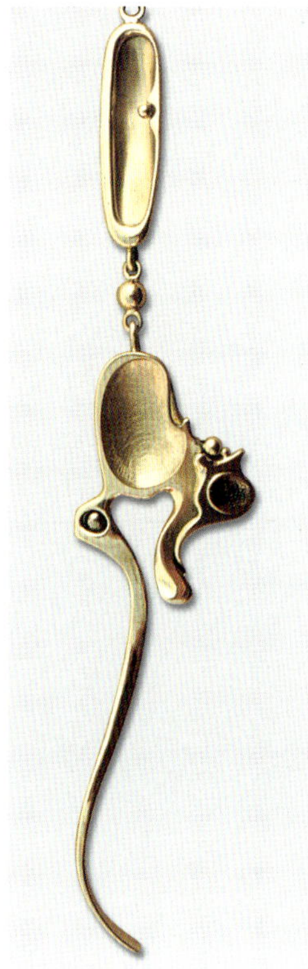

This and opposite page, clockwise from top left:

3.44 Amitai Kav, brooch from the series "Bird", 1995, 18-ct white and yellow gold, h. 10.0 cm. The integration of pin and stem is inspired by the fibula form.

3.45 Amitai Kav, sketches for brooches and rings from the series "Bird", 1990, pencil on paper

3.46 Amitai Kav, *Kandinsky Pendant No. 1*, 1974, 18-ct white and yellow gold, h. 10.0 cm

3.47 Amitai Kav, *Kandinsky Pendant No. 2*, 1974, 18-ct white and yellow gold, h. 10.0 cm

3.48 Amitai Kav, bead bracelet, 1994, 18-ct white and yellow gold, sterling silver

3.49 Amitai Kav, *Dove of Peace*, pin, 1994, sterling silver, 18-ct gold, h. 3.0 cm. Presented to the wives of the participants in the Israel–Jordan peace treaty ceremony, 1994.

3.50 Amitai Kav, pendant from the series "Bird Clasp", 1998, 18-ct white and yellow gold, h. 3.0 cm

Innovative visitors from abroad, 1970s

The 1970s saw great changes in the Israeli jewellery scene, much of it thanks to initiatives by **Arie Ofir**, who headed Bezalel's newly named gold- and silversmithing department from 1972 to 1984. Ofir was born in Israel in 1939 to parents who had fled Poland a few years previously. He graduated from Bezalel in 1964 and perfected his craft working as David Gumbel's assistant (from 1963, when Ofir was still a student, to 1965). From 1967 to 1968 he worked at the Georg Jensen Company in Denmark. On his return to Israel, he established an independent studio and joined the metalwork department faculty in Bezalel until, in 1972, he took on its directorship. He divided the department into two sub-divisions, one devoted to jewellery design and the other to hollowware design, including Jewish ceremonial objects. He himself made both ceremonial objects and jewellery (figs. 3.51–3.53). Another innovation of his was to set up a teaching faculty comprised, in addition to jewellers Benny Bronstein, Israel Dahan, Shaul Seri and Amitai Kav, of artists in other disciplines, such as sculpture, painting and architecture. Among these were notable Israeli artists Pinchas Cohen-Gan, Osvaldo Romberg, Gideon Gechtman, architect Nahum Meltzer and others.

Another of Ofir's remarkable initiatives was inviting guest lecturers from abroad and setting up student exchange programmes with schools in Europe and the United States. The list of personages who came to Jerusalem from abroad, featuring some of the foremost innovative artists on the international scene, is most impressive. Fritz Falk, then the director of the Schmuckmuseum (Jewellery Museum) Pforzheim in Germany, was the department's academic consultant (see box on page 96). Jewellery designers who came as guest lecturers included Stanley Lechtzin and Kurt Matzdorf from the United States; David Watkins, Wendy Ramshaw, Pierre Degen and Tony Laws from Britain; Gijs Bakker and Emmy van Leersum from the Netherlands; and Cornelia Rating and Claus Bury from Germany. Most guest lecturers taught at Bezalel for one trimester. Undoubtedly, these encounters with some of the most radical expounders of the New Jewellery movement left their mark on the students. Breaking jewellery-making conventions and stretching boundaries, these artists used a large variety of materials – including non-precious ones – to make pieces with simple, minimalist forms, often with some playful element (Dormer and Turner 1985).

A 1978 exhibition of works by students of the Bezalel gold- and silversmithing department travelled from the

3.51 Left: Arie Ofir, ring designed and made for H. Stern – Israel, 1973, 18-ct gold, synthetic diamond

3.52 Centre: Arie Ofir, ring designed and made for H. Stern – Israel, 1973, 18-ct gold, diamonds, pearl

3.53 Right: Arie Ofir, ring designed and made for H. Stern – Israel, 1973, 18-ct gold, pavé set diamonds

3.54 Left: Malka Cohavi, bangle inspired by New Guinea tribal art, 1975, wood, copper, included in the exhibition "Bezalel Academy Jerusalem", Schmuckmuseum Pforzheim, 1978

3.55 Right: Malka Cohavi, bracelet, 1975, silver, brass, copper, nickel silver, included in the exhibition "Bezalel Academy Jerusalem", Schmuckmuseum Pforzheim, 1978

Schmuckmuseum in Pforzheim to Hanau, Antwerp and the Electrum Gallery in London. Leafing through the catalogue of the exhibition, one notes a plethora of innovative works that could easily find their place on the contemporary, global art jewellery scene (Bezalel Academy 1978). Notable among the students showing in this exhibition was Vered Kaminski, who would become one of the leading jewellers in Israel (see below, Chapter 4). Malka Cohavi showed an architectonically inspired bracelet made of various metals (fig. 3.55), and an arm bracelet inspired by New Guinea tribal art (fig. 3.54). The bracelet was included in Oppi Untracht's book *Jewelry: Concepts and Technology* (1982, p. 213, fig. 6–166).

In addition to guest lecturers, many leading figures on the international scene of art jewellery were invited on visits to the department, allowing students the opportunity to forge international connections. Among them were Helen W. Drutt English, owner of the Helen Drutt Gallery in Philadelphia, Pennsylvania, USA, and Barbara Cartlidge, founder of the Electrum Gallery for contemporary art jewellery in London.

Outstanding among the designers who came to Bezalel as guest lecturers was **Claus Bury**, who left a significant mark on the department's creative spirit and thinking processes (Strauss 2007, pp. 96–107). Bury was a key participant in the New Jewellery movement. His jewellery merged gold and acrylic and he employed unique techniques to combine various metal alloys. He visited the Bezalel department twice, in 1975 and 1978. On his first visit, he took the students on a trip to the Judean Desert where, under his guidance, they created geometric human formations in the landscape. These served both the students and himself as inspiration for their jewellery making (figs. 3.56 a–g) (Bezalel Academy 1978; Dormer and Turner 1985, pp. 8–9). On his second visit to Israel, in 1978, Bury took the department teachers and students on a trip to the Sinai Desert. He lined up the students, who were holding sheets of fabric attached to wooden poles, in systematically changing variations. In this way he created fascinating forms in the desert landscape (figs. 3.57 a–d). The photographs of these human installations in the desert then became the starting point for a search for artistic forms that could be translated into the language of jewellery. In an article about the project, Bury describes it as a novel learning experience for both students and himself (Ofir and Bury 1978, pp. 31–38). Bury has left jewellery

3.56 a – g Scenes from a Bezalel trip to the Judean Desert guided by guest lecturer Claus Bury, 1975, courtesy of Claus Bury. Geometric human formations were created by the students in the open landscape.

3.57 a–d Scenes from a Bezalel trip to the Sinai Desert, guided by guest lecturer Claus Bury, 1978, courtesy of Claus Bury. Bury arranged students and teachers, holding sheets of fabric attached to wooden poles, in systematically changing variations.

making altogether since 1979 in favour of sculpture. As he writes to Dirk Allgaier, the publisher at Arnoldsche Art Publishers, Bury considers his Israeli experience instrumental in establishing his own sense of freedom, and as his "first step towards sculpture".[14]

While leading New Jewellery artists were visiting Israel and leaving their mark on the local scene, some local artists chose to study abroad, where they were naturally exposed to global trends and influenced by them. One such jeweller was **Maury Golan**. Born in Israel in 1941 to parents from the United States and Canada, it was only natural for him to decide to study in the United States. He started out by studying product design at the Museum College of Art in Philadelphia (which later changed its name to the Philadelphia College of Art). Soon, however, he switched to the crafts department, where he studied under Olaf Skoogfors, a Swedish-born American jeweller (1930–1975) who influenced him greatly.[15] Skoogfors, considered one of the deans of American jewellery (Strauss 2007, pp. 288–293), had an interest in organic forms and surface patterns. Golan, too, had an interest in sculptural forms and in the relationship between soft forms and rigid mechanical shapes. Skoogfors's influence is also evidenced by Golan's juxtaposition of rough and polished surfaces (fig. 3.59).

Golan subsequently continued his studies in the graduate programme established at the Tyler School of Art at Temple University, Philadelphia, by jewellery designer Stanley Lechtzin. Lechtzin was famous for pioneering an extensive use of electroforming. With his organic aesthetics and belief in applying industrial technology to making jewellery, he soon became Golan's mentor. While there, Golan met Albert Paley, a fellow student who became known for jewellery made by forging. Golan, too, designed jewellery using this technique (fig. 3.60). However, he had already become more interested in developing affordable jewellery and industrial production. After graduation, he taught at the Moore College of Art and Design, Philadelphia, until in 1970 he decided to return to Israel. On his return, he taught for a while at Bezalel and joined Maskit, where he developed the high-end gold-jewellery department. At the same time he set up

14_ Claus Bury in an e-mail to Dirk Allgaier, 13 March 2013.
15_ Maury Golan in an interview with the author, Tel Aviv, Israel, 2012.

Memories of Bezalel's gold- and silversmithing department under Arie Ofir

Fritz Falk Former director of the Schmuckmuseum Pforzheim (1971–2003), academic consultant to the department 1974–1980

Suddenly one day, in the summer of 1973, Arie Ofir – head of the gold- and silversmithing department at the Bezalel Academy of Art and Design in Jerusalem – appeared without advance notice in the lobby of the Schmuckmuseum Pforzheim, of which I was the director. He wanted to visit the international exhibition "Jewellery 73 – Trends" on view in the museum, and that is how we became personally acquainted. Our first encounter took place in my office. The answer to my queries about how long he hoped to stay in Pforzheim and whether he was already engaged for the evening were answered by Ofir arriving, flowers in hand, for the evening meal at my home. (Later, when I told the story in Jerusalem, the fact that he had brought flowers was met with a great deal of light-hearted interest, for in his home country it was not usual for him to observe such "conventional" practices.) The following day, Ofir went to Hanau, where he met Claus Bury (a meeting that would have far-reaching repercussions for both Bezalel and Bury). Shortly thereafter the Yom Kippur War broke out. Arie and I would not hear from one another again until the following March. In a letter, he wrote about the war – "it was terrible" – but at the same time invited me "to become a consultant to our department." My first trip to Israel took place just a few weeks later (fig. 3.58).

Bezalel's gold- and silversmithing department was quite well equipped with the necessary tools but hardly had any of the usual new technical aids available by then in other places. However – and this is what really mattered – it was bursting with unbridled enthusiasm, energy and drive. These can be credited to the charismatic personality of the head of the department, Arie Ofir, who had then only held the post for a year. Thanks to his charisma, the young people, despite their inexperience and lack of hands-on knowledge of what was happening in their field abroad, were nonetheless enthusiastically doing their best to try out things that were new to them. The simple tools and lack of a foundation training course (hardly any of the students had served a thorough apprenticeship in the German sense of the term or had had similar professional experience) cried out for basic crafts training alongside schooling in art and aesthetics. Yet the sheer boundless creativity of the individual students was remarkable even in those early days.

In my opinion, the department presented a successful balancing act between tradition and modernism. Ofir never tired of instilling in his students the need to accept the challenges of the present while at the same time developing one's own personal, individual "style". Since the time Ofir took over the department, distinguished exponents of the field from around the world shared their knowledge and skills with the Bezalel students. Under his management, a strong sense of Israeli identity and self-awareness was combined in the department with open-mindedness to global art. Most of the students were born in Israel, but young people from other countries were also among their numbers. Ofir described this special situation in his introduction to the little catalogue accompanying the 1978 exhibition "Bezalel Academy Jerusalem: Jewellery and Silversmithing Department", which travelled from Pforzheim to Hanau, Antwerp and London. "Thanks to the presence of exceptional cultural diversity," he writes, "Israel is fortunate in being in a special situation, which is also attested to by the broad range of nationalities within our student body and a corresponding plurality of artistic influences" (Falk 1978). That is how it was then, and so it seems to have remained to the present day!

3.58 Fritz Falk (second from right) at Bezalel, Jerusalem, 1974, with Prof. Dan Hoffner (on his right) and Arie Ofir (on his left)

a Maskit workshop to produce silver jewellery, some of which he himself designed in a modernist line, using local raw materials, such as Eilat stones. This series of jewellery won two of the Israel Export Institute prizes. Golan also travelled to international fairs in order to market the pieces abroad. His early designs in Israel still show the influence of his Philadelphia years. Another strong influence is found in a 1974 brooch that looks like a burst sphere (fig. 3.61). Golan made several versions of this brooch, which also lent its form to his company's logo. The burst-sphere motif, which recalls a split fruit revealing its seeds, received its inspiration from Arnaldo Pomodoro's sculpture *Sphere within Sphere* (also made in several versions). The brooch makes evident Golan's interest in sculptural forms and in contrasts – both the contrast between the smooth surface and the torn edges, and between the form's exterior and what is happening within (figs. 3.62, 3.63).

From functionalism to expressiveness and decorativeness

The 1960s and 1970s were crucial in the formation of new directions in jewellery making in Israel. After many years of severe formal and functionalistic design, a young generation of jewellery makers in search of new possibilities developed different concepts. They moved from rigid formalism to a free style character-

This and opposite page, clockwise from far left:

3.59 Maury Golan, brooch, 1970s, forged 18-ct gold, moonstone

3.60 Maury Golan, necklace, 1960s, cast and forged sterling silver, moonstone

3.61 Maury Golan, brooch, 1960s, sterling silver, 14-ct gold, constructed

3.62 Maury Golan, man's ring, 1970s, 14-ct gold cast from balsa wood

3.63 Maury Golan, brooch, 1960s, sterling silver cast from Styrofoam, citrine crystal

ised by romantic expressiveness. After years of modernism, jewellery artists in Israel allowed themselves to look back on tradition for inspiration. In a country of immigrants like Israel, diverse ethnic traditions on which one could draw were prevalent. At the same time, the arrival in Bezalel of some of the foremost designers of the New Jewellery movement also left its mark on the local jewellery scene.

In a way, the little-known jewellers of the 1960s and 1970s paved the way for the international recognition gained in the late 1970s and 1980s by leading Israeli jewellery artists. Four internationally renowned Israeli artists will be discussed in detail in the fourth chapter of this book.

Proliferation, 1980s

Israeli industrial jewellery manufacturers began proliferating in the 1980s and continued to do so through the 1990s. They also gained recognition among international buyers (as evidenced by Export Institute catalogues published during those years).

A remarkable company established in the 1980s prospers to this day, and its story is heart-warming. **Yvel** (an anagram of Levy) was established in Jerusalem in 1986 by Orna and Isaac Levy. In 2010 they moved their enterprise to Motza Tachtit, on the outskirts of Jerusalem. Orna comes from a long line of jewellers from the Moussaieff family. Her great-grandfather was a goldsmith in Bukhara, Uzbekistan. When he immigrated to Palestine over a hundred years ago he opened a jewellery shop in the Old City of Jerusalem. Her grandfather imported pearls from Japan to Europe and Israel, and her mother also sold jewellery in the shop she opened at the King David Hotel in Jerusalem. As Orna Levy puts it, she was "born into the jewellery scene."[16] Her childhood love of the pearls imported by her grandfather is manifested in the company she opened with her husband,

3.64 Yvel, brooch, 2007, natural white, wild freshwater pearls, set with diamonds in 18-ct white gold. Winner of the *Town and Country* Couture Design Award, 2007.

which specialises in designing and manufacturing high-end gold and pearl jewellery. The design of Yvel pieces is bold, free and breaks tradition. Orna and Isaac Levy prefer amorphously shaped pearls to round ones and design their pieces around them. The conceptual design is theirs, and they are helped by other designers and silversmiths. Apart from casting, the company produces every stage in the pieces' manufacturing. Yvel has thrice received the prestigious *Town & Country* Couture Design Award for its unique designs – in 2005, 2006 and 2007 (fig. 3.64).

Yvel employees – about fifty professionals – are mostly newly arrived immigrants from various countries, and this ties in with the life story of Isaac Levy. He himself immigrated to Israel with his family at the age of four. As newcomers, they lived in a transit camp and experienced hardship. This has made him sensitive to the needs of immigrants. Wishing to give back to society, the Levys established a jewellery-making school adjacent to the workshop, where immigrants – mostly of Ethiopian extraction, the most disenfranchised among immigrants to Israel – learn a profession that allows them to be gainfully employed. Each student gets a monthly stipend and on graduating, receives a certificate from the Ministry of Industry and Commerce. Some leave for jobs in other places, and some find employment in the adjacent Yvel workshop.

Another company which was immensely successful in the 1980s and 1990s was **Golan Fine Crafts**. After Maury Golan (whose work as a jeweller was discussed earlier in this chapter) left Maskit, he established the company in 1977 with two partners. It became a leading company in the industry, producing cast, embossed and electroformed gold jewellery designed by Golan (fig. 3.65). The company's products ranged from "lightweight" pieces, through jewellery inlaid with semi-precious stones, to diamond-studded pieces. The jewellery was sold mainly in the United States and Japan. Gili Golan, Maury's daughter, also a jewellery designer, joined the company in 1994. The company flourished, reaching a turnover of 22 million dollars a year by the end of 1995. Unfortunately, the economic climate at the turn of the century meant that many companies had to shut down. One of the companies which suffered this fate was Golan Fine Crafts. By the end of the 1990s it encountered liquidity problems and was finally dissolved.[17]

3.65 A page from the 1997 catalogue of Golan Fine Crafts, a company engaged in designing, manufacturing and marketing 8-ct to 18-ct gold jewellery, using casting, stamping and electroforming

16_ Orna Levy in an interview with the author, Jerusalem, Israel, 2012.

17_ In 2003 Maury Golan made another attempt at a new company, Golan Goldex, co-founded with David Tiber of Goldex. It produced varied collections in silver and fashion jewellery. Lately, unable to compete globally, it too was dissolved.

4 International Recognition

Bianca Eshel Gershuni
Vered Kaminski
Esther Knobel
Deganit Stern Schocken

4 International Recognition

Bianca Eshel Gershuni
Vered Kaminski
Esther Knobel
Deganit Stern Schocken

This chapter is devoted to four internationally renowned Israeli jewellery artists: Bianca Eshel Gershuni, Vered Kaminski, Esther Knobel and Deganit Stern Schocken. Each of these artists has her own unique language. They have all participated in international exhibitions and their work has been included in various books on contemporary jewellery, as well as in private and public collections around the world.[1]

Bianca Eshel Gershuni

Bianca Eshel Gershuni spearheaded the breakthrough in the field of art jewellery in Israel. In the 1970s she started making pieces that freely combined gold with feathers, tar, plastic, aluminium foil and pearls, often incorporating found objects as well. This innovative mixture of precious, "high" materials and common, "low" ones was a breath of fresh air on the local scene, which until then had only featured either ethnic jewellery from Islamic lands or the pure forms of modernist and Scandinavian design. Eshel Gershuni made large, colourful, expressive pieces, to be worn in unusual ways – extremely large pendants and brooches, rings for several fingers, bracelets for the back of the hand (from wrist to fingers) and earrings that partially covered the face. The pieces were mostly figurative and narrative and had a ritual aspect which touched on the ancient role of jewellery as an amulet with magical powers.

Eshel Gershuni was born in Sofia, Bulgaria, in 1932. She immigrated to Israel with her parents in 1939, escaping from the Nazis after her father, a textile industrialist, had been blacklisted by them. Like many immigrant children, she made every effort to become integrated into her new land and break away from her country of birth. From 1958 to 1964 she studied art at the Avni Institute of Art and Design in Tel Aviv. She started making jewellery for her own use. While still a student at the Avni Institute, a friend showed her how to work with metal, and from that point on she continued as a self-taught artist. On graduation, she stopped sculpting and turned to jewellery making even though she had never had any formal training in metal work.

1_ In 2006 they held a joint exhibition, "Women's Tales: Four Leading Israeli Jewelers", organised by the Racine Art Museum in Racine, Wisconsin, in collaboration with the Israel Museum, Jerusalem. It was on view in both museums and travelled to several US venues (Taragin, Ward and Drutt English 2006).

4.1 Bianca Eshel Gershuni, necklace, 1966, silver, glass, corals, 24.0 × 24.0 cm

4.2 Bianca Eshel Gershuni, pendant, early 1960s, silver, copper, glass beads, 9.0 × 3.0 cm

Eshel Gershuni immediately gained acclaim, participating in exhibitions and being awarded prizes for her work. She won First Prize at a competition for designing bracelets which was held by the Israel Export Institute in the late 1960s. Professor Karl Schollmayer, director of the Schmuckmuseum Pforzheim in Germany, became acquainted with her work during a visit to Israel. He was impressed by it and bought several pieces for his museum, also referring to her work in his book *Neuer Schmuck* (New Jewellery) (Schollmayer 1974, pp. 97–102, pls. 303–305). In 1971 she won the Gold Medal at the Sonderschau in Munich (fig. 4.7), and in 1977 she participated in the exhibition "Trends" in Pforzheim, Germany. In Israel, she showed and sold her work at the Spilo-Yaglom Gallery in Jaffa and in Maskit. Despite being a self-taught jeweller, she taught at the gold- and silversmithing department in Bezalel from 1986 to 1997. Throughout her career, she has intermittently pursued painting, ceramic sculpting and jewellery making. These pursuits are manifested in the contents and visual language of her jewellery pieces. They are functional and wearable yet also have an autonomous presence as sculptural objects.

Eshel Gershuni's first pieces, from the 1960s, were made of silver or copper (Fischer 1966, pp. 28–37). She started out with ethnically-flavoured flat pendants made of copper wire (fig. 4.2), at times incorporating blue ceramic beads and leather straps. Gradually, she made the transition to more volumetric, imaginary organic forms (fig. 4.1). Influenced by her friend Shmuel Mestechkin, a Bauhaus graduate who designed many buildings for the kibbutz movement, she also made architectonically inspired pieces: *Castles* with medieval motifs (fig. 4.3) and a piece she called *Saddle* (fig. 4.4), inspired by the saddle roof of the Hebrew University swimming pool, which was designed by Mestechkin.[2]

Eshel Gershuni showed her first silver pieces (figs. 4.5, 4.6) in a 1966 one-person show at the Masada Gallery in Tel Aviv. By the 1970s, she was already working in gold, which became her signature material. Her treatment of gold is primal and sensuous, showing the imprint of her manual work process (figs. 4.7, 4.11). Although her work is quite different from his, Griegst's influence is quite evident in Eshel Gershuni's pieces. During his stay in Israel she became acquainted with his style, and his influence is manifested in her fascination with the Baroque and Romanticism and in her softly curved, lively forms. In 1977 Yona Fischer, then the curator of contemporary Israeli art at the Israel Museum, Jerusalem, curated a show of Eshel Gershuni's jewellery pieces at the museum, which later travelled to the Museum of Decorative Art in Copenhagen (Fischer 1977).

As mentioned above, Eshel Gershuni's assemblages combine uniquely fabricated gold with common materials and found objects that are not habitually used in jewellery making (figs. 4.8–4.10, 4.13–4.15). A fine

2_ All remarks by Bianca Eshel Gershuni are from an interview with the author, Ra'anana, Israel, 2008.

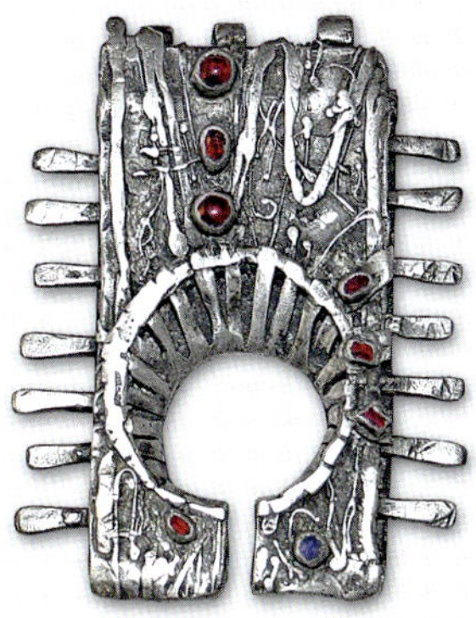

4.3 Top left: Bianca Eshel Gershuni, pendant from the series "Castles", early 1960s, silver, 9.0 × 9.0 cm

4.5 Bottom left: Bianca Eshel Gershuni, pendant, 1960s, silver, garnets, 8.0 × 6.3 cm

4.4 Top right: Bianca Eshel Gershuni, *Saddle*, pendant, early 1960s, silver, opals, 9.5 × 10.0 cm

4.6 Bottom right: Bianca Eshel Gershuni, *Bird's Nest*, brooch, 1960s, silver, agates, diam. 9.0 cm

4.7 Bianca Eshel Gershuni, necklace, 1971, 24-ct and 18-ct gold, pearls, rubies, 20.0 × 15.0 × 3.7 cm. Gold Medal winner at the Sonderschau in Munich.

4.8 Bianca Eshel Gershuni, earring, 1976, gold, feathers, plastic, mirror, coral, pearl, 20.0 × 17.0 cm

4.9 Bianca Eshel Gershuni, two-finger ring, 1977, 18-ct and 24-ct gold, white coral, feathers, mirror, plastic, 6.6 × 7.6 × 3.5 cm

4.10 Bianca Eshel Gershuni, *My Grave*, ring, 1977, 18-ct and 24-ct gold, plastic, plaster, feathers, pearls, paint, 6.3 × 12.0 × 3.8 cm

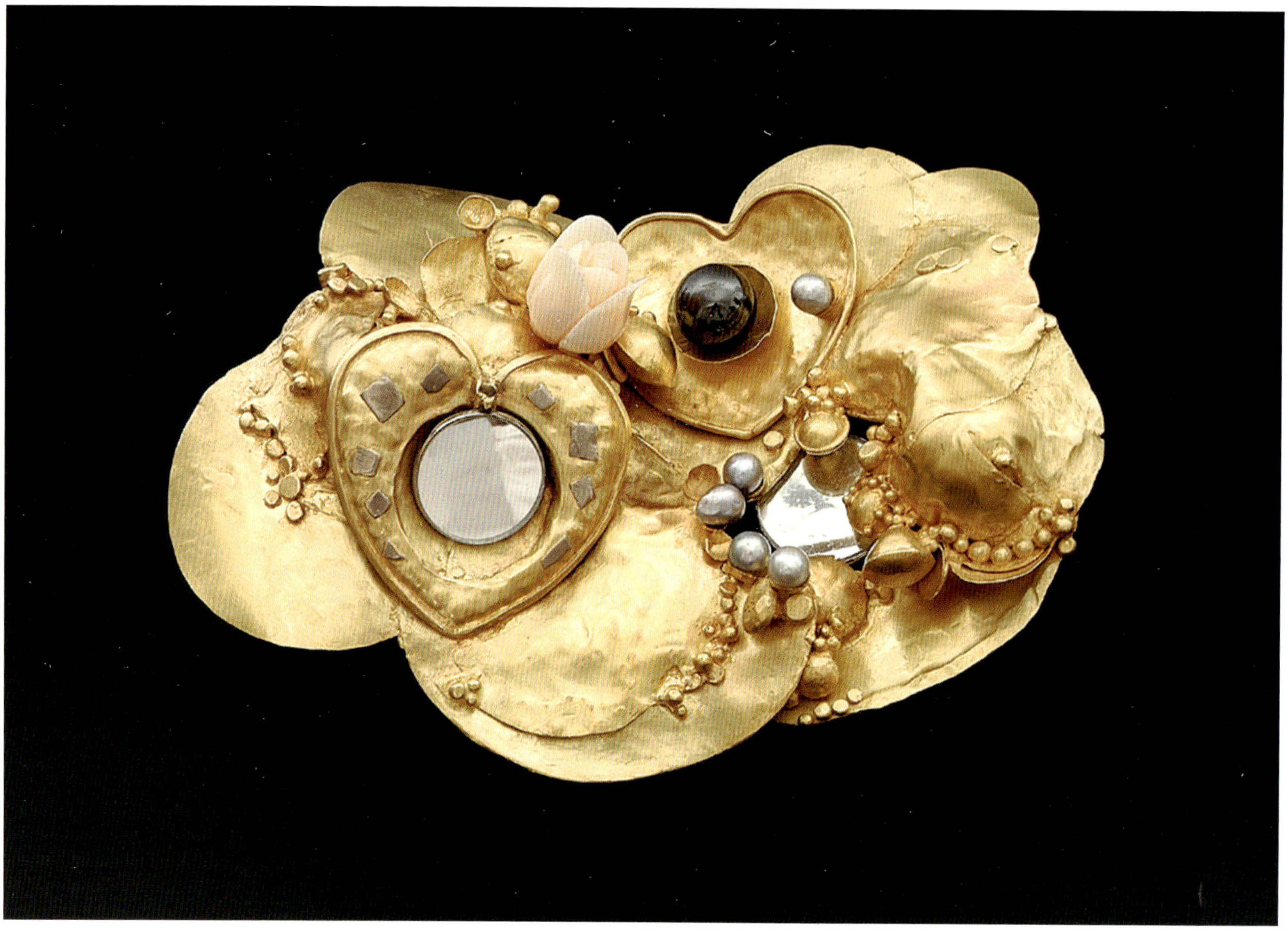

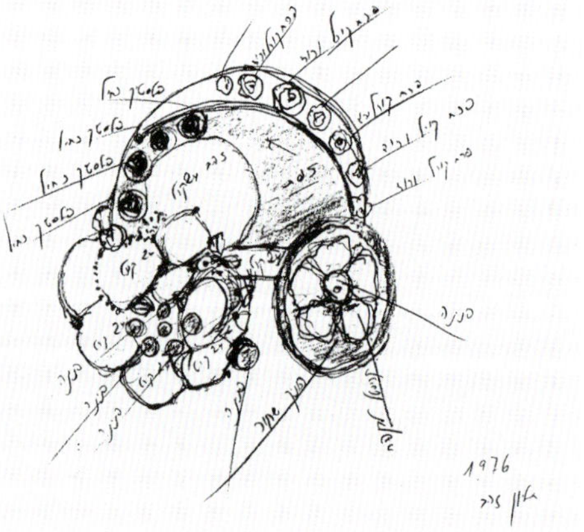
1976

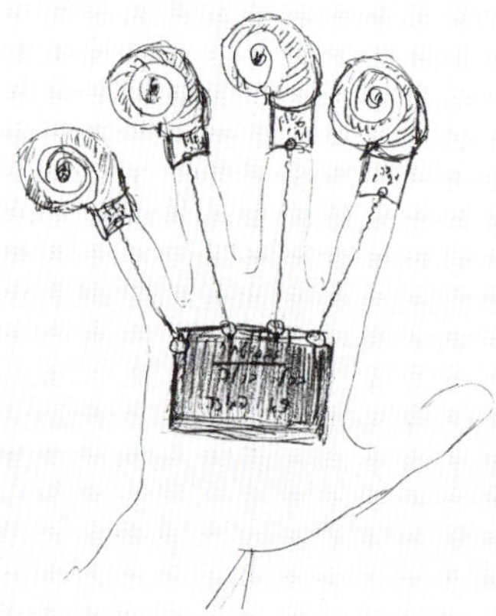

This and opposite page, clockwise from top left:

4.11 Bianca Eshel Gershuni, pendant, 1974, 18-ct gold, black pearl, coral, mirrors, white gold, 11.2 × 15.0 × 4.0 cm

4.12 a, b Bianca Eshel Gershuni, bracelet (two views), *c.* 1970, 18-ct to 24-ct gold, coral, pearls, collection of Helen W. Drutt English, Philadelphia, Pennsylvania

4.13 Bianca Eshel Gershuni, pendant (detail), 1976, gold, lapis lazuli, 11.0 × 13.0 cm

4.14 Bianca Eshel Gershuni, sketch for *Snail Rings* (glove and snail shells), 1976, pencil on paper (Fischer 1977, no. 29)

4.15 Bianca Eshel Gershuni, sketch for a pendant, 1976, pencil on paper (Fischer 1977, no. 26)

4.16 Top: Bianca Eshel Gershuni, brooch, 1995, silver, 18-ct and 24-ct gold, snail shell, pearls, paint, 10.0 × 10.0 cm

4.17 Bottom: Bianca Eshel Gershuni, brooch, 1995, silver, glass, red crystals, 18-ct gold, paint, 8.0 × 8.0 cm

example of her early gold pieces with corals and pearls is a bracelet, recently acquired by Helen Drutt English (figs. 4.12 a, b).[3] The imagery of her early pieces is fascinating, combining diverse images such as animals (sheep, dogs, snails, rabbits) and tombs (figs. 4.10, 4.14, 4.16). Gideon Ofrat (1978) offers an in-depth analysis of her work in the article "Longing for the Good Forest". He points out her fascination with decadence and claims that "a morbid aspect … informs her pieces", adding that the domesticated, cute animals and flowers express, in his view, "a longing for the lost paradise that was her distant childhood" (Ofrat 1978, p. 29). Eshel Gershuni's free use of materials and original, unconventional craft work has left a considerable impact on the Israeli jewellery scene, and her influence is still in evidence in the work of young jewellery artists, such as Shirly Bar-Amotz (see below, Chapter 5) (Fishof 2012a, p. 103).

Like her work in other media, Eshel Gershuni's jewellery pieces are laden with autobiographical elements, mixing personal stories with pagan, folklore and Christian motifs. Her work emits an aura of shamanistic healing, combining tribal elements, such as voodoo feathers, and Christian symbols, such as the cross and the Lamb. Two painful events have left their mark on her. In 1956 her first husband, an Israel Defence Forces pilot, died in the Sinai War. She was left a young widow, the mother of a young girl. In the 1980s her second husband, renowned painter Moshe Gershuni and father of her two sons, left her on realising his attraction to men. Eshel Gershuni coped through artistic creation. In 1985 she held an exhibition at the Tel Aviv Museum of Art, showing large sculptural platforms and small works, which the exhibition curator, Sarah Breitberg-Semel, dubbed "fetishes". "These were make-up chests of sorts (*vanitas* chests)," Breitberg-Semel (1995, p. 18) recalls a decade later, "which contained animal furs, bloody, dead plastic animals pierced by pins, and photographs of you and your ex-husband Moshe Gershuni, marked with a bloody cross." Subsequently Eshel Gershuni returned to jewellery making, creating a series of round brooches, some with erotic imagery, each of which told a personal, emotive story (figs. 4.16, 4.17).

3_ This bracelet, which was exhibited at the Electrum Gallery, London, was later in the possession of Kurt Egger, a German collector of contemporary jewellery, and Drutt English acquired it from his estate.

4.18 Bianca Eshel Gershuni, brooches, 1991, silver, shell, mirror, paint, photograph, found objects, pearl, plastic. These fish-airplane brooches were made during the Gulf War.

The series was exhibited at the Sara Levi Gallery in 1990 (Ron 1990, pp. 12–13). Art critic and psychotherapist Mordechai Geldman (2007, p. 20) wrote about these brooches: "It seems that following the tumultuous crises in Bianca Eshel Gershuni's life, which were reflected in her work, she has striven to 'return to herself', reorganise and regroup. This was facilitated by her return to jewellery and the Mandala form, which has lent her work an aspect of healing and reconstruction."

4.19 Bianca Eshel Gershuni, brooch, 1985, 18-ct and 24-ct gold, jade, pearls, enamel, turquoise, coral, onyx, 11.4 x 11.4 x 3.2 cm

Crises in the local public arena have also found expression in Eshel Gershuni's work. At the beginning of 1991, during the Gulf War, when missiles were falling in central Israel and TV news was full of images of military aircraft dropping bombs, she tried to calm herself by making fish-shaped brooches. Soon, however, the fish turned into bomber aircraft (fig. 4.18). In one of the brooches, the bombs were made of bottles of Givenchy perfume for men. As Eshel Gershuni recounts, the events of that evening triggered a resurgence of the feelings of grief over her first husband's death.

In the 1990s, Eshel Gershuni adopted the tortoise as a key motif in her work, which figured in many of her sculptures and mixed-media brooches (fig. 4.19). The first intimations of this motif had already appeared in her 1960s silver brooches, as well as in her 1980s work. The artist identifies with the tortoise's slowness, its burrowing under the home it carries on its back, and the wisdom it accumulates over many years of life.

In 2009 Eshel Gershuni was awarded the Israeli Ministry of Culture and Sport's Lifetime Achievement Award. In 2010 her son, photographer Uri Gershuni, curated an extensive retrospective of her work at Inga Gallery of Contemporary Art, Tel Aviv.

Vered Kaminski

Vered Kaminski's jewellery language is composed of fences, nets, stones, mosaics, trees, mobiles, loops and soap bubbles. She also uses branching and merging and visual models of exponential progression. Experimenting playfully, she builds models and explores flat and three-dimensional constructions. With meticulous, painstaking manual craftsmanship she constructs experimental objects, which are then realised as wearable jewellery pieces, such as brooches, pendants, bracelets, rings and earrings. In the 1990s, she also made bowls and baskets, and occasionally Judaica objects (Jewish ceremonial art), but jewellery making has always been her main pursuit.

Kaminski often incorporates common, inexpensive materials in her work, such as wire (at times unravelling metal wire mesh and using the unravelled wire), or gravel stones found on the streets of Jerusalem. She treats simple stones as if they were precious ones, setting them in a way that endows them with a prestigious appearance (figs. 4.20, 4.21). Kaminski is inspired not only by the most banal objects around her but by the overall aesthetics of her surroundings – the pale, soft hues of the stone of which all Jerusalem buildings are built is reflected in her work. But her main source of inspiration is nature. She is enchanted by both stones and metals (while living in Paris, she says, she used to spend a lot of time in a shop where building materials were sold).[4]

Kaminski was born in 1953 on Kibbutz Revadim, to Holocaust survivors from Poland. She studied at Bezalel's gold- and silversmithing department from 1975 to 1979, when Arie Ofir headed it. Thanks to the department's international connections forged by Ofir, her work gained global exposure when she was still a student. In 1978 she participated in the department's exhibition at the Schmuckmuseum Pforzheim (Bezalel Academy 1978). The exhibition later travelled to other venues in Europe – Hanau, Antwerp and London (see above, Chapter 3).

Kaminski went on to study in the jewellery department of the Gerrit Rietveld Academie in Amsterdam

4.20 Top: Vered Kaminski, brooch, 2010, silver, turquoise, 7.0 × 7.0 × 1.0 cm. Presented by Israel's President Shimon Peres to German Chancellor Angela Merkel, 2010.

4.21 Bottom: Vered Kaminski, brooch, 1991, stones, brass, 6.0 × 6.0 × 1.0 cm

4_ Vered Kaminski in an interview with the author, Jerusalem, Israel, 2012.

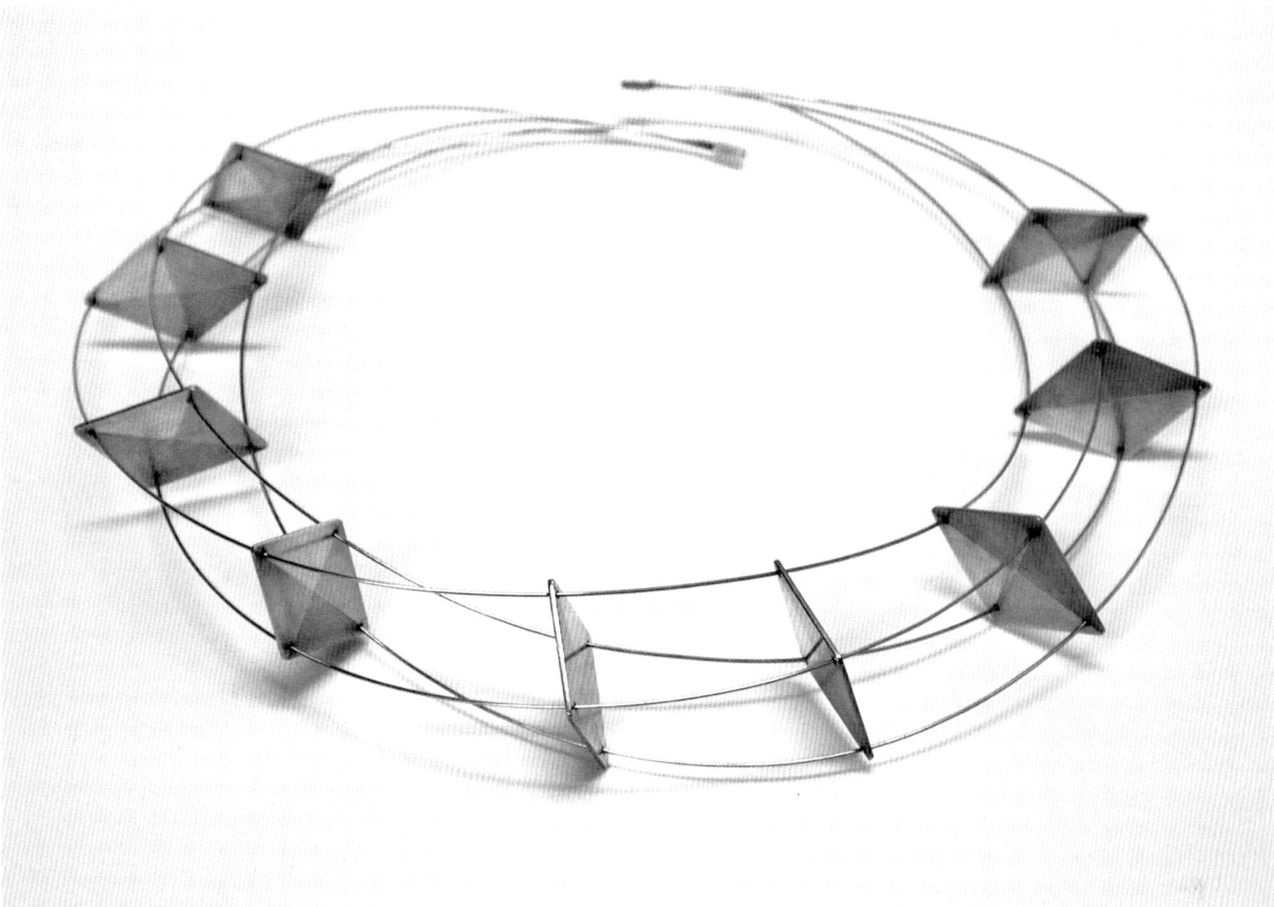

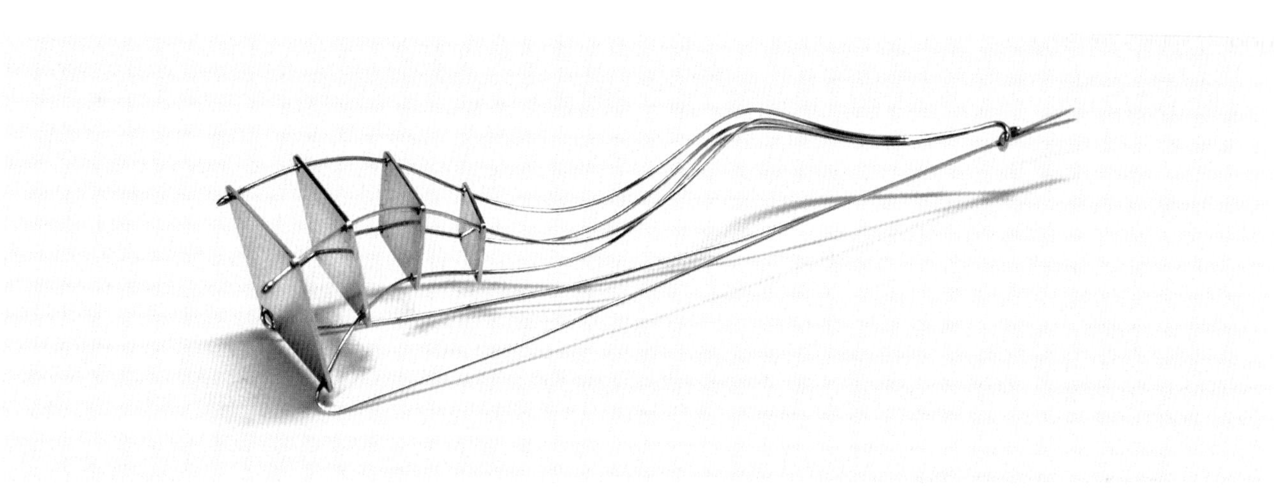

4.22 Top: Vered Kaminski, necklace, 1981, stainless steel, silver, brass, copper, nickel silver, 17.0 × 17.0 × 3.0 cm

4.23 Bottom: Vered Kaminski, brooch, 1981, silver, 13.0 × 2.5 × 2.4 cm

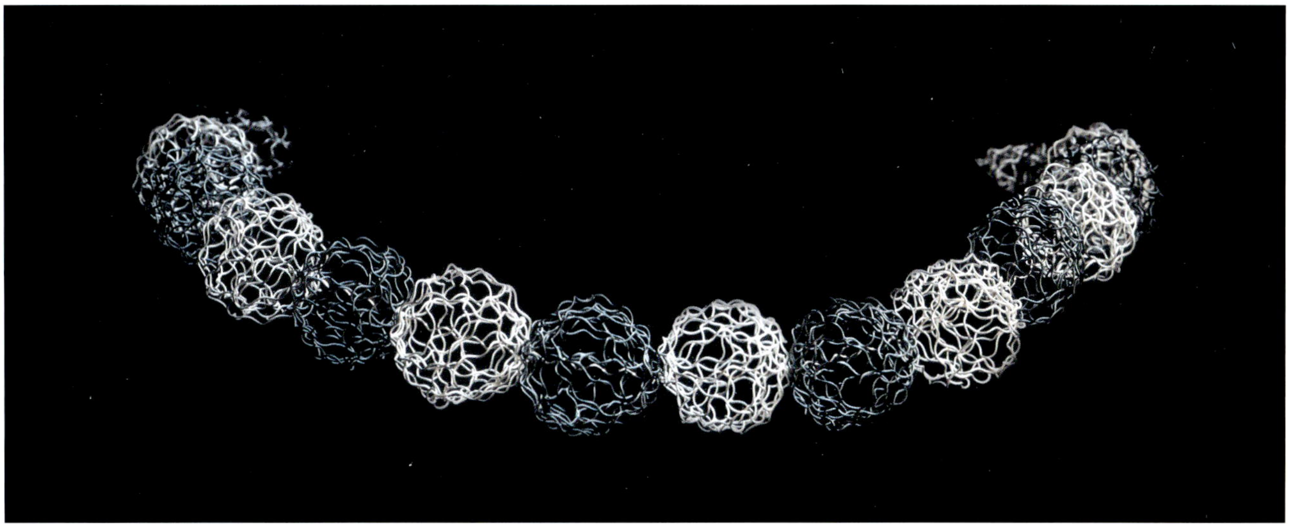

4.24 Top: Vered Kaminski, necklace, 1985, silver, 25.0 × 2.0 cm

4.25 Bottom: Vered Kaminski, bracelet, 1987, silver, diam. 13.5, h. 3.0 cm

from 1979 to 1980, where she met several members of the New Jewellery movement in Europe. The department was then headed by Onno Boekhoudt,[5] and Joke Brakman[6] was a faculty member.

Kaminski was gaining recognition in Europe already in 1980. She was invited to participate in the Schmuck International 1900–1980 exhibition in Vienna, where she showed, among other pieces, a sophisticated, shape-changing bracelet. In 1981 she had a joint show with Esther Knobel at the Ra Gallery in Amsterdam, where she showed works that were a further development of a series she had made in Claus Bury's workshop at Bezalel (figs. 4.22, 4.23) (see above, Chapter 3).

Kaminski's interest in visual and material textures became more focused during her studies for a master's degree at the University of Paris VIII from 1986 to 1988. As part of her final work, she researched the formal components of Paris's fences, lattices and gates. A silver necklace and a bracelet she made during this period reflect this research (figs. 4.24, 4.25). The knotted, variously coiled silver wire of the lattice forms are an intimation of the knots and loops that would become a recurrent motif in her later work. On her return to Israel in 1988 she became a teacher at the gold- and silversmithing department, which was then headed by Alex Ward.

Kaminski's work process involves meticulous planning. In order to make a bracelet of woven silver wire, for instance, she first sketches a three-dimensional model in flattened form and then weaves it without any soldering (fig. 4.26). In a similar way, she approached the making of her series "Branchings and Mergings"

5_ Onno Boekhoudt (1944–2002) was a Dutch jewellery designer known as an inspiring teacher, who was more interested in the work process than in the end result.

6_ Joke Brakman (born 1946) was one of the leading Dutch jewellery artists in the 1980s, known for her wearable fabric pieces.

4.26 Vered Kaminski, bracelet, 2003, silver, 10.0 × 1.5 cm. This bracelet was made without any soldering.

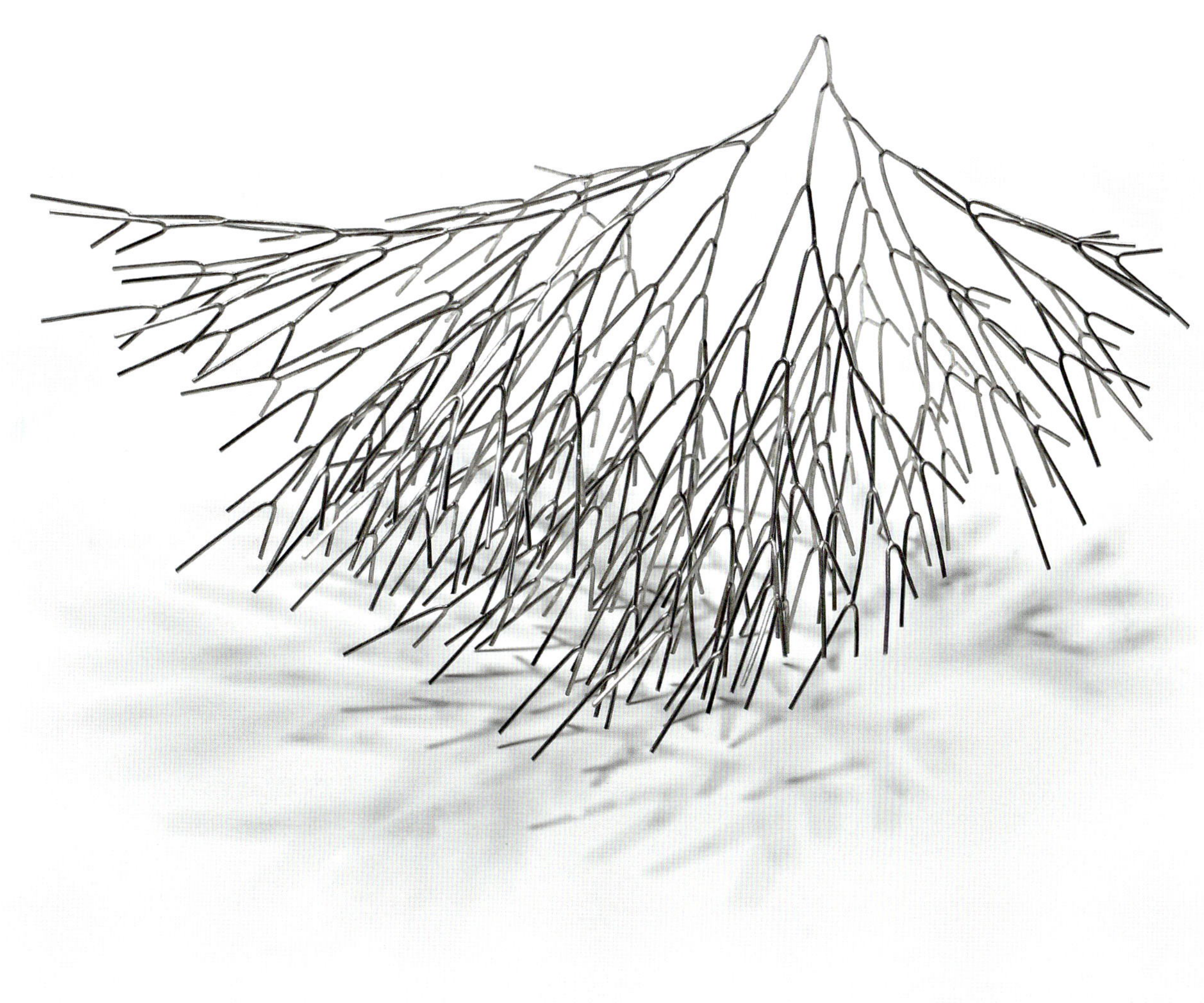

4.27 Vered Kaminski, *2⁸*, object, 2000, silver, 15.0 × 12.0 × 9.0 cm

4.28 Vered Kaminski, *2×2*[7], earrings, 2005, 18-ct gold, 9.5 × 4.0 × 3.5 cm

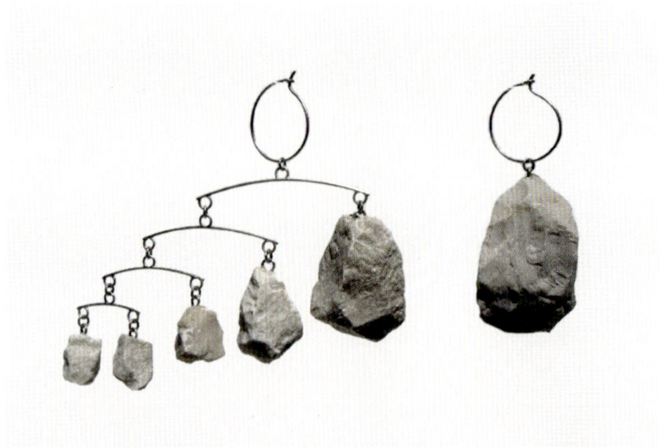

4.29 Top: Vered Kaminski, earrings, 2008, silver, stones, 5.0 × 6.5 × 1.5 cm, 5.0 × 2.0 × 2.0 cm

4.30 Bottom: Vered Kaminski, earrings, 2012, olive wood, stainless steel, 7.0 × 7.0 × 2.0 cm. Made from a readymade olive-wood camel.

(2007) like a mathematician formulating a model of exponential progression (Tamir 2007; Tamir 2010). This theme engaged her for several years. In the mid-1990s she started building models that explored the phenomenon of branching in nature. For instance, she made an upside-down tree of brass wires that branched out from one another – an object conforming to the model of 2^8 (fig. 4.27). She also applied the notion of branching to functional jewellery, such as the *2×2*[7] earrings (fig. 4.28) or the *Mobile* earrings, which were based on a precise calculation of weight and distance in order to produce balance (figs. 4.29, 4.30).

But alongside this planning, the element of surprise is also an important part of Kaminski's creative process. It is only on splitting open a stone, for instance, that she learns what colours or streaks are hidden within. It takes countless attempts to discover one that contains an interesting shape, attractive "veins" or unexpected colourful stains. Thus came into being the brooches whose split-open stone is reminiscent of the shape of butterfly wings (fig. 4.31). In addition, Kaminski created works of art that consisted of large surfaces on which the split (or broken) stones were arranged according to their colours.

4.31 Vered Kaminski, brooches, 2008, stones, silver, stainless steel, 2.0–3.0 × .5–4.0 cm

The duality of planning and surprise is also evident in a recent series of pendants by Kaminski, made in 2011 (figs. 4.36, 4.37).[7] Woven in silver and copper wire, these are figurative yet somewhat abstracted figures. The faces are featureless and the hair is connected to the hands. Kaminski's work process adheres to the rules of weaving: wires must go above and below one another as in warp and weft, and the holes must be of approximately equal size. She says that she is guided by the weaving process. Thus, although the works were originally flat (fig. 4.34), technical issues and chance "mistakes" led her to an exploration of three-dimensionality. Recognisable forms ensued, but as soon as her work became too mimetic she changed it, purposely avoiding figurativeness or narrative that was too explicit.

In June 2012 Kaminski showed some works from this series in the exhibition "Cycles of Mishap" at the Ra Gallery in Amsterdam. In an introductory essay to the exhibition, Paul Derrez (2012, n.p.) notes her "playing with order and spontaneity", a combination of "uncompromisingly arranged … geometric patterns" and "unexpected images and three-dimensional, abstract forms [that] occurred spontaneously."

7_ The series was exhibited at Gallery Loupe, Montclair, New Jersey, in 2011 (Taragin 2012, p. 55).

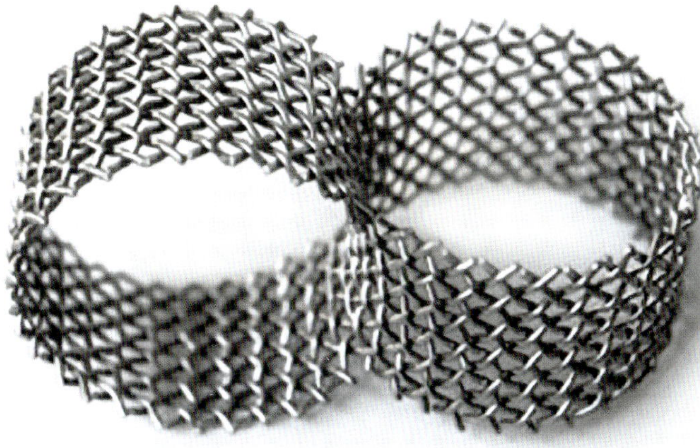

4.32 Left: Vered Kaminski, necklace, 2010, nickel silver, bronze, 18.0 × 13.0 × 0.5 cm. Inspired by an ancient Greek necklace from 400 BC.

4.33 a, b Right: Vered Kaminski, bracelets, 1998, stainless steel, 14.0 × 14.0 × 7.5 cm, 10.0 × 10.0 × 7.0 cm

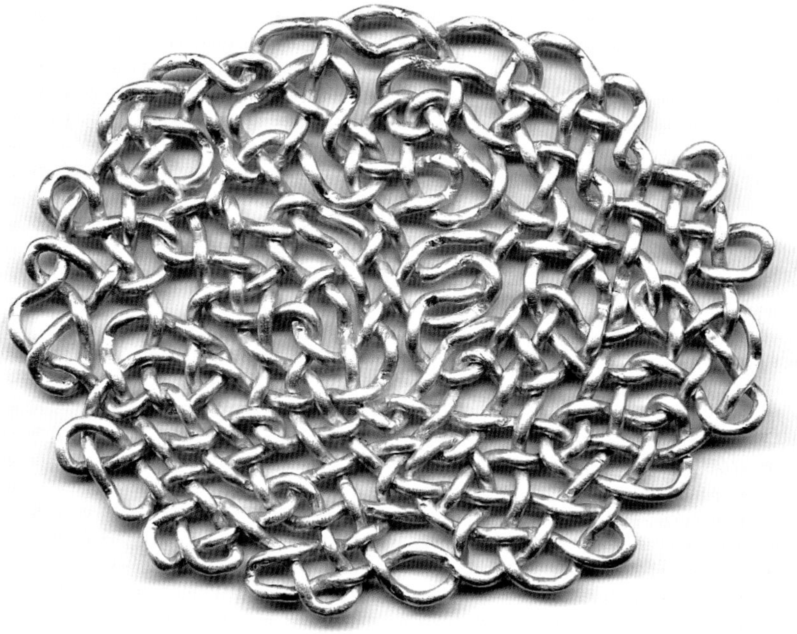

4.34 Vered Kaminski, brooch, 2011, silver, stainless steel, 7.2 × 5.6 × 0.3 cm

During one of our meetings, in early 2012, Kaminski told me about her fascination with the repetitive aspect and the aesthetics of knots. Her exploration of repetitive patterns has led her to the knot theory in mathematics.[8] This interest ties in with the appeal that the Hercules Knot – a key motif in ancient Hellenistic and, prior to that, Egyptian jewellery – holds for her. Kaminski often draws inspiration from the history of jewellery, a subject she is very familiar with and teaches at Bezalel. In her own words, she "draws on historical motifs and notions." Magical powers of healing were attributed to the Hercules Knot, a symbol of strength and protection. Believing the function of jewellery to have remained the same throughout history, Kaminski, too, regards some of her pieces as having the power to protect and strengthen their wearer.

In setting stones through metal wire Kaminski is also inspired by the history of jewellery, but in her

8_ When Kaminski showed this recent series in the "Israeli Jewellery 6" exhibition (June 2012), the exhibition's curator Nirith Nelson referred in her catalogue article to Kaminski's interest in the knot theory. She quotes Israeli mathematician Robert J. Aumann (2005 Nobel laureate in economic sciences), who has studied this theory, as expressing surprise at the practical applications of this purely scientific theory (Nelson 2012, pp. 63e, 128–130).

4.35 a, b Vered Kaminski, pendants, 2010, silver, copper, 8.5 × 8.5 × 0.5 cm (left), 9.0 × 9.0 × 1.0 cm (right)

case, the stone settings are usually made up of simple Jerusalem stones, such as may be found in the street. Her head-pendants necklace (fig. 4.32), too, draws on historical precedents, Greek pendants of heads which may possibly symbolise the decapitation of enemies. Kaminski's female heads dangle from a choker like heads on a boastful hunter's belt (Fishof 2012b, pp. 13–14, 96).

Kaminski's use of repetitive Islamic ornamentation is related to several of her interests. The repetitive patterns and knots (figs. 4.35 a, b) draw both on the history of art and on her immediate environment. As she explains it, this Islamic ornamentation is a means of connecting with her Arab neighbours. She finds that her work has a lot in common with Islamic art: meditative repetitiveness, and great investment of labour rather than costly materials.

In Kaminski's work, a banal element of public space turns into a new, unexpected aesthetic. Likewise, she

4.36 Left: Vered Kaminski, pendant, 2012, silver, copper, 12.5 × 11.0 × 3.5 cm

4.37 Right: Vered Kaminski, pendant, 2010, silver, copper, 10.5 × 11.0 × 3.0 cm

4.38 Vered Kaminski, brooches and locket, 2000, silver, stainless steel, 1.5 × 1.0 × 0.5 to 3.0 × 2.5 × 1.5 cm

adopted the idea of the large steel nets which were affixed to car windscreens during the first intifada to protect travellers from the stones thrown at them by Palestinian protesters (Gaon 1991). She used this protective net – in steel or silver – to create stools as well as jewellery, such as "protective" bracelets (figs. 4.33 a, b). In the mid-1990s she also wove nets that combined brass, copper and steel wires, making flat brooches that evoked geometrically patterned textiles.

The stone aggregates in the terrazzo tiles typical of Israeli floors are another source of inspiration, evident in several of Kaminski's series. She broke the tiles into pieces and set these fragments into her jewellery. These tiles also inspired a series of pieces cast in concrete (fig. 4.41). She constructed bowls and jewellery from sharp-angled pieces of metal, whose form recalls the stone patterns in these tiles. She continues to be fascinated with mosaic patterns, creating brooches whose patterns are composed of elements of varying sizes and densities (fig. 4.42), described by Alex Ward (2006, p. 54) as "kaleidoscopic 'snowflake' designs". In a 2011 exhibition at Gallery Loupe for Contemporary Art Jewelry, Montclair, New Jersey, she showed female figures composed of soldered pieces of metal, which she describes as "mosaics". Another variation on the stone theme is her stones cast in silver, which mimic the form of gravel stones (fig. 4.38). These she uses to make brooches, necklaces and rings.

"Soap Bubbles", as one of Kaminski's series is called, is a motif that manifests her interest in chance images.

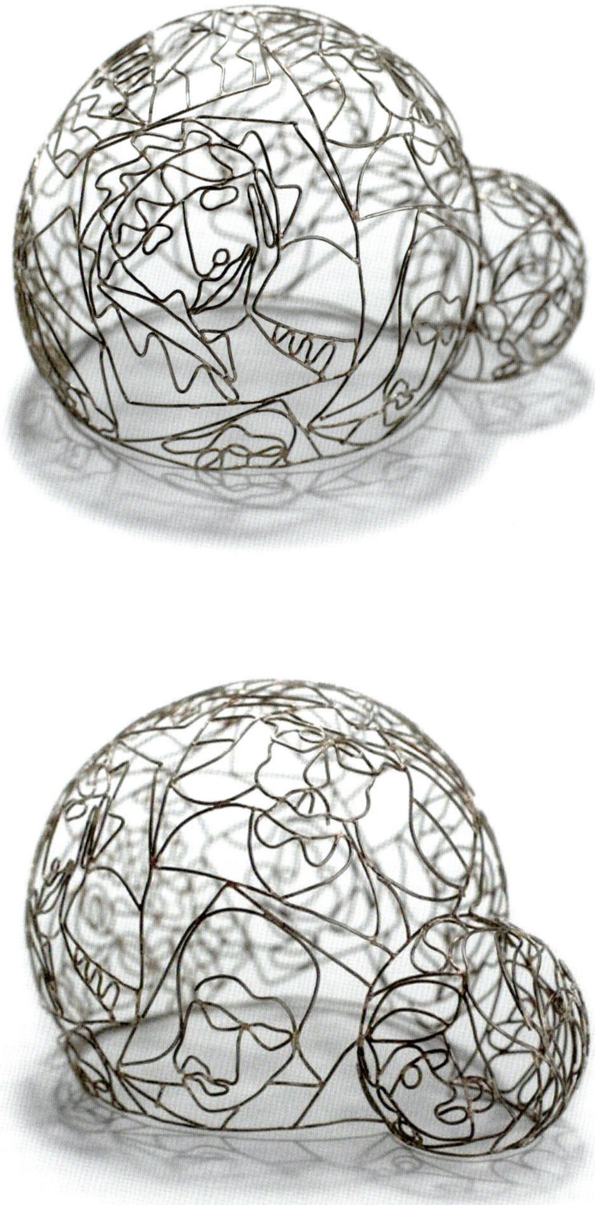

4.39 a, b Left top and bottom: Vered Kaminski, earring from the series "Soap Bubbles" (two views), 2007, nickel silver, 4.5 × 4.5 × 4.5 cm

4.40 a, b Right top and bottom: Vered Kaminski, earring from the series "Soap Bubbles" (two views), 2007, nickel silver, 6.0 × 4.0 × 3.5 cm

4.41 Vered Kaminski, brooches, 1995, concrete, stones, stainless steel, 3.5 × 3.5 × 1.0 cm

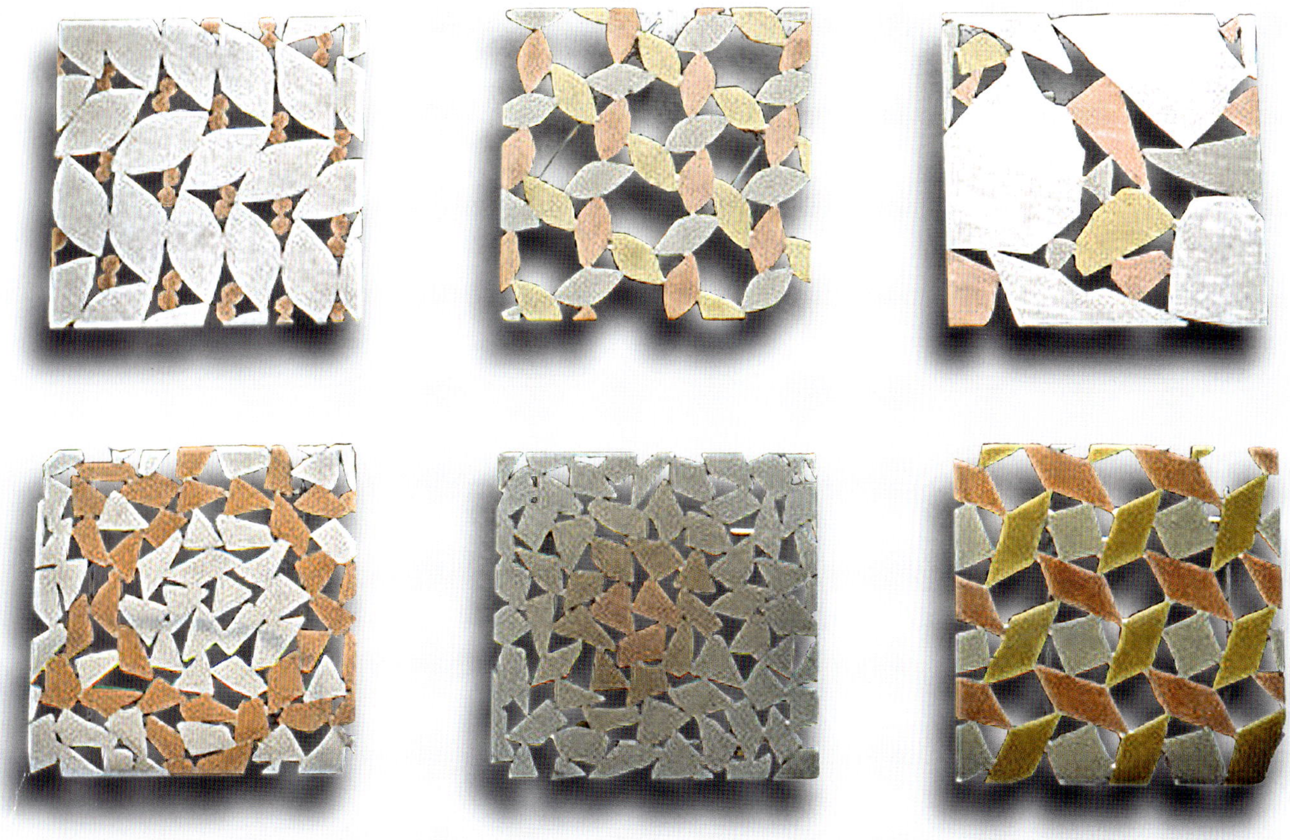

4.42 Vered Kaminski, brooches, 1997, silver, copper, brass, nickel silver, stainless steel, 4.0 × 4.0 × 0.5 cm

She solders convoluted, twisted nickel silver or gold wires into bubble forms, which at second glance reveal images such as a female face or flowers (figs. 4.39 a, b) (Vardimon 2007, pp. 38, 60–61). As she explains, they reflect her childhood memories of life on the kibbutz.[9] These delicate, airy bubbles, mostly made in 2007, are in fact wearable earrings (figs. 4.40 a, b).

Kaminski's colour scheme is subtle, featuring the natural hues of the stones and metals that she uses. She prefers to use ordinary, modest materials and only occasionally uses gold. Over the last ten years she has returned to experiment with some of her favourite themes in an innovative thought process. In a recent series of brooches, the curved line has been developed further, combining with the net imagery and the artist's fascination with patterns. The amorphous, winding forms have the appearance of loops. Kaminski filled in some of the spaces delineated by the wire with flat dark silver and left others empty. This results in a negative-positive, black-and-white pattern.

9_ Vered Kaminski in an interview with the author, Jerusalem, Israel, 2012.

Esther Knobel

In 1994, Esther Knobel was the first non-European to receive the prestigious Françoise van den Bosch Prize.[10] Since 1980, the prize has been awarded every two years to a designer of jewellery and objects who lives in the Netherlands. However, as Ra Gallery owner Paul Derrez (1994, n.p.) points out, "Despite the advice given by the Board of the Foundation to select a designer from the Netherlands, the jury's unanimous choice was the Israeli designer Esther Knobel." This honour reflects the wide acclaim Knobel has gained in Europe. She took an active part in the New Jewellery movement and participated in its exhibitions, and her work has been included in some of the most important books on the movement, such as Peter Dormer and Ralph Turner's *The New Jewelry: Trends & Traditions* (1985, pp. 121–123, figs. 122–124; p. 131, fig. 135). Since the early 1980s, works by Knobel have been acquired by major jewellery collections around the world.

Knobel was born in Poland in 1949 and immigrated to Israel with her parents when she was one year old. In the late 1960s she studied painting at the Institute of Plastic Art, Bat Yam, under Raffi Lavie, one of Israel's most influential artists and art teachers. As Meira Yagid-Haimovici (2008, p. 74) writes in the catalogue published on the occasion of Knobel's exhibition at the Tel Aviv Museum, Lavie had a significant influence on Knobel. In this context, Yagid-Haimovici quotes Yona Fischer's (1973, p. 240) observation that the purpose of painting "is not the finished product but the creation of a situation that reveals the processes themselves." In 1970 Knobel started her studies at Bezalel's metalwork department (headed by Arje Griegst), which was renamed the gold- and silversmithing department two years later (under Arie Ofir's directorship). From 1975 to 1977 she continued her studies in London, taking a master's degree at the Royal College of Art. She then left for Amsterdam, where she lived until 1979. At the time, Amsterdam was the global hub of avant-garde jewellery, and living there contributed greatly to Knobel's artistic development. In 1978 she held a joint exhibition with Pierre Degen, a radical Swiss-born jeweller, at the Ra Gallery. On her return to Israel, Knobel continued to be in touch with her European colleagues of the New Jewellery movement. She participated in the major exhibitions of the 1980s and 1990s and continues to do so to this day (Cohn 2012, pp. 41, 78, 91). After winning the Françoise van den Bosch Prize she held a one-person exhibition at the Ra Gallery. A year later, in 1995, the curator of design at the Israel Museum, Jerusalem, Izzika Gaon, curated a show of her works at the museum. In 2008 Knobel won the Andy Prize for Contemporary Crafts and held a solo show at the Tel Aviv Museum of Art.

4.43 Esther Knobel, *Pine Tree Needles*, chain, 1977, anodised aluminium, l. 60.0 cm

Knobel's work is inspired by childhood memories and daily life in Israel. During her studies at the Royal College of Art in London, in 1977, she made the aluminium *Pine Needle Necklace*, shaped like the actual pine needle necklaces habitually made by children in Israel (fig. 4.43). In a conversation with Israeli curator Tamar Manor-Friedman, she explains: "The choice of this

10_ Other non-Dutch artists have won the award before her, Otto Künzli and Manfred Bischoff among them.

'anti-necklace' represented an alternative proposal for the concept of a piece of jewellery; it was a synthesis of poetic memory – of a world of childhood and pine groves – with materials and technology borrowed from the world of industrial design" (Manor-Friedman 2008, p. III). In the series "Immigrants" (late 1980s), Knobel cut out figures from old tea boxes and posed them as travellers on rickety vehicles (fig. 4.44). "Family" (1989–1992) is a series of works (some of which are portable objects) made of nickel silver (fig. 4.45), based on family snapshots. She took apart flowers and laminated petals for a series of jewellery pieces entitled "Flora Palestina" (1998–2000) (figs. 4.46 a, b), which drew on images of Israeli flora in a botanical field guide – illustrations of which she had produced for Professor Michael Zohari in the early days of her studies at Bezalel.

Knobel often uses simple materials such as tin, and available materials not associated with precious jewel-

4.44 Top: Esther Knobel, brooch from the series "Immigrants", 1987, recycled tin, painted fabric, nickel silver, 14.0 × 8.0 × 1.5 cm

4.45 Bottom: Esther Knobel, *Whistle-Car*, brooches, 1987, painted fabric, nickel silver, 4.5 × 11.5 × 2.0 cm

4.46 a, b Esther Knobel, studies and rings from the series "Flora Palestina", 1998–2000, nickel silver, silver, laminated leaves, 18.0 × 10.0 cm

lery, as well as aluminium, titanium, nickel silver, copper, and, lately, silver. Her palette is rich and her use of materials inventive and daring. In the *Snail* brooches Knobel manually imprinted a metal wire into a piece of recycled tin can (figs. 4.47a–e). In this case, she used the print on the recycled tin as decoration. In some cases, she paints decorative, colourful patterns onto her pieces. She made several of the *Snail* brooches out of titanium and painted them with decorative patterns using a process of anodising. The works are mostly figurative and fraught with meaning and many of them have a toy-like, humorous quality as well as a more serious significance. These qualities not only serve to communicate Knobel's complex outlook on human existence but are also an exploration of questions related to jewellery making as art or craft.

Decorative surfaces are the key feature of Knobel's subsequent three series, "Wreaths", "Athletes" and "Warriors". She started working on these series, all of which are made of painted tin, during and following the 1982 Lebanon War. The "Wreaths" series included a *Camouflage Necklace* shaped like the wreaths placed on the graves of fallen soldiers. Her "Athlete" necklaces (fig. 4.49) – female swimmers and male rowers or tennis

4.47 a–e Esther Knobel, brooches from the series "Snails", 1981, recycled tin can, stainless-steel wire, 5.0 × 3.5 cm

players – were inspired by the circular, kaleidoscopic compositions of swimmers in Busby Berkeley films (Manor-Friedman 2008, p. X).

The colourful, vivid "Warriors" series (figs. 4.48 a–e) left a great impression on the New Jewellery scene and was included in many books and exhibitions. According to Knobel, the decorative, colourful aspect of the series was inspired by David Hockney's work (Manor-Friedman 2008, p. XI). In these pieces, the warriors seem to belong to a different age, as they use medieval lances and bows and arrows. They give expression to an existence informed by military conflict. It appears that Knobel chose to comment on current Israeli reality through the distancing effect of images from another period. At the same time, the series expresses the artist's personal outlook on life. As British writer and historian Rosemary Hill (1992, n.p.) points out, Knobel's identification with her country and "anxiety about its 'strange fate' is consistent with her remark (about some brooches of fighting figures) that she identifies herself with warriors and works best out of a sense of conflict. It is these aspects of her character and circumstances, as much as her physical distance from Europe, that make her work appear in a tangential,

4.48 a–e Esther Knobel, brooches from the series "Warriors", 1983, recycled tin can, paint, stainless-steel wire, elastic thread, 15.0 × 12.0 cm

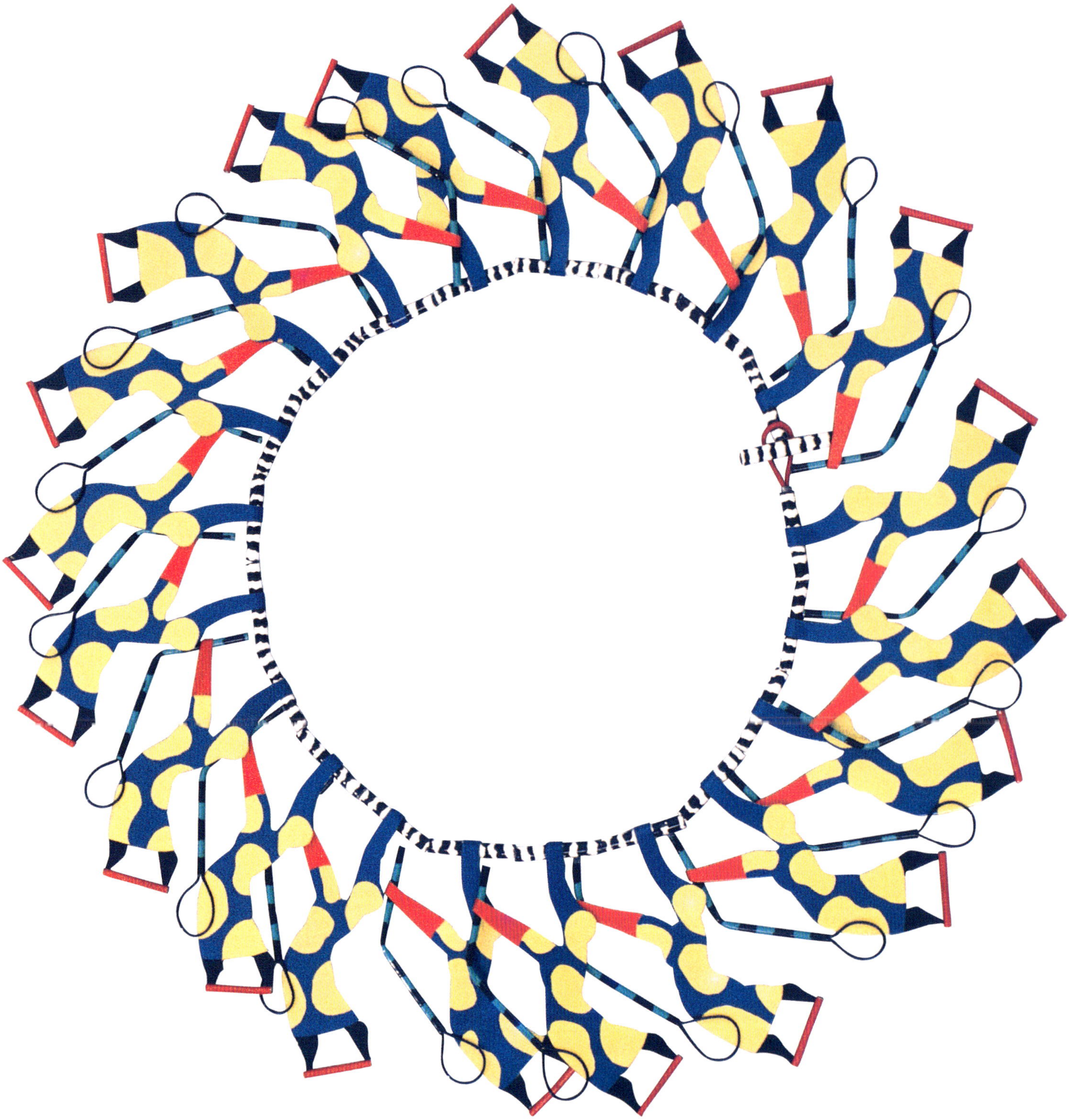

4.49 Esther Knobel, neckpiece from the series "Athletes", 1984,
recycled tin, paint, diam. 22.0 cm

4.50 Esther Knobel, *Requiem*, box pendants, 1994, copper, brass, cotton thread, 5.0 × 3.0 to 5.0 × 2.0 cm

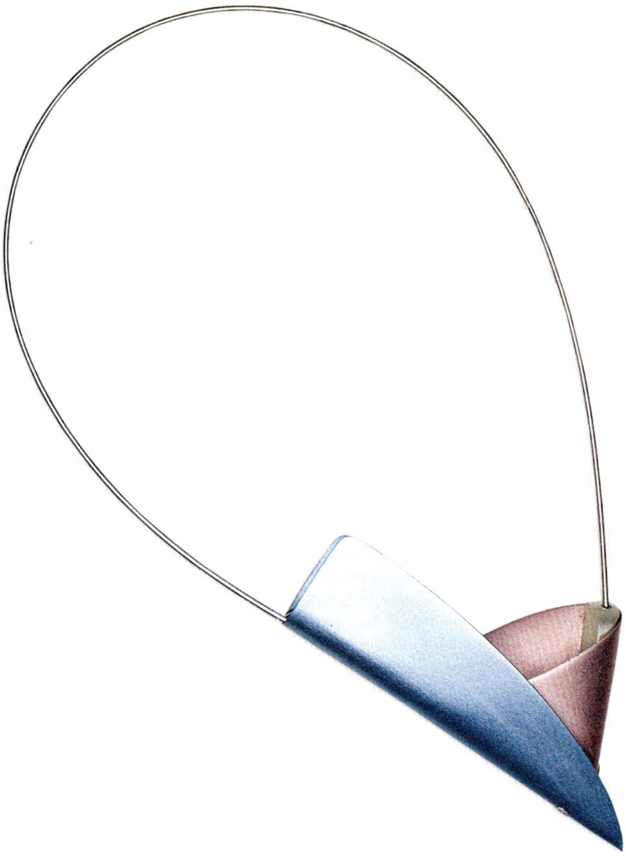

4.51 Left: Esther Knobel, *Safety Pin*, 1980, stainless steel, anodised aluminium, 10.0 × 2.0 cm

4.52 Right: Esther Knobel, *Safety Pin*, 1979, stainless steel, anodised titanium, 10.0 × 2.0 cm

sometimes dialectical, relationship with that of other jewellers."

Despite the serious subject matter of these brooches, both "Warriors" and "Athletes" convey lightness and joy. This duality is typical of Knobel's creative output, which runs the gamut from humour and playfulness to the harsh realities of war and grief, even touching on the Holocaust. The latter is most in evidence in her "Requiem" series of jewellery (fig. 4.50). Consisting of schematic portraits embossed and cut out on metal boxes, these pieces convey a sense of disaster. The succinct images in the series, she says, attest to "the existence of archetypical images that suddenly appear in diverse contexts and at various times" (Manor-Friedman 2008, p. XVII).

Knobel's work process is spontaneous and unpretentious. In an interview with Liesbeth den Besten (1994, n.p.), a Dutch scholar specialising in contemporary jewellery, Knobel says, "I see my jewellery rather like sketches in raw material which I dress up nicely." In Knobel's *Safety Pins*, made in 1977, the functional clasp is in fact the design (figs. 4.51, 4.52). As Den Besten points out, Knobel was not the only jeweller to be interested in this subject at the time. "However," she comments, "her work was so subtle and rarefied that it blew through the Netherlands like a breath of

4.53 Top: Esther Knobel, "My Grandmother Is Knitting Too", 2000, enamel on copper, pliers, 16.0 × 9.0 × 3.0 cm (teddy bear)

4.54 Bottom: Esther Knobel, *Deck Chair*, brooch, 1978, anodised titanium

fresh air when the Ra Gallery showcased her work in Amsterdam in 1978" (Den Besten 1994, n.p.) (fig. 4.54).

Knobel devised a unique technique for her work "My Grandmother Is Knitting Too" (1996–2002) (fig. 4.53). She knitted teddy bears and other objects from plastic-coated copper telephone wires she found in the street, then fired the objects in a kiln to melt down the plastic, recoated them in enamel and fired them once again. The teddy bear, which is usually a soft object, is consequently made of a rough, hard material, which provokes unease. Knobel says she started making this series after the death of her mother, who used to knit a lot. It was then that Knobel also started tackling

4.55 Esther Knobel, *Tene* (basket), 1992, nickel silver, dried peppers, 25.0 × 23.0 cm

4.56 Esther Knobel, *Magnet*, brooch, 2011, copper, found objects, enamel, 7.0 × 5.5 × 1.0 cm

the subject of the Holocaust, which was suppressed in her parents' home (Manor-Friedman 2008, pp. XIX–XXI).

Knobel's series "The Mind in the Hand" (2007–2008) (figs. 4.57–4.60) combines printing and jewellery techniques. She draws an image on paper – mostly an image of working hands employing tools. She transfers the image to a metal panel and then embroiders it with iron wire through premade perforations (Den Besten 2011, pp. 102–103). She inserts the embroidered metal panel in a folded aluminium plate and then runs them together through a press. Thus a double image (the front and back of the embroidery) is imprinted onto the aluminium plate. Finally, she uses this plate to print the double image on paper. Knobel is fascinated by the expressive power of the tangled wires on the back of the embroidered panel (Manor-Friedman 2008, p. XXVI).

Knobel developed a personal language informed by original techniques and unique aesthetics (figs. 4.55, 4.56), at times metaphorical and poetic (fig. 4.61). She is an artist of international acclaim, yet her work is deeply rooted in Israeli daily existence. Her pieces draw on childhood and personal memories, as well as on the collective realities of life under the shadow of ongoing military conflict.

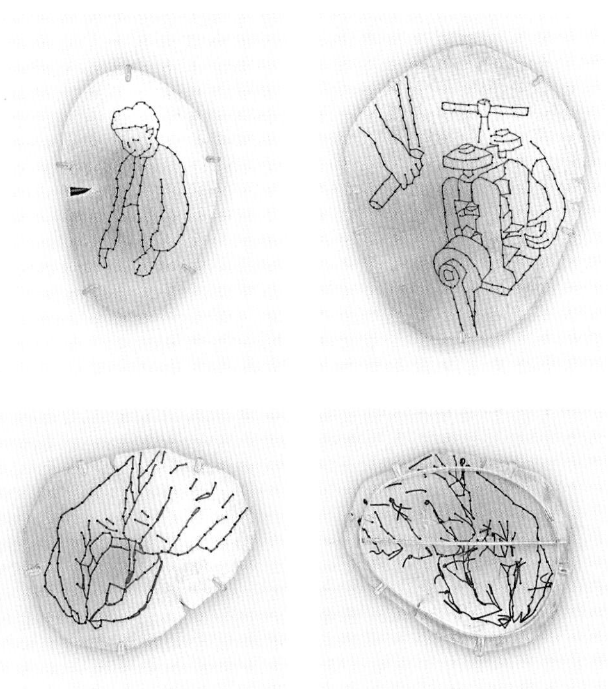

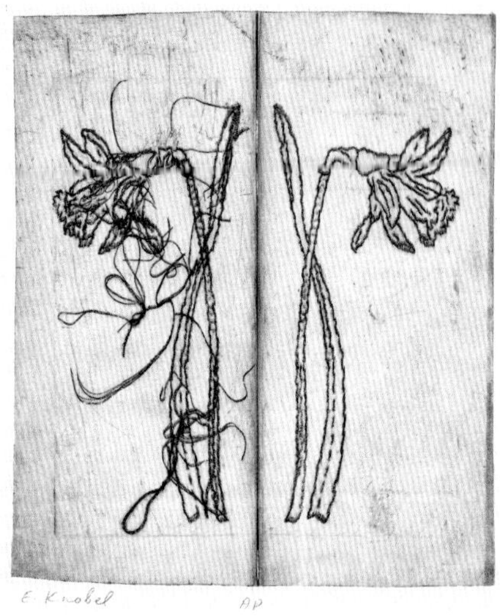

4.57 – 4.59 a, b Top: Esther Knobel, brooches from the series "The Mind in the Hand", 2007, silver, iron thread, approx. 6.0 × 4.0 × 0.7 cm (bottom left and right: front and back)

4.60 Bottom right: Esther Knobel, print from the series "The Mind in the Hand", 2007, etching on paper

4.61 Esther Knobel, *Kit for Mending Thoughts*, 2005, 18-ct and 24-ct gold, silver, paper, tin, 3.0 × 18.0 × 8.0 cm

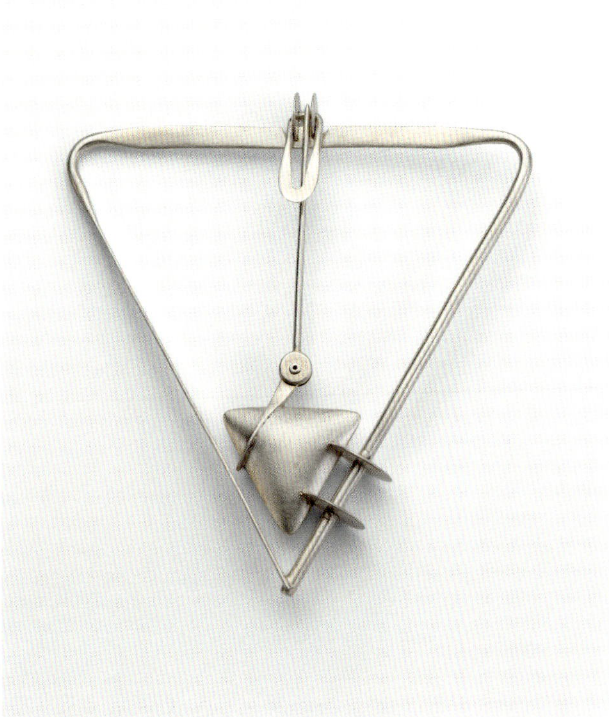

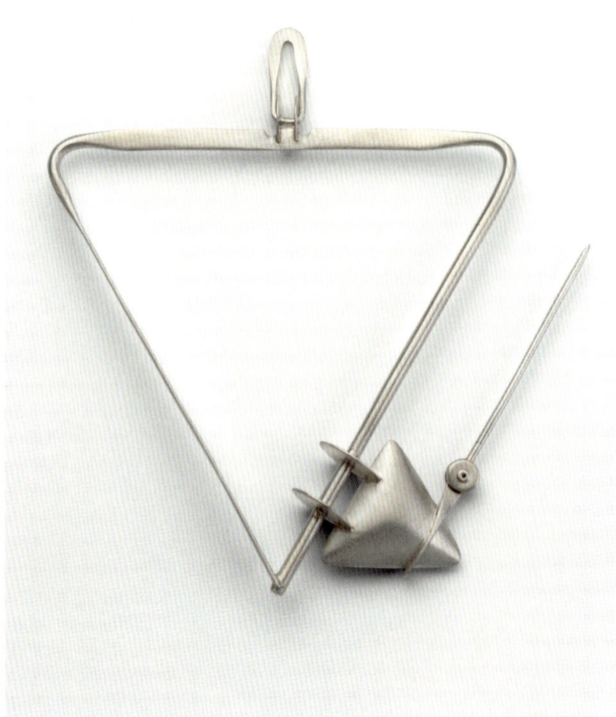

4.62 a, b Deganit Stern Schocken, brooch (open and closed), 1981, silver, 7.0 × 6.0 × 0.6 cm

Deganit Stern Schocken

In the course of her career, Deganit Stern Schocken has created a wide gamut of jewellery ranging from functional to conceptual, from figurative to abstract, from intellectual to expressive. She has gained international recognition since the 1980s and has exhibited widely in the United States and Europe.

Stern Schocken was born in 1947 on Kibbutz Amir in Galilee. She studied in the environmental and industrial design department at Bezalel from 1968 to 1972 and then moved to the gold- and silversmithing department, where she studied from 1972 to 1973. She continued her jewellery studies in London, first studying at the Sir John Cass School of Art (1974–1976), then at the Middlesex Polytechnic (Hornsey School of Art) (1977–1978), and finally took a master's degree at Middlesex University (2001–2002).

Stern Schocken's environmental and industrial design studies are evident in her early jewellery work. The motivation behind her early "Urban Jewellery" (1980s) series was architectural. As she describes it, the brooches are designed in terms of body and sign: the pieces of jewellery are placed like signs on the body of the wearer and an analogy is drawn between the signs in urban architecture, or the way buildings are arranged on streets, and the pieces of jewellery arranged on the body. During this period in her creative career she was mostly concerned with function as an expressive means. To Stern Schocken's mind, the act of fastening the brooch is the focus of interest, as meaningful as entering or leaving a building.[11] The fastening mecha-

11_ Deganit Stern Schocken in an interview with the author, Tel Aviv, Israel, 2008.

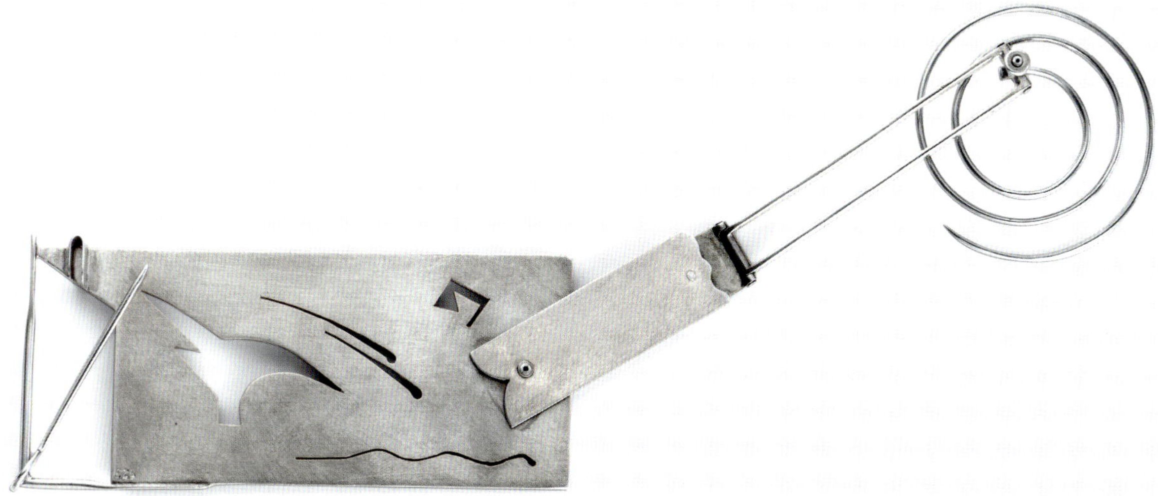

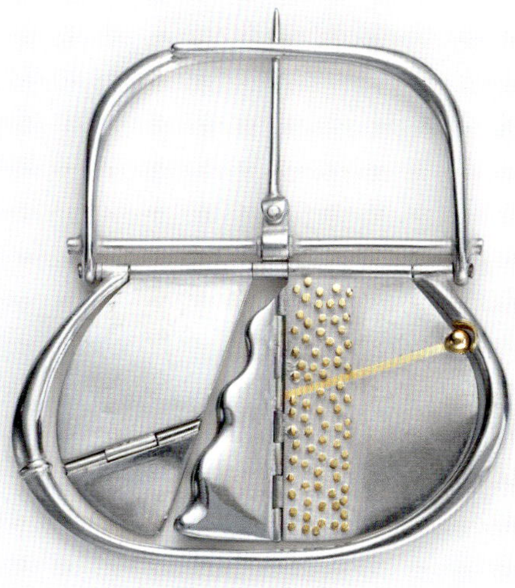

4.63 Top: Deganit Stern Schocken, brooch, 1988, silver, nickel silver, stainless steel

4.64 Bottom: Deganit Stern Schocken, brooch, early 1980s, silver, gold

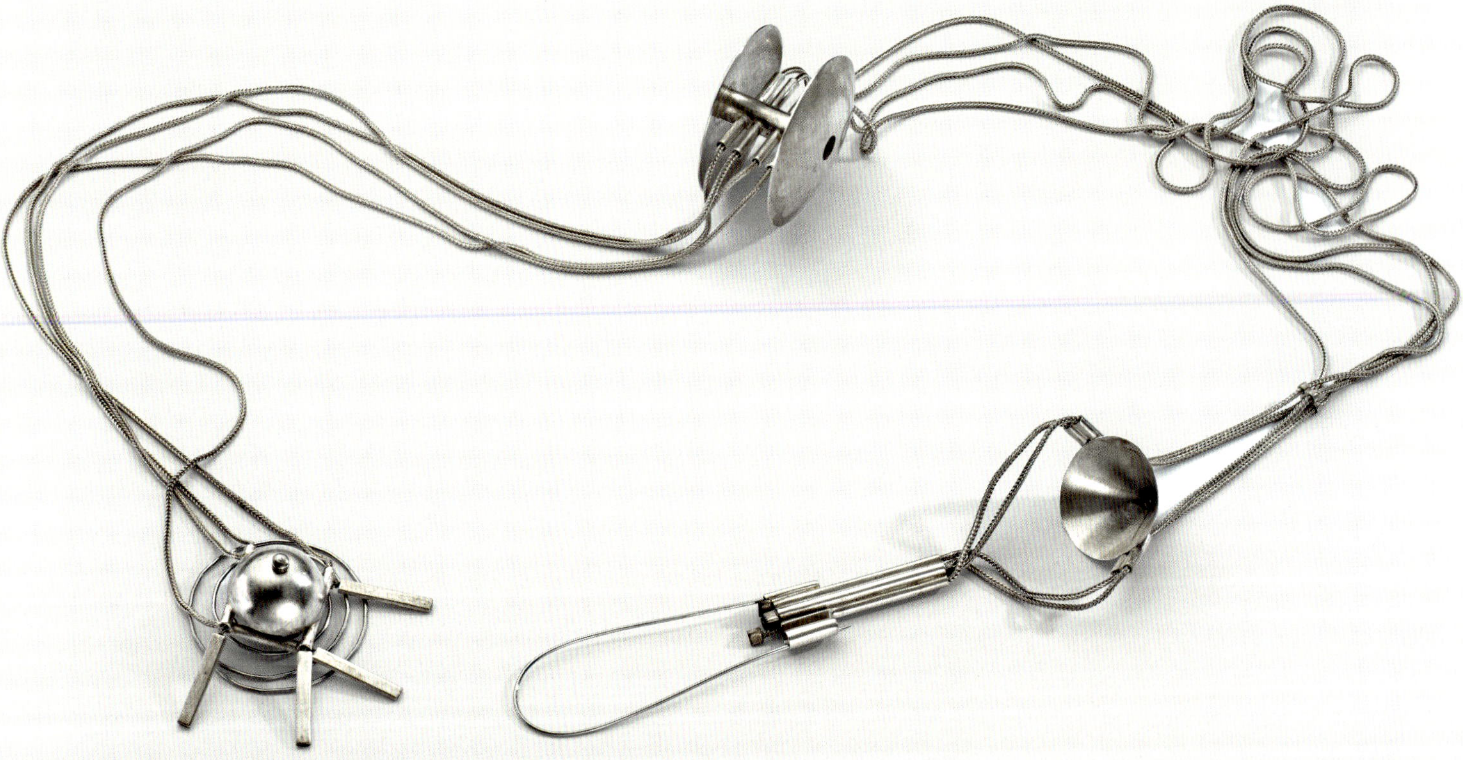

4.65 Deganit Stern Schocken, body jewellery, late 1980s, silver

4.66 Deganit Stern Schocken, body jewellery, 1980s, silver, gold, nickel silver

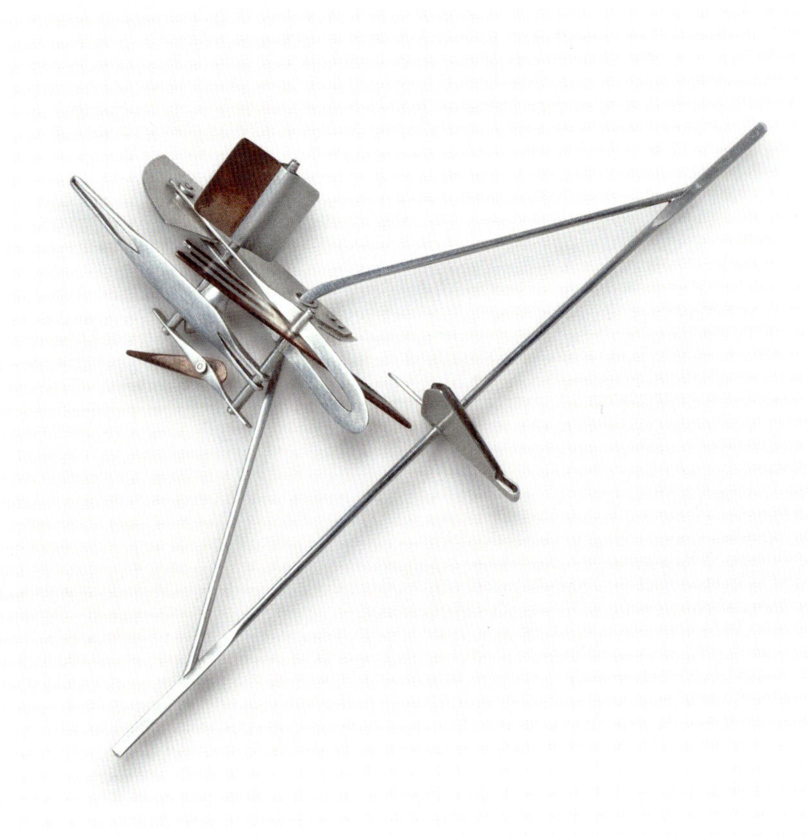

4.67 Deganit Stern Schocken, brooch, 1987, silver, copper, 17.0 × 16.5 × 2.2 cm

nism is in fact the entire brooch (figs. 4.62–4.64). Her notion of function that underlies form draws on the Greek and Roman fibula used for fastening garments. These early brooches are composed of a linear frame and a pin which turns on an axis. When fastened, the fabric beneath the brooch fills in the frame and becomes part of the form. The fibula is two-sided, and its form changes when closed or open. Making habitually concealed elements visible and affording them a central place as aesthetic elements is a familiar feature of modern architecture.

A similar outlook is evident in Stern Schocken's necklaces. Continuing her exploration of the fastening method, she adds a large spiral form to the necklace (fig. 4.65). This allows the necklaces to be worn in various forms, depending on the place where the necklace clasp is located on the wearer's body. In this way, the mode of wearing becomes the subject of the work. These pieces are mostly abstract but some have figurative elements, such as a tree, a bird, or a house, cut out in positive or negative form on a silver plate. The majority of the works created during this period are in silver and gold, but some incorporate other materials, such as porcelain. In 1984 Stern Schocken held a show at the Helen Drutt Gallery in Philadelphia and another in 1989 at the Helen Drutt Gallery in New York (Strauss 2007, pp. 280–283). David Gerstein (1989, p. 7) wrote about these early pieces, "The charm of these works stems from a synthesis between emotion and intellect, to which elements of surprise and mystery are added.

Deganit Stern Schocken combines ideas like beads on a never-ending necklace" (translation slightly modified).

Stern Schocken's necklaces develop into large body jewellery extending from the head to the front, back and shoulders (fig. 4.66). Like the fibula, there is a long tradition of large body jewellery from the Roman period onwards. When worn, these necklaces are never seen in their entirety. Each perspective reveals a different aspect. As Stern Schocken (2000, n.p.) writes, "The body, the basis for the piece of jewellery, is three-dimensional. It has a front, back and sides. The piece on the body – the sign – cannot be experienced as a whole but as a series of events – a system – in much the same way as we experience the city. The gaze, always rooted in a particular time, place and angle, only sees fragments and what is between them." Art historian, collector and author Arturo Schwarz (2001, p. 325) writes about Stern Schocken's large body jewellery, "If one wishes to speak of body art, we have here a beautiful example that proves that the body need not be altered (as is done in offensive practices, so fashionable today, such as piercing, tattooing, scanning, and the like) in an effort to beautify it. Her necklaces, when worn, do not assail the body's sacredness, but become one with it, lending it their own moving grace and beauty."

Movement is a key element in Stern Schocken's work. In the second half of the 1980s, exploring the movement of geometric forms in space, she started adding a third dimension to the brooches she designed (fig. 4.67). Helen Drutt English compares her works to Iraqi-born British architect Zaha Hadid (born 1950). "Neither woman knows the other, neither is affected by the work of the other," she writes, "but the linear, planar and spatial geometries are remarkably similar" (Drutt English and Dormer 1995, p. 69).

In the 1990s Stern Schocken focused on and explored materials – specifically stones – and containers, breaking conventions and offering novel alternatives. Challenging the status-awarding role of precious stones in traditional jewellery, she creates "stones" by folding and rolling off-white pieces of silk and then setting them in a silver frame (figs. 4.68, 4.69). Or else she drips green, blue or red water into organically shaped silver

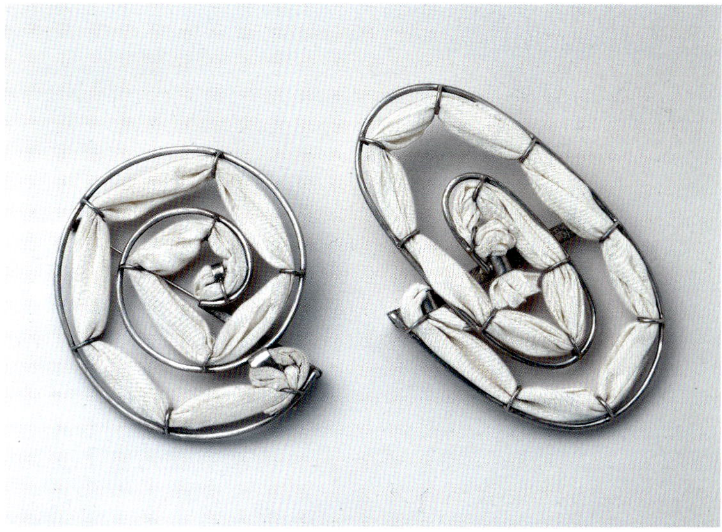

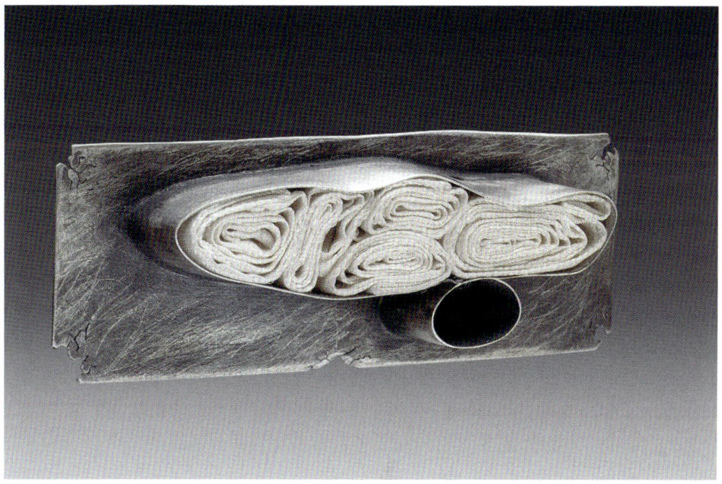

4.68 Top: Deganit Stern Schocken, brooches, 1990, silver, silk, 7.3 × 8.2 × 1.5 cm; 6.3 × 10.4 × 1.5 cm

4.69 Bottom: Deganit Stern Schocken, brooch, 1992, silver, silk, 2.5 × 3.5 × 10.8 cm, the Museum of Fine Arts, Houston, Helen Williams Drutt Collection, museum purchase funded by the Caroline Wiess Law Foundation

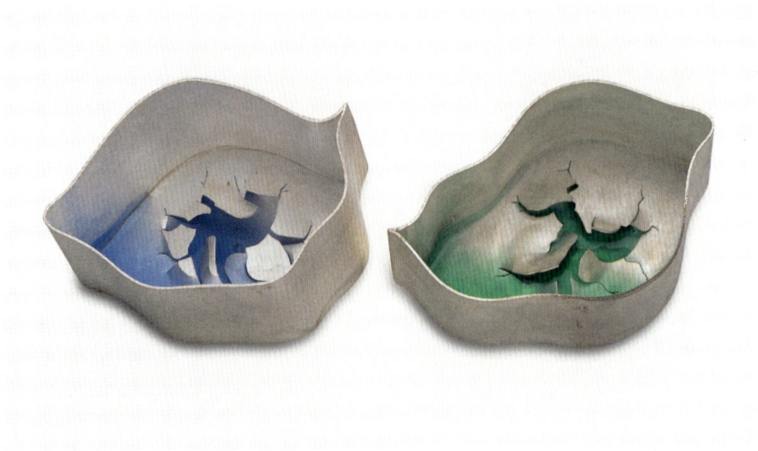

4.70 Top left: Deganit Stern Schocken, *Pool*, object, 1993, silver, coloured water, 6.5 × 6.2 × 2.5 cm

4.71 Top right: Deganit Stern Schocken, *Pools*, objects, 1993, silver, coloured water, 7.0 × 5.0 × 4.0 cm each

4.72 Bottom: Deganit Stern Schocken, *Landscape*, brooches, 1996, silver, cotton thread, quartz, 4.7 × 11.0 × 2.0 cm (left); 4.4 × 11.4 × 1.5 cm (right)

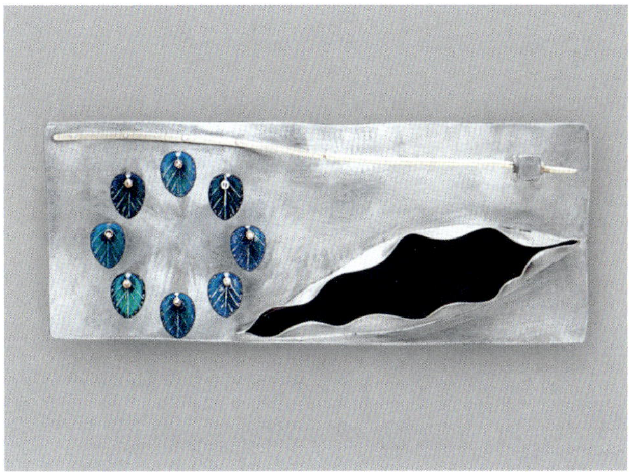

4.73 Left: Deganit Stern Schocken, *Territories*, brooch, 1995, silver, cloth, 5.7 × 9.5 cm

4.74 Right: Deganit Stern Schocken, *Territories*, brooch, 1995, silver, jade, 5.0 × 12.2 × 2.0 cm

containers, creating small decorative pools (figs. 4.70, 4.71). "I made a stone out of water," Stern Schocken says (Sukman 1995, n.p.). Indeed, the coloured, shimmering water functions as a precious stone. It is a temporary one, but the setting or container into which she poured the "stone" is permanent. Stern Schocken refers to it as a pool (Sukman 1995, n.p.). These pools are an integral part of her conceptual urbanism. Beads, buttons and other ready-mades serve as additional landscape elements (fig. 4.72).

In 1998 Helen Drutt English organised an exhibition as a tribute to the first woman to serve as American Secretary of State, Madeleine K. Albright. The latter was known for wearing brooches to meetings as a sign of her views and intentions. Stern Schocken showed two brooches entitled *Territories* (1995) (figs. 4.73, 4.74). They depicted landscapes and objects seen from a bird's-eye view: a lake with green trees, a fabric bag, and a pool filled with gravel. She wrote in the catalogue, "We share olive trees and sand in the Middle East. We must reconcile our differences" (Drutt English and Steiner 1998, pp. 106–107). This was perhaps Stern Schocken's first use of jewellery to express a political stance, a precursor to her political works in later years.

In 1997 Stern Schocken held the exhibition "Replacements" at Periscope Gallery in Tel Aviv. In an artist's statement, she wrote, "'Replacements' is an attempt to join different places, to make new connections between different signs; to create a territory; to integrate and interrogate a city" (Stern Schocken 2000). In this exhibition, the pieces were displayed on maps drawn by the engineering department of the Tel Aviv Municipality (laid out over long wooden tables), with brooches serving as buildings and pools. The exhibition also included a large-scale pool installation.[12] This form of display served as an exploration of boundaries and definitions. Where does the body end and the city begin? Are jewellery pieces architectural structures attached to the body?

Stern Schocken's 2003 one-person exhibition "How Many Is One" at the Tel Aviv Museum of Art, curated by Meira Yagid-Haimovici, was also presented as a large installation (designed by Studio de Lange) (Yagid-Haimovici 2003; Miron 2003, pp. 72–73). Uncovered

12_ From the 1990s onward, Stern Schocken showed several large-scale art installations at various art venues.

4.75 a, b Deganit Stern Schocken, brooches from the series "How Many Is One", 2003, silver, paint, 7.0 × 4.5 cm (top), 5.5 × 3.0 cm (bottom)

4.76 Deganit Stern Schocken, *City*, object from the series "How Many Is One", 2003, silver, 35.0 × 35.0 cm

4.77 Deganit Stern Schocken, pendant from the series "Kalandia Checkpoint", 2007, smashed beverage cans, silver, stainless steel, diamonds, 14.5 × 18.0 cm

4.78 Deganit Stern Schocken, *Mouth*, pendant from the series "Figure of Speech", 2011, stainless steel, polystyrene, gold, silver, zircon, nylon, cotton thread, 11.0 × 8.5 cm

4.79 Deganit Stern Schocken, pendant from the series "Holiness", 2011, silver, paint, 7.0 × 15.0 cm

4.80 Top: Deganit Stern Schocken, brooch from the series "In the Air", 2013, stainless steel, dice, 7.0 × 3.0 cm

4.81 Bottom: Deganit Stern Schocken, brooch from the series "In the Air", 2013, stainless steel, silver, citrine, 6.0 × 3.0 cm

silver jewellery and small wax objects travelled on an oval conveyor belt, around which high chairs were placed for viewers. The starting point for this exhibition was the lost-wax method for casting jewellery, used for industrial mass production. Stern Schocken combined ready-made industrially produced jewellery parts and purposely miscast ones, and then recast them. Unlike the usual casting process, however, she did not cut off the thin long sprues through which the wax and molten metal are poured (called *Angüsse* in German). Rather, she made them part of the final silver pieces. Some of her cast pieces were painted with industrial paint and turned into brooches (figs. 4.75 a, b). Others were left as enigmatic, branch-like, imaginary objects. Of special interest was a cluster of variously dispersed objects, creating a small-scale urban vista which once again manifested the artist's fascination with architecture and urbanism (fig. 4.76).

In 2009 Stern Schocken created the installation *Ants* for the group exhibition "Natural History Museum" at the Petach Tikva Museum of Art. It was a further development of ideas which were already apparent in her previous exhibition. She mounted thousands of individual "ants", which were in fact tiny pieces of jewellery, on the museum walls. Some were cast from the same rubber moulds as pieces in "How Many Is One". But the subject and look of *Ants* was quite different. As Uriel Miron (2013, n.p.) describes it, "If 'How Many Is One' was about production, *Ants* was about infestation." One may draw a connection between this army of ants raiding the museum space and political pieces of jewellery created by Stern Schocken over the past years. Her preoccupation with the Israeli-Palestinian conflict finds expression in her work. Visiting the Kalandia military checkpoint, through which Palestinians seeking work, medical care and so forth must pass in order to get to Jerusalem from Ramallah or adjacent villages and refugee camps, she was touched by their hardship. She collected crushed soft-drink cans with Arabic writing that were thrown as garbage by the roadside. In 2007 she turned these smashed cans into precious pendants set with diamonds, a series she titled "Kalandia Checkpoint" (fig. 4.77) (Vardimon 2007, pp. 48–49). This was her way of protesting against military checkpoints and the way Palestinians are treated by the Israeli army. The Arabic writing on the cans makes this political reference to their neighbours immediately apparent to Israeli viewers.

In her 2009 series "Figure of Speech" (fig. 4.78) Stern Schocken once again used ready-made objects with Arabic writing. She made these pieces from the plastic plaques used to teach Palestinian children how to read. Simple, colourful images show body parts, such as a hand, leg, or eye, and bear the relevant inscription. Stern Schocken cut out images from the plaques, mounted them on a stainless-steel support and added jewellery parts made of gold and zircon gems (Fishof 2010b, pp. 40–43). Through these pieces, Stern Schocken refers to the basic similarity between Israeli and Palestinian children, who all learn to read with the same visual aids (made in China…), thereby expressing a hope for a change in the situation between the two peoples. She does so by combining precious metal and stones with mass-produced plastic, thereby making the "unworthy" as valuable as any precious jewellery.

In 2011 Stern Schocken was invited by German jewellery artist Gisbert Stach to participate in a group exhibition which took holiness as its theme. She responded by making the series "Holiness", in which she reused several yellow-painted Stars of David from her exhibition "How Many Is One", adding to their flower-like form "stamens" in the blue and white colours of the Israeli flag (fig. 4.79). A clear reference to the Holocaust (yellow Stars of David), the work bears a dual significance of destruction and disintegration on the one hand and optimistic revival on the other.

In a new series of works by Stern Schocken, "In the Air" (figs. 4.80–4.82), on view in 2013 at Gallery Loupe for Contemporary Art Jewelry, Montclair, New Jersey, she returns to her early 1980s works. Setting aside political references, she turns once again to pure design. Thematically, these works deal with weightlessness. Theoretically, they were inspired by Branko Lukić and Barry M. Katz's book *Nonobject* (2011), in which the authors challenge the accepted dogma that form follows function.[13] In this book, they imagine what would have

13_ Deganit Stern Schocken in an interview with the author, Herzliya, Israel, 2013.

4.82 Deganit Stern Schocken, pendant from the series "In the Air", 2013, stainless steel, polystyrene, silver, diam. 9.0 cm

happened if design had started not from the object but from the space between people and the objects they use. Stern Schocken's brooches and pendants are inlaid with semi-precious stones, which are attached to axes and are therefore movable. Elevated and hovering away from the body, the stones seem light. Some pieces are inlaid with dice, which are by definition throwable objects. The dynamic spiral form of her early works is revisited in the brooches, with a stone attached to its end. The series also includes pendants made of cut-out flight safety instructions, which literally deal with "staying in the air". In this way, Stern Schocken explores and challenges our relation to the world.

Impact on the contemporary jewellery scene in Israel

The four leading jewellery artists who are the subject of this chapter and whose work has made Israeli jewellery famous worldwide were invited to become faculty members in the gold- and silversmithing department at Bezalel by Alex Ward, who headed it from 1984 to 1991. Consequently, their influence on contemporary Israeli jewellery artists became even more meaningful.

Alex Ward (1945–2012) was born in Scotland. He earned his first degree in art from the University of Dundee, Scotland, and his master's degree in textile design from the Royal College of Art in London. Prior to his arrival at Bezalel he was senior lecturer and design coordinator in the Sir John Cass Faculty of Art, Architecture and Design, London. Ward first arrived in Israel for a faculty exchange programme. As head of the gold- and silversmithing department, he fostered both technical skills and conceptual aptitude. To strengthen methodological technical studies, which were not as developed in Israel as in European countries, he invited teachers such as Carol Hirtenstein to teach hollowware and forging, and Willie Bloch to teach engraving and stone setting in jewellery making, and reinstated Vera Ronnen as an enamel teacher. At the same time, he also invited Israeli visual artists to join the faculty. Among them were Dina Hoffman, Gary Goldstein and Avi Siton, as well as Bianca Eshel Gershuni who had arrived at jewellery making after starting out as a visual artist. Prominent Israeli jewellery maker and Bezalel professor Vered Kaminski remarks, "The works which emanated from the department when Alex was the director were of an entirely different class; forceful, rich in imagination and executed in varied and exceptional forms of craftsmanship, works the likes of which I hadn't seen previously, either in Israel or abroad."[14]

Like his predecessor Arie Ofir, Ward cultivated connections with the international jewellery scene. He invited renowned guest jewellery artists to give workshops at Bezalel. Among them were Wilhelm Tasso Mattar (who was also the owner of Galerie Mattar in Cologne, Germany) and South African-born Daniel Kruger from Germany. Michael Rowe and Richard Hughes (who gave a workshop on metal colouring, bronzing and patination, having published a book on the subject) and master enameller Jane Short came from Great Britain. Thanks to his recommendation, the noted Swiss jewellery artist Otto Künzli was awarded an Honorary Fellowship of the Bezalel Academy in 1992. Ward also encouraged students to continue their studies abroad. In this way, he exposed Bezalel students to enrichment from other countries while fostering the exposure of Israeli output among new audiences as well. Quite a few of the younger generation of Israeli jewellery artists represented in the next chapter studied at Bezalel while the department was under Ward's directorship.

In later years, Ward continued to exert an influence over the jewellery scene in Israel in his capacity as the curator of design and architecture at the Israel Museum, Jerusalem (1998 to 2012). He held two important jewellery exhibitions at the museum. In 2000 he organised a solo exhibition of works by Dutch jeweller Onno Boekhoudt entitled "Why Not Jewellery?" In 2006, when asked to curate an exhibition of Israeli jewellery, he proposed the concept of a joint exhibition by the four jewellers who are the protagonists of this chapter – which became the travelling group exhibition "Women's Tales: Four Leading Israeli Jewelers"

14_ Vered Kaminski in an interview with the author, Jerusalem, Israel, 2013.

(co-curated by Ward and Davira Taragin). Indeed, Ward was the first to draw attention to the strength of Israeli female jewellery artists.

I would like to conclude this chapter by quoting Izzika Gaon, who was the curator of design at the Israel Museum, Jerusalem from 1973 to 1997, regarding the lack of recognition of Israel's internationally renowned jewellers in their own country. "It is most interesting that graduates of Bezalel's gold- and silver-smithing department, for instance, are not sufficiently known in Israel, although they are well known to gallery and museum visitors and to critics from Tokyo to Amsterdam," he comments. "Having gained great appreciation among their international colleagues, most of them have found their way back to the department as teachers educating the younger generation. Had there also been wider Israeli public interest in their artistic output, their economic potential would also be affected. This would most certainly have resulted in the development of one of the most interesting phenomena on the international jewellery scene" (Gaon 1988, p. 6).

5 The Contemporary Scene

1990s to the Present

5 The Contemporary Scene

1990s to the Present

A diverse and vibrant field

Since the 1990s Israel has witnessed vivid developments in the field of art jewellery. In addition to the Bezalel department in Jerusalem, a jewellery design department opened at Shenkar College of Engineering and Design in Ramat Gan in 1998. It was set up by Deganit Stern Schocken, who headed it for nine years. Another of Stern Schocken's initiatives is a group called Inyanim (the Hebrew word for "Matters") founded in 2009 (Stern Schocken 2010, pp. 4–5). Comprised of eleven members, all graduates of the two leading schools of design in Israel (Bezalel and Shenkar), the group meets regularly and holds exhibitions in Israel and other countries.[1]

Since 1998, an Israeli jewellery exhibition has been held every few years at the Eretz-Israel Museum in Tel Aviv. Since 2006, the Andy Prize for Contemporary Crafts, initiated by philanthropist Charles Bronfman, has been awarded annually to an Israeli decorative artist in various fields, including jewellery making. Among the recipients in the field of jewellery were Itay Noy, who makes timepieces (2007), Esther Knobel (2008), Tzuri Gueta, a textile designer who also makes jewellery (2010), Shirly Bar-Amotz (2012) and Attai Chen, who was awarded the 2014 prize. The winner is granted a solo exhibition at the Tel Aviv Museum of Art with an accompanying catalogue, and two of his or her works are purchased for the collections of the Tel Aviv Museum of Art and the Israel Museum, Jerusalem. Jewellery exhibitions are also held by privately owned galleries. One such gallery is Periscope Gallery in Tel Aviv, headed by Sari Paran, which focuses on contemporary Israeli design and routinely holds jewellery shows. Contemporary Israeli jewellery artists are often invited to hold solo shows and participate in group exhibitions in Europe and the United States. Public recognition of the field has also grown, and jewellery artists are supported by the Israeli Ministry of Culture and organisations such as the Association of Israel's Decorative Arts (AIDA), which connects artists with galleries, exhibits works at international art fairs and fosters the development of artists in many other ways.

1_ The members of the Inyanim Group are Vered Babai, Shirly Bar-Amotz, Rory Hooper, Aviv Kinel, Gregory Larin, Tehila Levi Hyndman, Michal Oren, Kobi Roth, Dana Seachuga, Deganit Stern Schocken and Edda Vardimon Gudnason.

Is there a concept such as Israeli jewellery?

One must consider whether there are specific characteristics that distinguish contemporary Israeli jewellery from contemporary jewellery production around the world. Is Israeli jewellery informed by unique thematic concerns, techniques or materials? Is there a local Israeli aesthetic?[2]

We have already noted the multiculturalism of Israeli society in previous chapters: Jewish immigrants from East and West live side by side with a native Arab population. Israel is also a country fraught with tensions. There is an underlying sense of threat in Israeli society which is related to a collective memory of the Holocaust as well as to a strong awareness of being a small Jewish state surrounded by Arab countries. The ongoing conflict between Israel and the Palestinians has resulted in bloody wars and waves of terrorism. In addition, there are growing social tensions between economic groups (as economic polarisation grows) and between ethnic groups (as the number of migrant workers and African refugees rises). As we shall see, jewellery making is an arena where all of the above find expression. While there are many similarities between local and global contemporary jewellery making, there are indeed unique characteristics to local production – particularly thematic ones. Since contemporary jewellery serves as an artistic medium for conveying personal, social and political ideas as well as for expressing emotions, it is no wonder that the particular issues with which Israeli society as a whole is concerned find expression in Israeli art jewellery.

Israeli jewellery makers employ a wide variety of materials and techniques, often experimental in nature. A return to craftsmanship is a notable tendency which is in keeping with global trends. Alongside some uses of precious metals and stones, one notes a marked

5.1 Shirly Bar-Amotz, brooch from the series "Zoo", 2009, sterling silver, copper, brass, Teflon plating, oxide, zircon gem, epoxy resin, epoxy chips, hot enamel, 5.5 × 5.0 × 1.5 cm

2_ For a discussion of this issue, see my article "Is There Contemporary Israeli Jewellery?" in the catalogue accompanying "Transit", an exhibition of contemporary Israeli jewellery presented in Germany (Fishof 2012, pp. 6–25), and my article "Facing Israel's Jewelry Today" in the catalogue *Inyanim Group* (Fishof 2010c, pp. 6–10).

5.2 Top: Shirly Bar-Amotz, brooch from the series "Happy Days", 2012, sterling silver, brass, Teflon plating, rhodium plating, oxide, pearls, coral gems, zircon gems, epoxy resin, 7.0 × 7.0 × 4.3 cm

5.3 Bottom: Shirly Bar-Amotz, pendant from the series "Happy Days", 2012, copper, Teflon plating, pearls, epoxy resin, 11.0 × 11.0 × 8.6 cm

tendency to use inexpensive and industrial materials, which is familiar from Israeli visual arts. The "want of matter" tendency was a significant style in Israeli art from the 1960s to the 1980s, and its influence is felt to this day. It was characterised by the use of cheap, industrial materials, such as plywood, industrial paint, collages and assemblages, and a "non-aesthetic" approach to painting.[3] Likewise, Israeli jewellery is informed by a purposely unpolished, "non-aesthetic" approach to style which utilises non-precious, modest materials. The palette is relatively monochromatic, with grey and brown as dominant colours. It reflects both the colours of the Israeli rural landscape and the lustreless colours of local urban landscapes. Metals are more often in matt finish and rough rather than shiny and smooth, and more often blackened rather than having a bright shine. However, one also notes a significant number of works with a bold palette – in enamel work or paint – which may reflect the gaudiness or unrestrained nature of Israeli popular culture.

Cultural heritage

In its endeavour to create a new culture, the Israeli Zionist society suppressed and erased cultural diversity for many years. However, in contrast with the "melting-pot" policy of Israel's early years, many of the country's younger generations have been pursuing a search for their ethnic identity and their family roots. Young artists often engage in a dialogue with a diasporic culture that they themselves, their parents or grandparents left behind on immigrating to Israel.

Shirly Bar-Amotz, who was born in Israel in 1974, is a 1999 Bezalel graduate and holds a 2006 master's degree from the same institution. Her grandparents were Zionist pioneers of Eastern European descent. Bar-Amotz's work attests to nostalgia for European landscapes – woods, lakes and animals that she became familiar with through photographs and her parents' stories and that she perhaps also remembers from a three-year childhood stay in Europe with them. Bar-Amotz laments the revolt of the early Zionists against their Jewish heritage, which resulted in their "trashing it all."[4] She regards this self-erasure as tragic and attempts to recapture something of that erased memory in her works (Fishof 2012a, p. 107). In her 2008 exhibition "Like in Europe" she showed white porcelain decorative objects and figurines of animals – such as swans, horses or camels – drowning in unglazed clay, stuck in a new, barren reality. These porcelain decorations represented her grandparents' European culture of origin. In the series "Zoo" (2009–2010) swans and rabbits were sunk into a rocky land, overwhelmed by their burden (fig. 5.1). In her exhibition "Happy Days" (2012) at the Tel Aviv Museum of Art she developed this theme further with brooches and pendants of animals, which at first sight convey a sense of merriment. A second glance, however, reveals that under the guise of carnivalesque vibrancy the animals, drowning in mounds of paint which prevent them from moving, are deeply stuck in the reality surrounding them (figs. 5.2, 5.3).

Aviya David-Shoham, born in Israel in 1979, is a ninth-generation descendant of a family of silversmiths from the community of Beihan in south-east Yemen. Her grandfather was jeweller Zadok David and her father is jeweller Moshe David, nephew to Moshe Ben David, who ran the silversmithing department in Maskit

5.4 Aviya David-Shoham, brooch from the series "Memories from Grandma's Home", 2005, sterling silver, nylon fibres

3_ The theoretical underpinning of this artistic tendency was established by the curator Sarah Breitberg-Semel, who in 1986 curated the group exhibition "The Want of Matter: A Quality in Israeli Art" at the Tel Aviv Museum of Art.

4_ Shirly Bar-Amotz in an interview with the author, Kibbutz Ma'abarot, Israel, 2012.

5.5 Left: Tehila Levi Hyndman, *Subala*, 2012, organic material, bone glue, mixed media, 8.0 × 3.0 × 7.0 cm

5.6 Right: Tehila Levi Hyndman, *Comb Bracelet*, 2008, nickel silver, mixed media, diam. 6.0 cm

(see above, Chapter 2). David-Shoham is a Bezalel graduate (2005). During her bachelor's degree she also studied in an exchange student programme in the Sir John Cass Faculty of Art, Architecture and Design in London. She then earned a master's degree in the department of industrial design at Bezalel (2009). David-Shoham vividly recalls the woven baskets her grandmother would prepare from the *lulav* – the ceremonial palm fronds used during the Jewish holiday of Sukkoth. Together with other women from her ethnic background, she would dye the palm fronds in vivid colours, submerging them in large wash tubs to do so. They would then be woven into huge baskets and trays which were used in the traditional henna ceremony held about a week before a wedding.[5] David-Shoham's final project in Bezalel's jewellery and accessories department (as it was then called) was inspired by these baskets. She called the series "Memories from Grandma's Home" (fig. 5.4). The series consisted of pendants, bracelets, brooches and rings reminiscent of woven baskets and made of silver and colourful nylon threads. These pieces garnered a lot of attention and travelled to a gallery in the United States.[6]

Tehila Levi Hyndman, born in Israel in 1982, is a 2008 Shenkar graduate. Her creative process involves meticulous craftsmanship. She made *The Last Feather* necklaces of her 2009 series "Ventricular Fibrillation" by soldering thin silver chains together (fig. 5.7). Both the necklace *Barbarian Tiara* and the bracelet entitled *Comb Bracelet* (fig. 5.6) were made with endless patience by manually hammering brass nails. These pieces bring to mind the Norwegian artist Tone Vigeland, with her steel "feathers". Levi Hyndman ascribes this quality to her parents' Yemeni heritage. Her father immigrated to Israel in 1949 from Sana'a, Yemen, a country of strong silversmithing tradition. While her family wasn't directly part of this tradition, Levi Hyndman (2012, p. 83) believes that her heritage entails a particular sensitivity which affects her work. She refers to this heritage in her works, which seem brittle and fragile, as if they are covered with the patina of time, like archaeological findings (Fishof 2010a, pp. 28–31). Her work *Subala* (2011) is an enigmatic, cross-breed creature: a dried gecko with beautiful butterfly wings (fig. 5.5). Putting it together required great patience and precision (Nelson 2012, pp. 56e–57e).

5_ Aviya David-Shoham in an interview with the author, Ness Ziona, Israel, 2009.

6_ One day, quite by chance, David-Shoham saw the then Secretary of State, Hilary Clinton, on TV wearing one of these pieces. Apparently, Bill Clinton had bought the whole collection for his wife.

5.7 Tehila Levi Hyndman, *The Last Feather*, necklace from the series "Ventricular Fibrillation", 2009, fired and soldered silver and glass powder, 20.0 × 8.5 cm

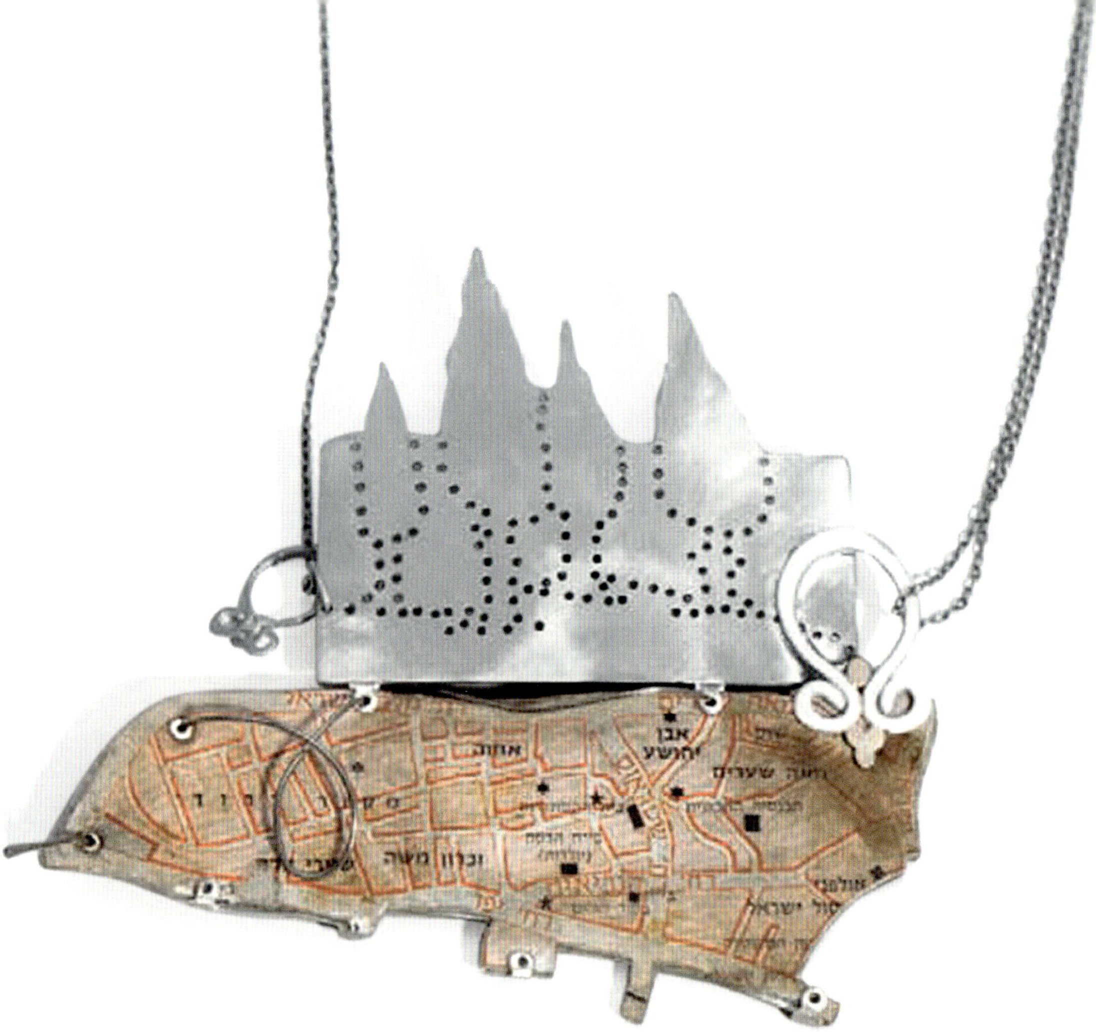

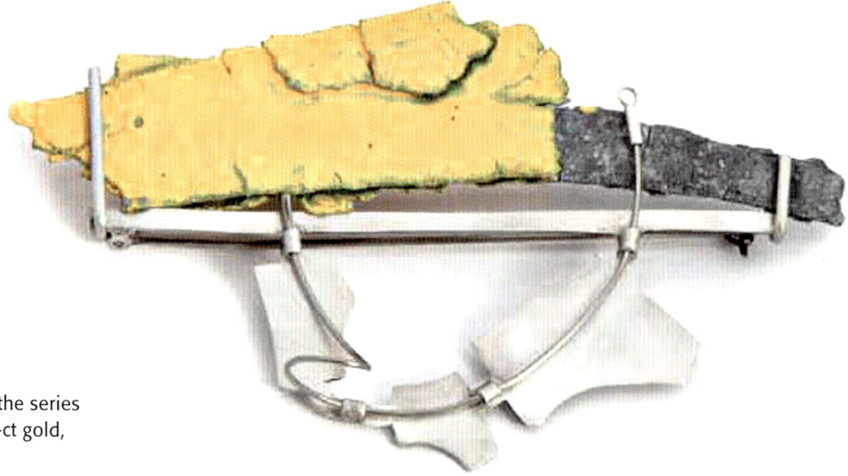

5.8 Top: Anat Aboucaya Grozovski, pendant from the series "Land(e)scape", 2011, silver, nickel silver, paper, 14-ct gold, 11.0 × 10.0 × 1.2 cm

5.9 Bottom: Anat Aboucaya Grozovski, brooch from the series "Land(e)scape", 2011, silver, found metal, paint, nickel-coated iron wire, 10.4 × 6.0 × 2.0 cm

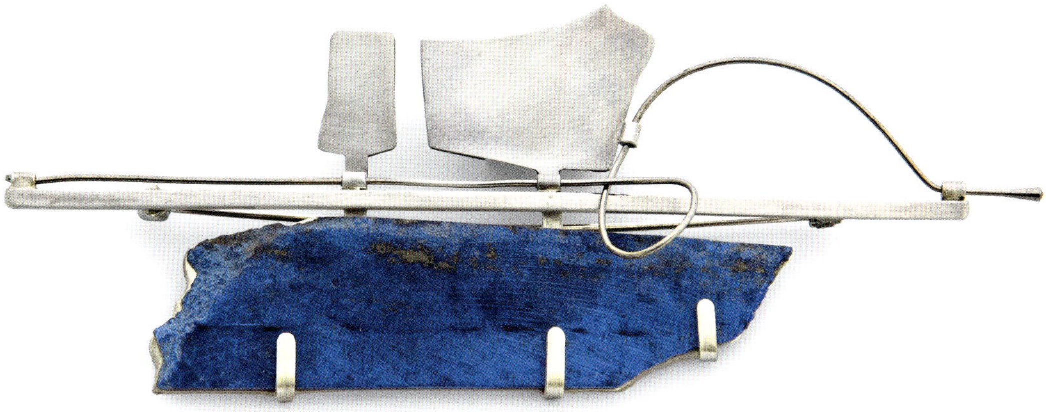

5.10 Anat Aboucaya Grozovski, brooch from the series "HomeLand", 2013, silver, lapis lazuli, 11.0 × 4.6 × 0.8 cm

Israeli nature and landscape

Israel's rural and urban landscapes are recurrent themes in jewellery made by Israeli artists. These themes often relate to childhood memories. They frequently involve overt or implied criticism regarding the erosion of natural landscape due to progress and development. While the Israeli jewellery makers' treatment of nature and landscape is quite local, it also ties in with global environmental concerns.

Anat Aboucaya Grozovski was born in Israel in 1959. She studied at the Omanit Jewellery School in Jaffa from 1984 to 1986 and art history at Tel Aviv University from 1986 to 1989. She returns to the landscape of her childhood and laments its loss in her 2011 series of brooches and pendants "Land(e)scape" (figs. 5.8, 5.9). She writes, "In the brooch series ... I purposely decided to move away from details and elevate the design to a wider-angle panoramic view, to offer a bird's eye perspective on landscapes. ... Ultimately, only forms remain, and a whole new vision emerges, born from the distance ... This is the essence of my take on nature" (Grozovski 2012, p. 51). Aboucaya Grozovski continues to develop this concept of landscape in a more recent series, "HomeLand". Here, the landscape is more abstract, incorporating stones such as lapis lazuli (fig. 5.10). In these works, she explains, geographic memory turns into geologic memory.[7] In her own neighbourhood, beautiful hills have been eaten up by bulldozers in order to prepare the infrastructure for new high-rise buildings. She sets her pieces with raw stones as a souvenir of the lost landscape around her in which mountains have been splintered into stones.

A recurrent motif in Aboucaya Grozovski's jewellery is the cypress tree. It is one of the most common trees in Israel, scattered on hills, dividing orange groves and demarcating graveyards. In one of her pieces she included a fragment from the map of Jerusalem topped by a row of cypress trees (fig. 5.8). This instantly brings to mind traditional depictions of the city, especially in nineteenth-century souvenirs from the Holy Land, with a row of cypress trees above the Western Wall (see figs. 1.1 a, b and 1.3 in Chapter 1 above). However, Aboucaya Grozovski takes an opposite stand to the longing for Jerusalem, intimating that she would rather live without this heavy historical load.

7_ Anat Aboucaya Grozovski in an e-mail exchange with the author, May 2013.

5.11 a, b Left: Ella Wolf, *Cypress Hanging on the Wall* (opposite page: detail), wall object, 2009, glass beads, brass wire, 150.0 × 23.5 cm

5.12 Right: Ella Wolf, *House*, bracelet from the series "House and a Tree", 2007, glass beads, brass wire, 16.0 × 10.0 cm

The cypress tree is also a prominent motif in the work of **Ella Wolf**, who was born in Romania in 1960 and immigrated to Israel in 1961. Wolf is a Bezalel graduate from 1987. She continued her studies at the Royal College of Art in London, where she received a master's degree in 1989. She was only a year old when she came to Israel with her family. She grew up in Rehovot, a town famous for its citrus groves and where cypress trees are a common sight, dividing and delineating the groves. Wolf meticulously uses thread and glass beads (figs. 5.11 a, b) – echoing the folk art of Romania, her country of origin – to recount what she describes as "the roots and origins of my life. This life began in Romania but is deeply rooted in the Land of Israel" (Wolf 2012, p. 163). Since 2001, she has been pursuing the theme of "the house and the tree" in works that straddle art, craft and fashion. As the daughter of a family of immigrants Wolf was impressed by the cypress tree, which is very strong, firmly holding on to the soil and resistant to winds. The house in her works has an emblematic

5.13 Vered Babai, brooches from the series "DU BE", 2005–06, silver, copper wire, 5.8 × 4.4 × 0.5 cm

form and like the tree represents values of permanence and stability. Her house-shaped bracelet deliberately ignores the anatomy of the forearm, thereby creating immediate tension (fig. 5.12).

Vered Babai, a Bezalel graduate from 1993, was born in Petach Tikva, Israel, in 1967, in a neighbourhood surrounded by wild fields and groves. "I have a longing for childlike, direct contact with untended nature, where everything grows in season and dies in season," she says.[8] Her series "Open File" (2008) reflects the beauty she finds in the fragility of nature, as can be seen in her *Bare Trunk* and *Bandaged Trunk* (fig. 5.15). Babai's restraint and attention to detail show the influence of her teacher Vered Kaminski and Italian jewellery artist Giovanni Corvaja, whose work she admires. She ascribes her free approach to jewellery – creating small, expressive pieces that are not necessarily wearable – to the influence of Dutch jewellery artist Onno Boekhoudt. She works with silver, and variously toned copper wire which she acquires at an electrical transformer factory. In her recent series "Traces" (2011) she endeavours to give expression to natural harmony and to the logic inherent in nature, as in *Morning Dew* (fig. 5.16). She embroiders the works with copper wire, offering her own contemporary take on traditional "female" crafts to which she was exposed in her childhood through her grandmother's Gobelin embroidery. The same meticulous handcraft is also found in her earlier series "DU BE" (2005–2006) – *dooby* is Hebrew for "teddy bear" (fig. 5.13). Babai dressed the teddy bear in clothes made of copper wire which she cross-stitched on a silver industrial grid. The work, she says, toys "with terms such as rigidness, playfulness, discipline and openness on technical and conceptual grounds alike" (Babai, n.d., p. 12). In 2011 Babai also made the series "Circuits", made of twigs and palm inflorescence found in her neighbourhood (fig. 5.14). "While studying this new material, I noticed the many nuances of each twig and came to appreciate its beauty, simplicity and strength," she remarks (Babai, n.d., p. 38).

8_ Vered Babai in an e-mail exchange with the author, April 2013.

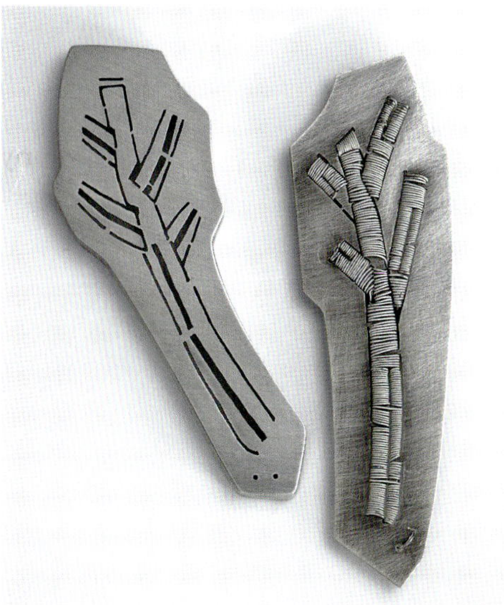

5.14 Top: Vered Babai, bracelet and ring from the series "Circuits", 2011, twigs, 11.0 × 11.0 × 5.5 cm (bracelet); 6.0 × 3.5 × 2.5 cm (ring)

5.15 Bottom left: Vered Babai, *Bare Trunk* and *Bandaged Trunk*, from the series "Open File", 2008, silver, copper wire, 9.0 × 3.0 × 0.5 cm

5.16 Bottom right: Vered Babai, *Morning Dew*, from the series "Traces", 2011, silver, 9.0 × 5.0 × 3.5 cm

Attai Chen was born in Israel in 1979 and today lives and works in Germany. A 2006 Bezalel graduate, he continued his studies in the Akademie der Bildenden Künste, Munich, under Otto Künzli, where he received a diploma in 2012. Chen is fascinated by natural processes of growth and decay. Towards the end of his studies at Bezalel, he made a series called "Redundancy of Matter" (2006), which explored the meaning of materiality and cycles of growth in the virtual world. He used a single ounce of pure gold to make three groups of jewellery pieces depicting plants at various stages of their growth cycle. He photographed the pieces, melted them and then made new pieces from the same piece of gold, repeating the process several times. Finally, he displayed the photographs as a slide show on a brooch consisting of a miniature digital screen (figs. 5.17 a–d). Similar concerns find expression in Chen's series "Forgotten Things" (2007–2010). These works refer to the little objects which are all around us but of which we usually take no notice. Resembling dry, peeling twigs, they are made of thin sheets of silver that are fused and soldered together (fig. 5.18). Chen (2012a) writes about this series, "I find that I am rarely attracted to the beauty of perfection in nature but rather to the imperfection, asymmetry, and intimacy of decay." Chen's treatment of this theme is further developed in the series "Compounding Fractions" (2010), which he made while studying under Otto Künzli in Munich. He uses pieces of recycled paper to create organic-looking forms that have a poetic, quivering appearance, as beautiful and vulnerable as flowers at the height of bloom, just before they start to wilt (figs. 5.19 – 5.23). His choice of material embodies the notion of cyclicality, for paper is a reincarnation of wood, giving it new life, yet is also perishable itself.[9] In addition, Chen (2012b, n.p.) recounts, these pieces are "self-portraits … made of drawings and writings of my intimate thoughts which I seal in an unreachable place, like a diary that is written in an encoded language."

9_ Attai Chen in an e-mail exchange with the author, January 2012.

5.17 a–d This and opposite page: Attai Chen, "Redundancy of Matter", digital-screen brooch, 2006, 24-ct gold, MP-player, nickel silver, stainless steel, 8.0 × 6.0 × 1.5 cm. Photographs of jewellery pieces, all made from the same ounce of pure gold (opposite page, left), are displayed as a slide show on the screen (opposite page, right).

5.18 Attai Chen, brooches from the series "Forgotten Things", 2007–10, silver, shibuichi, gold leaf, enamel, stainless steel, 3.0 × 0.7 × 0.5 to 9.4 × 2.4 × 1.8 cm

5.19 Left: Attai Chen, *Untitled (Coral Black)*, neckpiece from the series "Compounding Fractions", 2012, paper, paint, glue, coal, linen, mixed media, 12.5 × 7.0 × 6.5 cm

5.20 Right: Attai Chen, *Free Radicals (Part 3)*, brooch from the series "Compounding Fractions", 2013, paper, paint, glue, silver, brass, stainless steel, 11.0 × 9.0 × 6.0 cm

5.21 Opposite page: Attai Chen, *Untitled*, neckpiece from the series "Compounding Fractions", 2012, paper, newspaper, graphite, paint, glue, silver, cotton string, mixed media, 9.5 × 10.0 × 4.5 cm

5.22 Top left: Attai Chen, *Free Radicals (Part 8)*, brooch from the series "Compounding Fractions", 2012, paper, paint, coal, glue, silver, brass, stainless steel, mixed media, 9.5 × 5.3 × 4.8 cm

5.23 Top right: Attai Chen, brooch from the series "Compounding Fractions", 2010, paper, paint, coal, glue, brass, stainless steel, mixed media, 17.0 × 10.0 × 8.0 cm

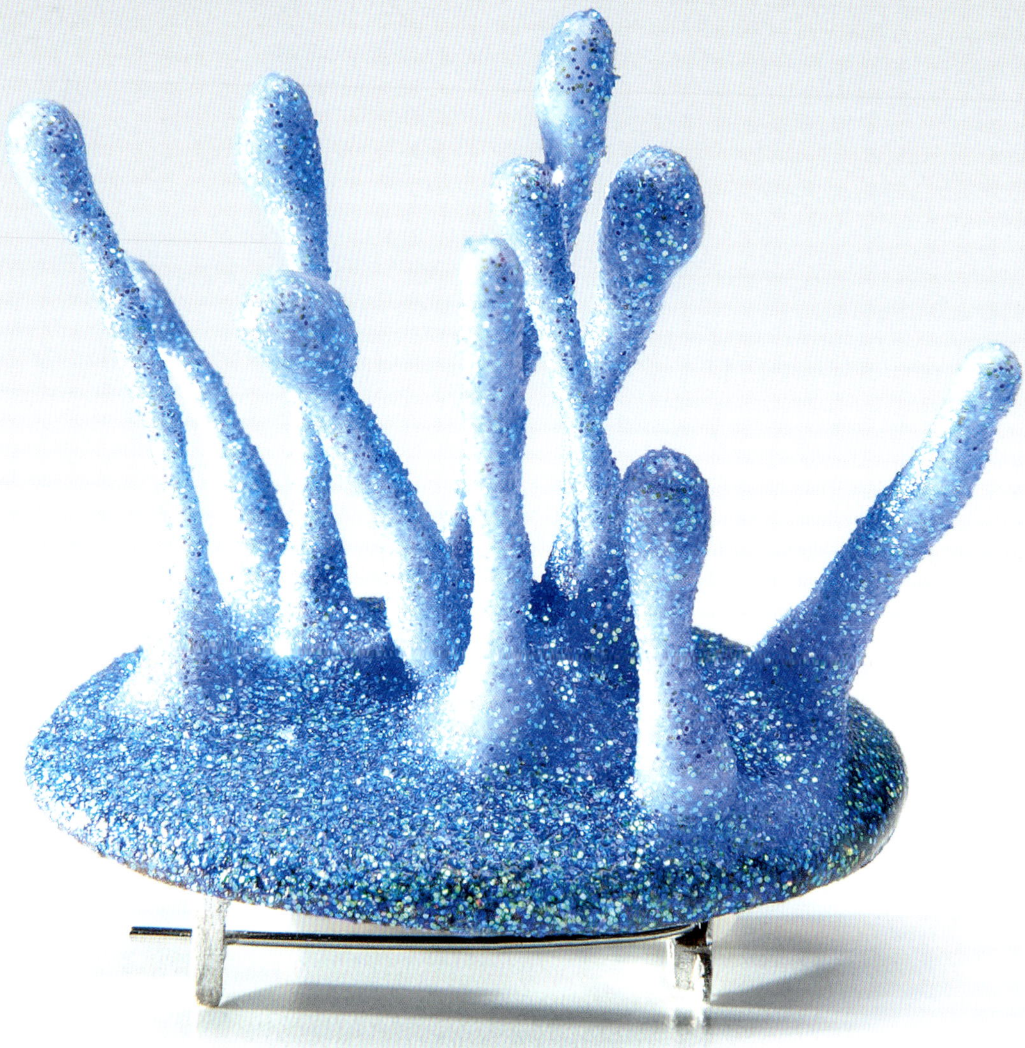

5.24 Shirly Bar-Amotz, brooch from the series "Weeds", 2011, copper, sterling silver, synthetic pearls, epoxy resin, epoxy chips, 3.7 × 4.1 × 3.2 cm

5.25 Shirly Bar-Amotz, brooch from the series "Weeds", copper, sterling silver, synthetic pearls, epoxy resin, epoxy chips, 5.6 × 5.5 × 4.3 cm

Shirly Bar-Amotz (see this chapter above) was born and raised on Kibbutz Ma'abarot. She is drawn to the weeds which those who tend fields and gardens consider undesirable and troublesome. Her 2011 series of brooches "Weeds" is made of synthetic pearls, paint drippings and epoxy chips (figs. 5.24, 5.25). These weeds "grow" freely on copper discs and in silver tubes. By making weeds worthy of integration into jewellery pieces, she challenges the normative view, but in doing so, she also offers a synthetic, faux alternative to the bourgeois tradition of flower lapel pins. These wild, colourful, synthetic weed brooches "suggest an alternative beauty standard" (Bar-Amotz 2012, p. 27).

Ido Noy, born in Israel in 1979, is a Bezalel graduate from 2006 and holds a master's degree in art history from the Hebrew University of Jerusalem. Noy's jewellery explores Tel Aviv's urban landscape. In his 2009–2011 series "Altneuland" he turns his gaze to electric poles, laundry hanging on clothes lines, satellite dishes, dumpsters and air conditioners (figs. 5.26 – 5.28). With a loving eye, he creates miniatures of these urban objects, gives them a corroded and neglected look and bestows a new kind of beauty on them. These miniatures can be held in one's hand as intimate playful objects or worn on one's body as an ornament. The series' name refers to a utopian novel by Theodor Herzl, founder of the Zionist movement, which describes an envisioned Jewish state in the Land of Israel. His novel was translated into Hebrew as "Tel Aviv", giving its name to Israel's major city founded in 1909. According to Noy, these miniatures are all extremely local Tel Avivian images and therefore tackle questions of identity. "By looking at the city and its unique characteristics, we learn about ourselves," he points out. "By looking at ourselves, we learn about the city's past and future" (Noy 2012, p. 115).

5.26 Ido Noy, *Dumpster*, brooch from the series "Altneuland", 2009, copper, stainless steel, 3.8 × 8.0 × 4.1 cm

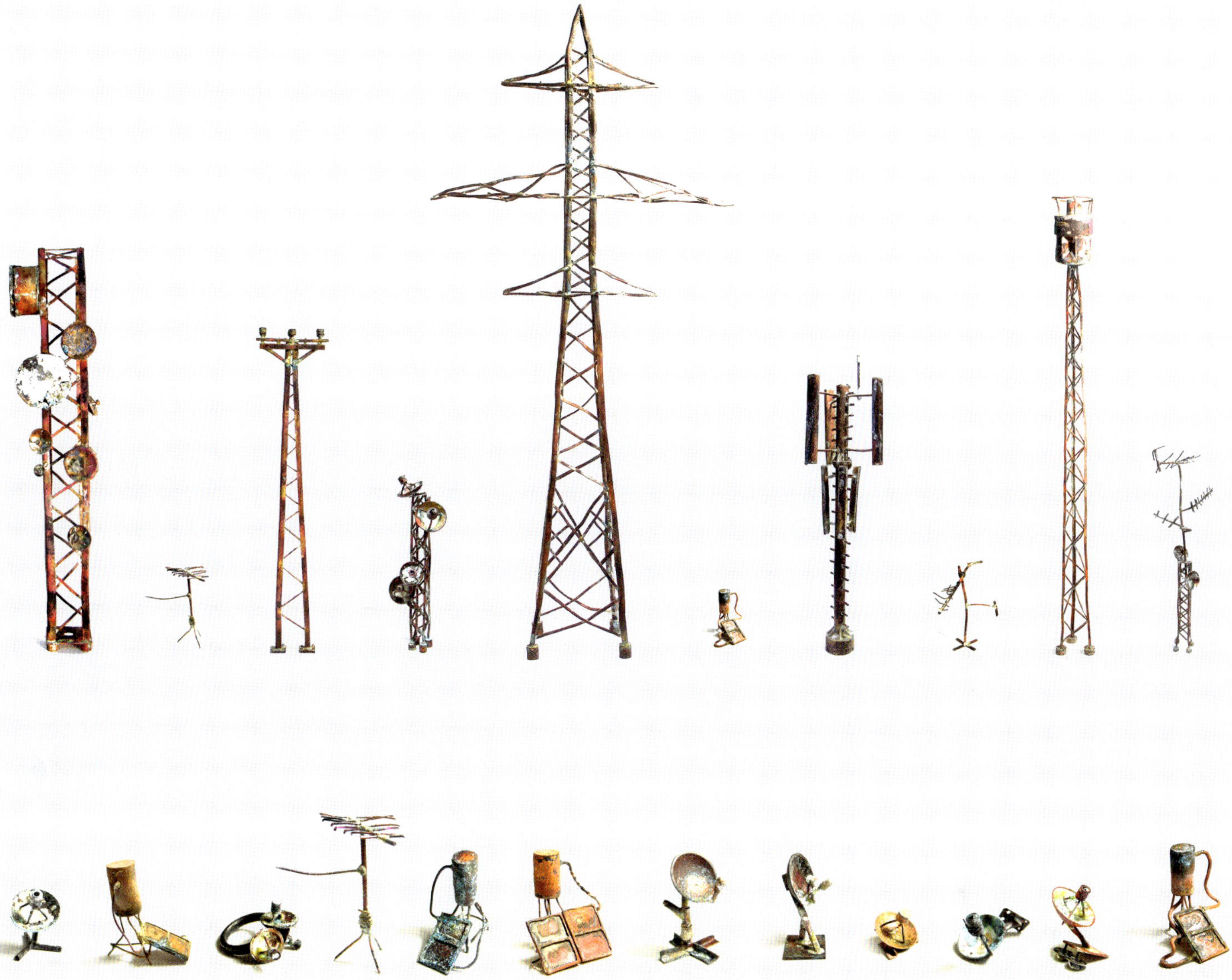

5.27 Left: Ido Noy, *TLV Ring*, from the series "Altneuland", 2010, copper, brass, silver, 14-ct gold, steel cable, 36.0 × 21.0 × 17.0 cm

5.28 Right top and bottom: Ido Noy, miniatures of electric poles, TV aerials, siren loudspeakers, satellite dishes and solar water heaters, from the series "Altneuland", 2009, copper, brass, silver, gold, h. 1.5–5.5 cm

5.29 Aviv Kinel, necklaces from the series "High Tide", 2011, wood, oxidised silver, feathers, crushed stones, steel, coral, paint

5.30 Opposite page: Aviv Kinel, necklace, 2012, silver plated with 18-ct gold, woven cotton threads, l. 26.0 cm

Aviv Kinel, born in Israel in 1983, is a Shenkar graduate from 2009. Kinel's recent jewellery pieces convey a sense of another time. Their creation entails meticulous craftsmanship, combining traditional silversmithing with manual weaving of cotton threads in a complex, intuitive process. She makes various small series of neck jewellery that bring to mind tribal ethnic pieces (fig. 5.30). For Kinel, weaving represents the world of traditional craft and places that have not been touched by technology. She imagines, for instance, women in remote places in Iran who weave carpets while sitting on the floor, peacefully singing a lullaby, their babies next to them.[10] Kinel combines the weaving with silversmithing. She continues the cotton threads with silver chains, and together they form one organic unit. The series "High Tide" (2011) is inspired by the low and high tides of the sea (fig. 5.29). It is perhaps interesting to note that despite Israel's many beaches, the sea is not a common theme among Israeli jewellery artists.

10_ Aviv Kinel in an e-mail exchange with the author, July 2013.

5.31 Malka Cohavi, brooches from the series "Unity", 2011, aluminium, silver, gold, ebony, 12.5 × 3.5 cm

Malka Cohavi, who was born in Israel in 1951, graduated from Bezalel in 1976 and from 1977 to 1992 was part of the faculty there. While still a student at Bezalel, she started working in the studio of David Heinz Gumbel, a mythological New Bezalel teacher (see above, Chapters 1 and 2), where she continued to work until his death in 1992.[11] Cohavi has been interested in the organic form of seashells since the early 1980s. She first used it to make a brooch that could be attached to one's clothing without making a hole in the fabric: a stick was pressed into a shell's form from underneath together with the fabric. Well aware of the seashell's use as a magical fertility charm since prehistoric times, she further developed the notion of its magical properties. She has incorporated variously coloured aluminium shell forms in items such as alms boxes, the case for the biblical Book of Esther in scroll form, and a Torah Pointer or *yad* (a pointer used by the reader to follow the text while reading the Torah scroll). In the 2011 series "Unity" she combined the shell form with other symbolic forms culled from diverse cultures – yin and yang, a circle with a dot at its centre (the astrological and astronomical symbol of the sun), a Star of David, and so forth (fig. 5.31). The series takes up the notion of the "unity of opposites" both in the pieces' forms and in their materials.[12]

Batia Wang was born in Samarkand, Uzbekistan, in 1945. She immigrated to Israel with her parents as a baby and grew up on Kibbutz Nir David. Wang earned her master's degree at the University of Applied Arts, Vienna, in 1971, specialising in metal processing. On her return to Israel she began making large gold jewellery pieces using the forging technique which was inspired by memories of her childhood landscape. Wang produces soft forms with rough surface textures and a matt finish (fig. 5.32) reminiscent of the open expanses of the desert landscape covered in "a blanket of sandy dust."[13] Wang's treatment of gold is unorthodox. She draws panoramic landscapes in charcoal and then hammers them in 18-carat or 24-carat gold. Until the late 1990s, her pieces were "one-offs" and clearly showed the artist's hand. She has since started casting her pieces to produce a small series of each model while continuing to make one-off pieces.

5.32 Batia Wang, *Mitzpe Ramon*, brooches, 2000, forged 18-ct gold, 3.5 × 3.5 cm. Design based on a series of charcoal drawings of the Ramon Crater in southern Israel.

11_ As the sole owner of the copyrights to Gumbel's designs, Cohavi continues to produce Gumbel's pieces in addition to pursuing her own artistic career.
12_ Malka Cohavi in an e-mail exchange with the author, May 2013.
13_ Batia Wang in an interview with the author, Tel Aviv, Israel, 2009.

The Holocaust

The Holocaust is one of the strongest collective memories in Israel. No wonder then that quite a few artists relate to it as subject matter.

Batia Wang's parents are Holocaust survivors from Lithuania who fled to Uzbekistan en route to Israel. In 2010 she made an object called *Everything's in Place, but Nothing's in Order* for the group exhibition "Sequences, Identities: Israeli Jewellery 5" (Barkai 2010, pp. 25, 33). On a 9 × 9 cm square of thick, worn felt she placed a leaf of pure gold and used sewing thread to tie the felt and the leaf together (fig. 5.34). In a text she wrote to accompany the work, she recounts, "I live in this country, carrying all the pain, deprivation and alienation, the wounded spirit of my parents' generation. They have all trickled down to us, to the second generation. And so we walk about, work, eat, drink, have children and raise them, go on vacations, as if everything's alright, but all the while, as Israeli singer-songwriter Zeev Tene says in one of his songs, 'Everything's in place, but nothing's in order'" (Wang 2010, n.p.). Wang explains that the work refers to the repressed memories of people who

5.33 *Stolpersteine* (Stumbling Blocks), Düsseldorf. Similar blocks commemorating Holocaust victims are found throughout Germany.

5.34 Batia Wang, *Everything's in Place, but Nothing's in Order*, object, 2010, woollen felt, gold, sewing thread, 9.0 × 9.0 × 1.5 cm

5.35 Zoya Cherkassky, *Jude*, brooch, 2001–02, 18-ct gold, 5.0 × 5.0 cm, edition of 18, courtesy of Rosenfeld Gallery, Tel Aviv. This brooch was part of the artist's 2003 exhibition "Collectio Judaica". It relates to the yellow badge made mandatory for Jews under the Nazi regime.

survived the horrors of the Holocaust, repression achieved through intense preoccupation with daily matters, carrying on as if nothing had happened.[14] She regards the square as a "single pixel in an endless image." Wang further points out that her use of felt refers to Joseph Beuys in whose work it was a key material,[15] while she sees the gold as a "metaphor of purity and innocence, of healing and the comfort of sunshine." During that same summer, Wang was invited by the municipality of Düsseldorf to work there in a studio in preparation for an exhibition that would be part of an extensive art event. She made another identical pixel object before she flew to Düsseldorf. During her first hour in the city she found herself stepping on golden metal, *Stolpersteine* (German for "stumbling blocks") created by Gunter Demnig to commemorate Holocaust victims throughout Germany (fig. 5.33). These plaques – embedded in pavements and identical in size and colour to the object she had made in Israel – moved Wang immensely. This was the starting point for her work on her Düsseldorf exhibition entitled "Pixel", which featured chalk paintings on paper, photographs and the gold-and-felt object.

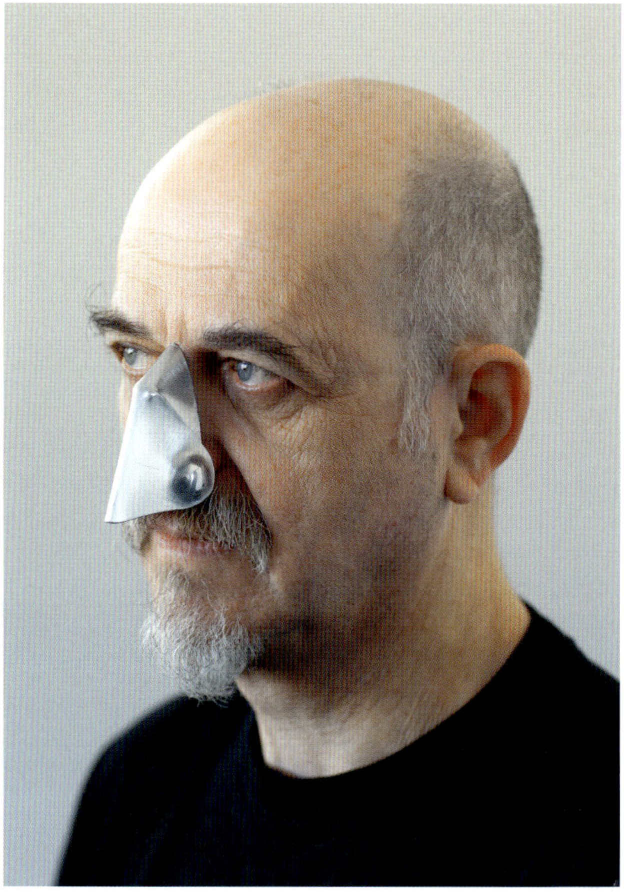

5.36 Yaacov Kaufman, *Who Nose*, nose clip made for the exhibition "I Am an Other", 2011, aluminium, 4.5 × 4.5 × 8.0 cm

Zoya Cherkassky was born in Ukraine in the Soviet Union in 1976 and immigrated to Israel 1991. She studied at Hamidrasha School of Art, Beit Berl College, from 1997 to 1999 and at the School of Visual Theatre, Jerusalem, from 1996 to 1997. Cherkassky is a multidisciplinary artist who is often engaged in questions of identity. In her 2003 solo exhibition "Collectio Judaica" at the Rosenfeld Gallery in Tel Aviv, she deconstructed the anti-Semitic stereotype of the Jew. Among the exhibits were two golden brooches shaped like a yellow star inscribed with the word *Jude* (fig. 5.35) – just like the yellow badge made mandatory for Jews under the Nazi regime, but in gold. "The centrality of this object within

14_ Batia Wang in an e-mail exchange with the author, April 2013.
15_ Beuys claimed that it was a reference to the felt in which his Tatar rescuers wrapped him after his plane crashed over the snowy Russian no man's land in WWII.

the 'Collectio Judaica' is inherent in the tragic meanings it bears and the dominance of its beauty," writes Diana Dallal (2004, p. 116), curator of the exhibition. Thus, Cherkassky turned a symbol of contempt and persecution into a decorative object and a symbol of pride. She herself wore one of the brooches to an opening reception of an exhibition in Aachen, Germany (while living there as part of an artist exchange programme between Germany and Israel). This provoked reactions ranging from appreciation to disapproval. "I wore it as an experiment," she recounts in an interview, "for this symbol, which was once worn mandatorily, currently holds opposite meanings. The word *Jude* itself is no longer problematic. It's only in a specific historical context that it's offensive" (Karpel 2004, n.p.).

Deganit Stern Schocken, too, addresses the subject in her series "Holiness" (2011). Her Star of David – a Jewish symbol such as is often featured in mass-produced jewellery – is stained yellow in dialogue with the Nazi yellow badge (see fig. 4.79 in Chapter 4 above).

Designer **Yaacov Kaufman** was born in Poland in 1945 and immigrated to Israel in 1957. He studied in the sculpture department of the Bat Yam Art Institute from 1966 to 1970 and took an industrial design course at the Tel Aviv branch of the Technion. From 1994 he has been a full professor at Bezalel. In a similar vein to Cherkassky, he turned the infamous anti-Semitic depiction of a Jewish hooked nose into a decorative object to be worn proudly (fig. 5.36) (Nelson 2012, pp. 61e–62e). His series "Who Nose" is rooted in a childhood memory from Poland, of his father asking a photographer to retouch his nose in a photograph so that it wouldn't be recognisably Jewish (Nelson 2012, p. 62e).

Political protest, war and conflict

Israel has experienced numerous wars since its establishment as a state. Military conflict is an emotionally fraught and ideologically charged aspect of daily life in this country. It is therefore no surprise that this is a recurrent theme in the work of many Israeli jewellery artists. Many works take war, terrorism and bereavement as their theme. Works by Israeli jewellery makers often express anxiety, loss, shame or outrage at wrongdoing or the infringement of human rights, but at the same time hope. These sentiments may be manifested in the form of anti-heroic symbolism, escapism (through childlike playfulness or reference to a different era) or outright political protest.

Following the 1973 Yom Kippur War, there was a wave of political protest in Israel. Artists, in particular, agitated against militarism. A seminal work from that time was a performance by artists Sharon Keren and Gabi Klezmer. Wrapped in bandages and wearing war medals, they positioned themselves just outside an official military award-giving ceremony (fig. 5.37). As we

5.37 Gabi Klezmer and Sharon Keren, performance outside an official military award-giving ceremony after the Yom Kippur War, Jerusalem, 1973, courtesy of Sharon Keren

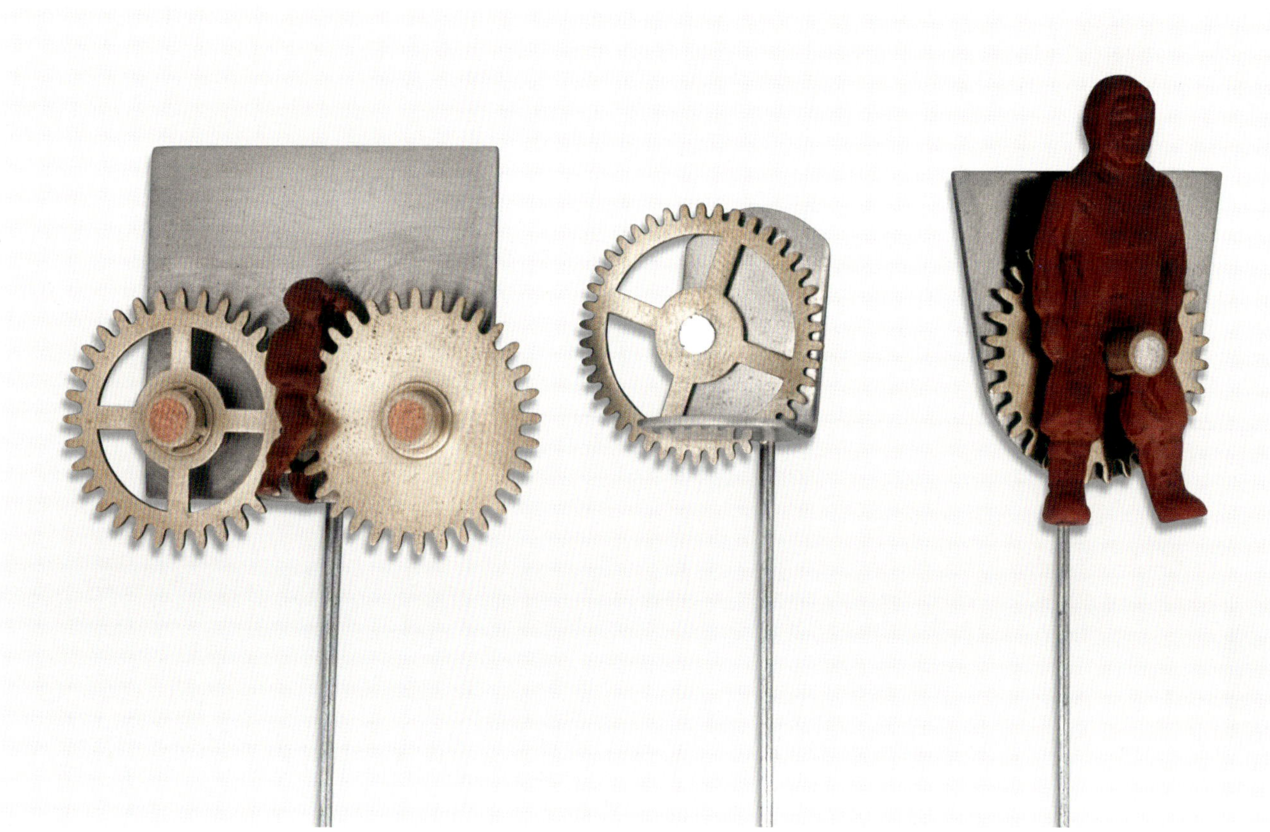

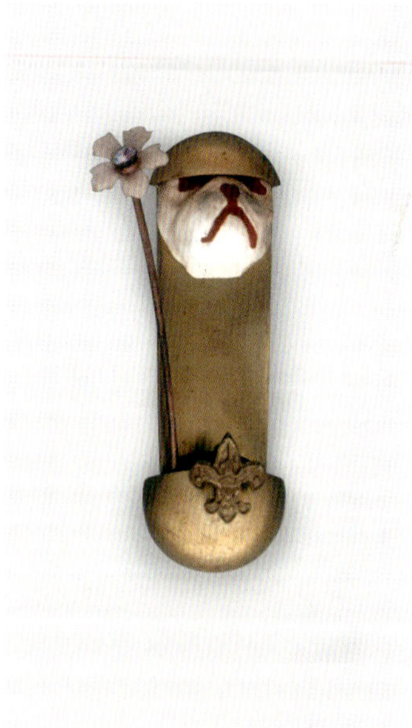

5.38 Top: Ron D. Grover, *Chocolate Soldiers*, lapel pins, 1982, silver, found objects, paint, 2.0 × 2.0 cm, courtesy of Bezalel Academy of Arts and Design

5.39 Bottom left: Ron D. Grover, lapel pin, 1982, silver, enamel, ivory, wood, paint, 2.0 × 1.5 cm, courtesy of Bezalel Academy of Arts and Design

5.40 Bottom right: Ron D. Grover, *Watch Dog*, lapel pin, 1982, brass, porcelain, enamel, paint, 2.0 × 0.5 cm, courtesy of Bezalel Academy of Arts and Design

shall see, medal-like jewellery was to become an anti-militaristic symbol aimed at undermining the values of a state at war. In the field of art jewellery, political protest became prevalent only in the 1980s, after the 1982 Lebanon War – possibly because that was the time when art jewellery became prominent in Israel. During that war, the Israel Defence Forces (IDF) invaded southern Lebanon and occupied it in order to expel the Palestine Liberation Organisation fighters who were attacking Israel from Lebanese bases. There was a heated debate in Israeli society regarding the necessity and righteousness of the war, which also found expression in the work of jewellery makers. Several Bezalel students and young graduates produced expressive jewellery that made an outright statement against militarism and the prevalent Israeli ethos of heroism. Since then, art jewellery in Israel has flourished as a medium by which

5.41 Top: Sean Avner Axelrod, *"What Are We Having for Breakfast Dear"*, jewellery installation, 1984, clay, print on paper, plastic doll, silver fork, knife, spoon, war decorations, 50.0 × 40.0 × 20.0 cm

5.42 Bottom: Sean Avner Axelrod, *Six National Heroes*, brooch, 1983, wood, felt, plastic, paint, glass, silk ribbon, 10.0 × 8.0 × 1.0 cm, collection of the National Gallery of Victoria, Melbourne, Australia

5.43 Sean Avner Axelrod, *2162564*, brooch, 1982, silver, print on paper, crystal, military dog tag, 6.0 × 9.0 × 1.0 cm

to express ideological and emotional responses to an ongoing state of military conflict.

Ron D. Grover, a 1982 Bezalel graduate born in Israel in 1956, made lapel pins that posed an ironic alternative to conventional badges of valour. Like most Israelis, Grover did mandatory military service and has experienced the terrible reality of military conflict from up close.[16] His works include chocolate soldiers, and medal-wearing figures whose limbs are made of painted wood shaped like matches (figs. 5.38 – 5.40).

Prominent among this group of jewellery artists was **Sean Avner Axelrod**,[17] who was born on Kibbutz Beit-Alpha, Israel, in 1954. He graduated from Bezalel in 1981 and continued his studies at the Pratt Institute, New York, where he received a Master of Fine Arts degree in 1986. Since 1988 he has lived in Melbourne, Australia, and pursued both sculpture and jewellery. Axelrod had no compunction in slaughtering sacred cows. For instance, in the exhibition "Contemporary Jewellery: The Americas, Australia, Europe and Japan", held in Kyoto National Museum of Modern Art in 1984, he showed a brooch called *Six National Heroes* (fig. 5.42), which depicted a cemetery with six graves (marked by arms holding guns) and a line of cypress trees typical of Israeli cemeteries, together with a hare – an anti-heroic symbol of cowardice – running between the graves. Axelrod's use of plastic toys in his pieces attests to Bianca Eshel Gershuni's influence (see above, Chapter 4). In the same exhibition Axelrod also showed an installation with war decorations in a blood-stained plate, surrounded by brooches shaped as expressive utensils: a knife wedged in a fissure, a fork stuck in an embryo and a spoon with a baby in it. A napkin bore the inscription "What are we having for breakfast dear" (fig. 5.41). He also made a pin with the symbol of the State of Israel – a Menorah (seven-branched candelabra) flanked by two olive branches – in which he replaced the Menorah with his own army dog tag (fig. 5.43).

We have already discussed **Esther Knobel**'s series "Warriors" (which she also called "Crusaders") (see above, Chapter 4). These decorative, cheerfully colourful brooches ostensibly depicted past warriors while in fact reacting to the Israeli reality of the time. Knobel herself referred to the "benevolent, cheerful exterior" of the series as "aesthetic camouflage" which served to "conceal its reprehensive tone" (Manor-Friedman 2008, p. XI). Knobel's *Camouflage Necklace* (1982) was made at the time of the first Lebanon War. Shaped like a wreath such as is placed on the graves of fallen soldiers and painted in camouflage colours, it clearly responds to the reality of war and the grief and bereavement which ensues.

Edda Vardimon Gudnason was born in Denmark in 1956 and immigrated to Israel in 1978. In Copenhagen she studied at the Danish Design School (1977–1978), and in Israel she first studied graphic design at Bezalel (1981–1984) and then took advanced studies in the gold- and silversmithing department there. Vardimon Gudnason tackled the pain brought on by topical events in Israel in her "Adhesive Band" series (1994),[18] such as the brooch *Plaster-X* (fig. 5.46). The series refers to a common response to children who have been hurt – putting a plaster on the wound to alleviate the pain – and to cartoon imagery. In 2011 she added Mickey Mouse figures onto these plaster-shaped brooches (fig. 5.44), reinforcing the absurdity of the notion that

16_ Ron Grover in a telephone interview with the author, July 2013.

17_ I am grateful to Esther Knobel for drawing my attention to Axelrod's work and helping me get in touch with him.

18_ The *Adhesive Band* brooches were first exhibited in the "Sign of Mine" exhibition at the Museum für Angewandte Kunst, Cologne, in 1994 and later in the Schmuck (Jewellery) show, Munich, in 1996.

5.44 Top: Edda Vardimon Gudnason, *Big Mickey*, brooch, 2011, silver, enamel, steel, 7.0 × 3.0 × 1.0 cm

5.45 Centre: Edda Vardimon Gudnason, *Yellow Strangers*, necklace, 2011, silver, enamel, cotton thread, 6.0 × 3.0 × 0.8 cm

5.46 Bottom: Edda Vardimon Gudnason, *Plaster-X,* brooch from the series "Adhesive Band", 1994, silver, 18-ct gold, 6.0 × 6.0 cm

5.47 Edda Vardimon Gudnason, *Flowers*, brooches, 2002, copper, enamel, diam. 5.0 cm

one may alleviate suffering as easily as with cartoon figures. Then she hung faceless heads in diverse colours from these adhesive bands (fig. 5.45), reflecting her empathy for the refugees of foreign nationalities who had become part of current Israeli reality. "Here the pain is on the inside," she points out. "The plasters do not cover the people but the other way around."[19]

The first intifada, which started in 1987 and lasted several years, was a violent but unarmed uprising of Palestinians in the occupied territories against Israeli occupation. The uprising involved widespread rock throwing against Israeli cars. Consequently, vehicles whose windscreens were covered with a protective steel mesh were a common sight at the time. **Vered Kaminski** (see above, Chapter 4) used that mesh (or one similar to it) to make bracelets – which she believed emitted a sense of security and strength when worn on one's wrist.[20]

Aggression was the subject of the exhibition "Arsenale: Aggression im Schmuck" (Arsenale: Aggression in Jewellery) in Frankfurt, curated by Wilhelm Mattar (Schepers 1991), in which several Israeli artists participated. **Vered Kaminski** showed jewellery made of rocks and metal wire mesh, and **Esther Knobel** showed a horseman brooch from the "Crusaders" series and a pomegranate belt made of nylon fabric and nickel silver, referencing a military belt. **Kobi Roth**, born in Israel in 1962, showed a series of insect-like brooches (or rather models for brooches) entitled *Bugs*, composed of knife blades, fishing hooks and watch parts inserted in aluminium foil (figs. 5.49 a – d). Roth, a 1991 Bezalel graduate, had been an IDF soldier and had known war personally. His series "I Try to Remember" (1997) is comprised of silver and gold foil figures of soldiers (fig. 5.48), some bearing arms, inspired by his collection of brass and lead soldier figurines. He grouped these soldier figurines, the likes of which he played with as a child, in diverse situations and compositions, thereby making a statement about the "game of war".[21]

In 2002 Vered Kaminski curated the exhibition "Chain Reaction: Israeli Jewellery 2" at the Eretz-Israel

19_ Edda Vardimon Gudnason in an e-mail exchange with the author, January 2012.

20_ Vered Kaminski in an interview with the author, Jerusalem, Israel, 2012.

21_ These works were later included in the exhibition "Good Kids, Bad Kids: 'Childliness' in Israeli Art", curated by Yigal Zalmona and Nirith Nelson at the Israel Museum, Jerusalem in 1998 (Zalmona and Nelson 1998).

5.48 Top right: Kobi Roth, *Toy Soldier*, from the series "I Try to Remember", 1997, silver foil, gold, 8.0 × 4.0 cm

5.49 a–d Centre and bottom: Kobi Roth, *Bugs*, sketches for brooches, 1991, aluminium foil, knife blades, fishing hooks, watch parts, included in the exhibition "Arsenal: Aggression in Jewellery", Frankfurt, 1991

5.50 Michal Bar-On Shaish, *Wire to Net*, brooch, 2011, silver, decal, enamel, 10.0 × 9.0 cm

Museum in Tel Aviv. The participants were called on to create pieces that would address "our lives here and now" (Kaminski and Tamir 2002, p. 5). In the foreword to the exhibition catalogue, Kaminski and art critic Tali Tamir (2002, pp. 6–8) point out, among the salient themes that emerged, "Military sources and weapons, self-protection, self-shielding, the threat of disintegration and annihilation, death and bereavement, the 'ostrich effect,' escapism." These subjects all reflect the upheaval in Israeli society brought about by the second intifada, which started in 2000. This Palestinian uprising was intensely violent, with many fatalities among military personnel and civilians, Jews and Arabs. For the first time, Palestinian methods of attack included extensive suicide bombings.

In this exhibition, **Edda Vardimon Gudnason** addressed the subject of fallen soldiers in her brass and enamel brooches, *Flowers* (2002). These flowers hovered like dark clouds over a puddle of blood (fig. 5.47). **Michal Bar-On Shaish**, a 1991 Bezalel graduate born in Israel in 1959, showed two *Black Wreath* brooches (figs. 5.51 a, b) made in 2001, which, like Knobel's *Camouflage Necklace*, refer to the wreaths placed on fallen soldier's graves. The *Black Wreath* brooches are designed in such a manner that the upper side is smooth and pretty, while the back side is prickly. The many pins protruding from its lower side render the brooch unwearable.[22] These brooches are made in silver, gold and enamel, a technique in which Bar-On Shaish has specialised. They mark perhaps the beginning of her experimentation with turning a weak wire into a strong net (Bar-On Shaish 2012, p. 147), which she did much later, in 2011 (fig. 5.50). Among the works first shown in the "Chain Reaction" exhibition were the *Merkava*

22_ Michal Bar-On Shaish in an e-mail exchange with the author, July 2013.

5.51 a, b Michal Bar-On Shaish, *Black Wreath*, brooches, 2001, silver, gold, enamel, diam. 9.0 cm (top), 8.0 cm (bottom)

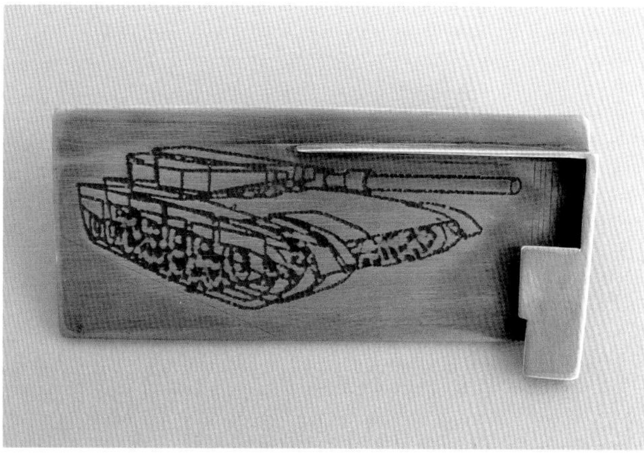

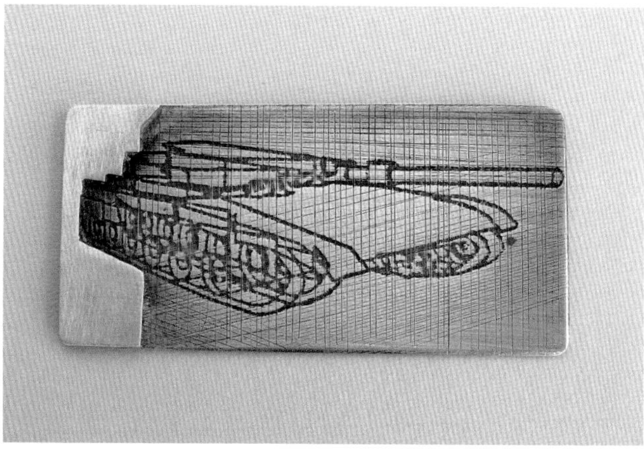

5.52 a, b Michal Oren, *Merkava*, brooches, 2002, silver, 3.1 × 6.5 × 0.3 cm (left), 2.7 × 5.7 × 0.2 cm (right)

silver brooches made by **Michal Oren**, born in Israel in 1972. Oren is a 1999 Bezalel graduate who went on to study art history at the Tel Aviv University, earning a master's degree in 2008. Her brooches were inspired by a press photograph of a Palestinian child throwing a rock at an Israeli Merkava tank in Gaza. This photograph became an iconic image of the uprising.[23] Oren used a computer program to depict the tank etched on silver, making the lines doubled and shaky, as though either the tank or the observer was trembling while looking at it (figs. 5.52 a, b). The image expresses the anxiety which is felt both by the men inside the tank looking out and by those who are faced by it.[24] Oren made the tank brooches in some variations, adding a magnifying glass, a viewing aperture or a target sign, hinting at the idea that we are all potential targets.

Oren's later works continue to tackle the notion of insecurity. In her 2009 series "Thinking about Places" she made an oxidised silver bracelet which she called *A Place to Hide* (fig. 5.54). It evolved from a series of charcoal drawings she made of bomb shelters and hiding places (Fishof 2010a, pp. 32–35). She then made a series of brooches with the words "Safe", "Home" (fig. 5.53) and "Sound". As she points out, "While thinking about 'home' or 'shelter', the private and the political intertwine" (Oren 2012, p. 123).

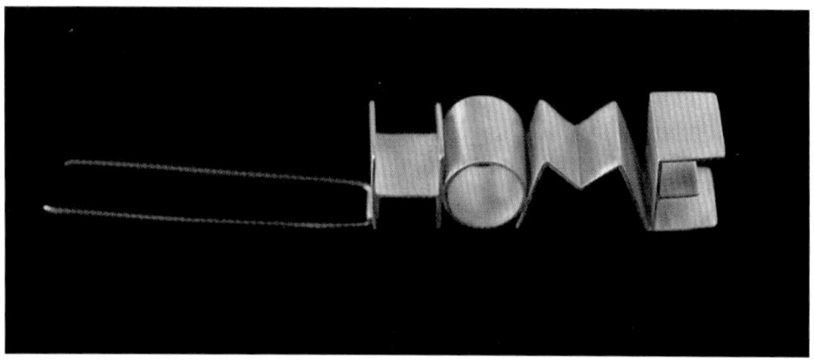

5.53 Michal Oren, *Home*, brooch, 2010, silver, stainless steel, 1.2 × 4.0 × 1.0 cm

23_ The photo was taken on 29 October 2000 by press photographer Laurent Rebours. The child, fourteen-year-old Faris Odeh, was shot to death a few days later.

24_ Michal Oren in an interview with the author, Tel Aviv, Israel, 2009.

5.54 Michal Oren, *A Place to Hide,* bracelet from the series "Thinking about Places", 2009, oxidised silver, diam. 6.0 cm

5.55 Einat Leader, *Fence 2*, ring from the series "Fences and Cameras", 2011, stainless-steel mesh, fine silver, steel screws, 4.2 × 6.0 cm

Anxiety and a search for safety in Israeli reality is also the subject of the series "Fences and Cameras" (2010–2011) by **Einat Leader**, born in Israel in 1966. A 1998 Bezalel graduate, Leader continued her studies in industrial design in the Faculty of Architecture and Town Planning at the Technion, Haifa, earning a master's degree. For the past eight years she has headed the department of jewellery and accessories (which later became the department of jewellery and fashion design) at Bezalel. Leader protests the excessive number of fences erected to curb people's movement through public space and the multitude of surveillance cameras that, under the guise of offering protection, invade our privacy. "The 'Fences' series deals with closure," Leader remarks. "The physical and legal barriers that are increasingly present in local political reality – obstructing the movement of too many groups of different people."[25]

In the current reality in Israel, Leader may have had in mind the fences that prevent the free passage of Palestinians, as well as the fences put up around African refugees. In her series "Fences and Cameras" (2011) she uses modest, simple materials such as aluminium mesh to build small, basket-like objects that can be carried on one's body. She also makes rings using stainless-steel mesh and silver (fig. 5.55). In "Fences and Minerals" (figs. 5.56 a, b), another series of the same year, she placed raw, unprocessed stones in the baskets. About this series Leader says, "The jewellery series 'Fences and Minerals' deals with the option of preserving minerals, which are used in the gem industry for inlaying, in their natural state as raw materials. Taking minerals from nature, even in small quantities, endangers the micro-ecological balance." These monochromatic works have an ascetic beauty.

25_ All quotations from Einat Leader are from an e-mail exchange with the author, July 2013.

5.56 a, b Einat Leader, *Fences and Minerals 6*, locket (in open and closed states) from the series "Fences and Minerals", 2011, aluminium mesh, aluminium thread, amber, 4.5 × 5.8 cm

5.57 Dana Hakim, neckpiece from the series "My Four Guardian Angels Blue Series", 2012, iron mesh, mirrored plastic, threads, reflective light threads, paint, lacquer, 29.0 × 24.0 × 7.0 cm

Dana Hakim, born in Israel in 1977, graduated from Bezalel in 2006 and continued her studies at the Konstfack University College of Arts, Crafts and Design in Stockholm, where she received a master's degree in 2010. In 2009, during her studies in Stockholm, she initiated (together with graphic designer Yosef Berkovich) an international online jewellery exhibition called "I Care a Lot: Middle East Portable Discussion".[26] Hakim resents the way governments use mass media to instil collective fear as a means of crowd control. In her amulet series "My Four Guardian Angels" (figs. 5.57–5.59) she comments on what she terms our "Fear Society", in which "we are constantly afraid of the 'other', of crime, terrorism, epidemics ..." (Hakim 2012, p. 67). The materials she uses are all related to protection measures. They include meshes, filters, ventilation covers, light reflectors and work gloves. She mainly recycles loudspeaker grilles to create her pieces. Her inspiration ranges from traditional talismanic elements, such as the *khamsa*, the blue colour and the eye symbol, to surveillance cameras and gas masks. In the process, most of the materials she uses lose their pro-

26_ See <http://www.icarealot.me/page1.html>.

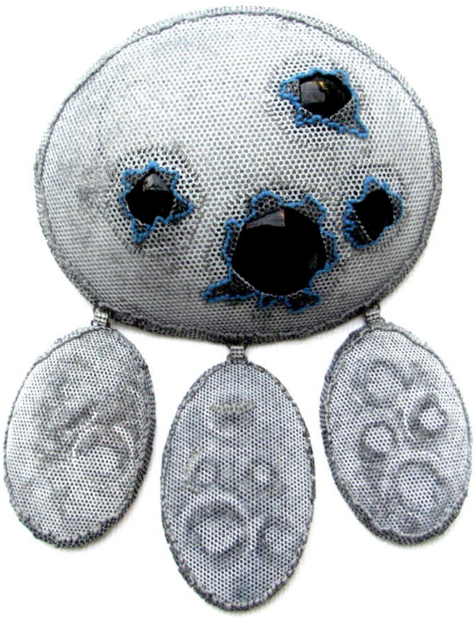

5.58 Top: Dana Hakim, neckpiece from the series "My Four Guardian Angels – Blue Series", 2012, iron mesh, threads, paint, lacquer, 33.0 × 22.0 × 5.0 cm

5.59 Bottom: Dana Hakim, brooch from the series "My Four Guardian Angels – Blue Series", 2012, iron mesh, black mirrored plastic, cotton thread, paint, lacquer, 25.0 × 18.0 × 2.0 cm

5.60 Gregory Larin, *Cork Ring*, 2012, 22-ct gold, black diamond, white diamonds, enamel, steel

tective properties, but these, she claims, are quite unnecessary to begin with (Hakim 2012, p. 67).

Gregory Larin was born in Tula, Russia, in 1977 and immigrated to Israel on his own in 1997, before he was twenty. He served in the army as an aircraft repairer, where he discovered his aptitude for building with different materials. In 2007 he graduated from the jewellery design department at the Shenkar College of Engineering and Design. Larin has developed unique techniques by which he creates his works (for instance, he invented a ring, *Cork Ring*, 2012, whose stone setting is achieved by the same principle as a lightning-type swing bottle closure) (fig. 5.60). Larin experienced the horrors of the second intifada up close, as he was living in the centre of Jerusalem where many suicide bombings took place. These events have left a deep impression on him. In 2009 he created the series "Fragmentation". It started off with an amputated porcelain doll entitled *Fragmentations: Venus Fragments* (Fishof 2010a, p. 27). He grafted what appeared to be malignant tumours made of a synthetic polymer mounted on a silver construction to each amputated limb. Each limb became an object in its own right, in addition to func-

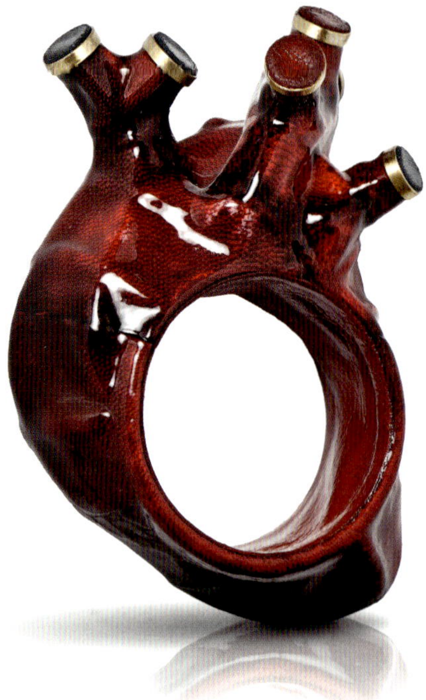

5.61 Left: Gregory Larin, *Anatomy Lessons,* 2012, bracelet, brass, synthetic hair, polymer, pigment, plastic teeth, zircon gems, 8.0 × 6.0 × 7.0 cm

5.62 Right: Gregory Larin, bracelet from the series "With All My", 2013, leather, polymer, brass, lacquer

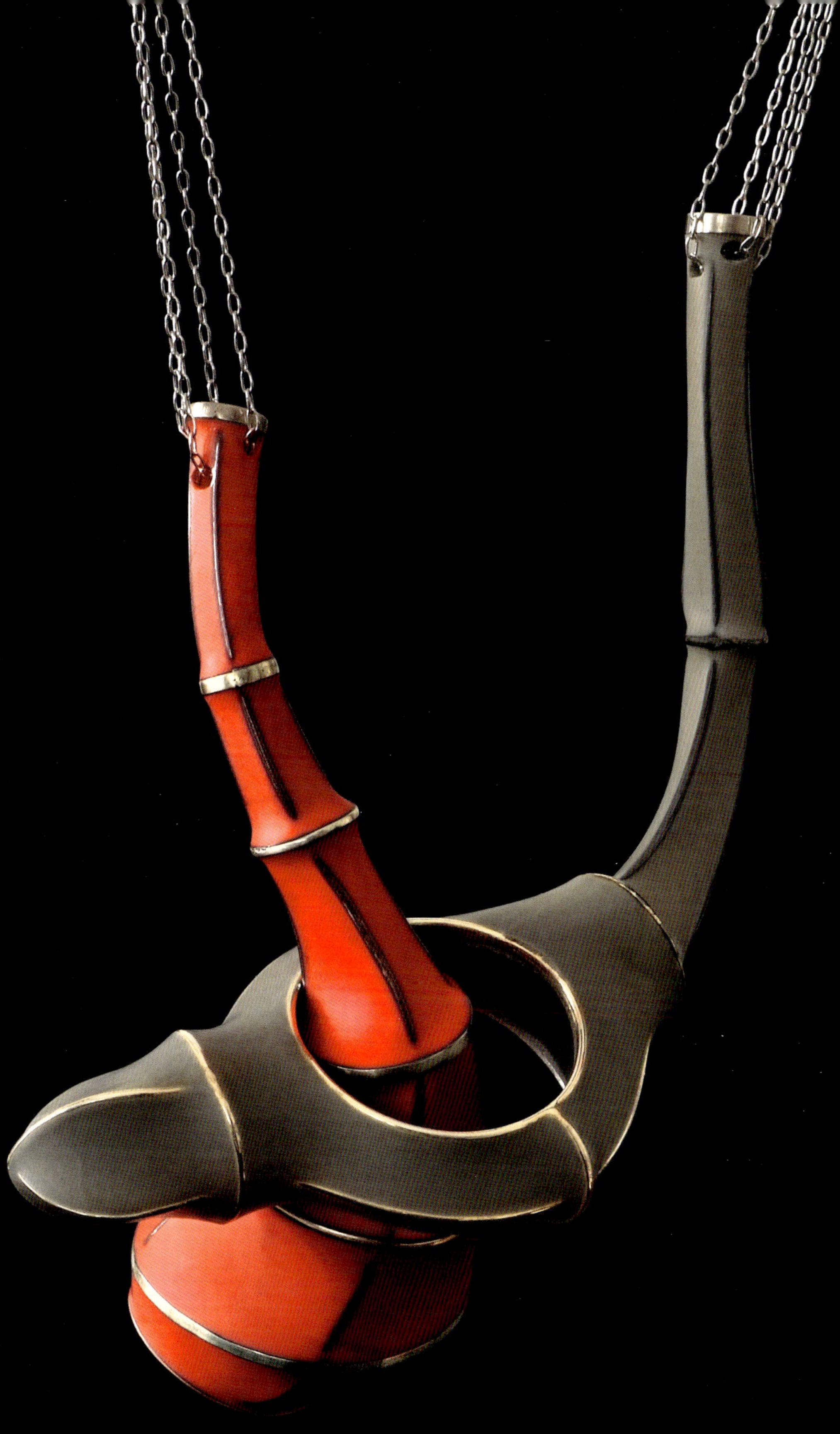

5.63 Gregory Larin, *Penetration,* neckpiece from the series "Fragmentation", 2009, silver 925, polymer, pigment, 11.0 × 5.0 cm

tioning as part of a doll. Drawing on his trauma, as well as on trash-metal music and album graphics, Larin's future works show the doll's distorted limbs gradually becoming more amorphous in form and turning into jewellery pieces, such as the neckpiece *Penetration* from the series "Fragmentations" (2009) (fig. 5.63). This was the case in rings and brooches as well.[27] Larin continued to develop this theme in series such as "Dismembered" (2011) and "Carcass" (2011), where he combined human or synthetic hair (Larin 2012, pp. 102–105), which he also used in *Anatomy Lessons* (fig. 5.61). In a recent series titled "With All My" (2013) – a bracelet and pendant shaped as an anatomically correct heart, with veins and arteries attached (fig. 5.62) – Larin explores various connotations of the heart. As he explains, it is a symbol of love, an engine that makes the human body run and a sacrificial organ as in Maya culture.[28]

Quite a few Israeli jewellery artists have used their creations to protest wrongdoings perpetrated by Israel against the Palestinian people.

Shirly Bar-Amotz's series "A Minor Bump on the Wing" (2006–2008) addresses what she perceives to be a value crisis. In 2002 Israeli Air Force High Commander and IDF Chief of Staff Dan Halutz was interviewed after an Air Force bombing in Gaza. The bombing had targeted the head of the military wing of the Palestinian Islamist movement Hamas, Salah Shehade, killing civilians, including children. When asked what a pilot feels when he drops a one-ton bomb on a residential neighbourhood, he replied, "A minor bump on the wing." This resulted in a public outcry in Israel against such actions, which Bar-Amotz joined through her jewellery. The pieces in this series, she explains, simulate remnants of a devastating process. The series includes three sub-groups. The "Airplane-Brooches" group (figs. 5.64 a, b) is made of silver or gold foil, die-cut with an image of an F-16 fighter jet, with some pieces embossed with gemstone settings that are filled with enamel and others set with zircon gems that bring to mind images of the bombs dropped by jets.

5.64 a, b Shirly Bar-Amotz, brooches from the series "A Minor Bump on the Wing", 2008, sterling silver, hot enamel, oxide, 5.0 × 9.0 × 0.02 cm (left), 5.0 × 8.0 × 0.02 cm (right)

27_ Gregory Larin in an interview with the author, Tel Aviv, Israel, 2010.
28_ Gregory Larin in an e-mail exchange with the author, May 2013.

Another group in the series, called "Gem Brooches" (fig. 5.65), is comprised of brooches cast in blackened silver on which gemstone settings are sketched and then filled with enamel. Blackened, torn and cut, these brooches bring to mind medals that have lost their original lustre, military decorations preserved in rock form like prehistoric fossils. The third group in this series, "Jet Debris Brooches" (fig. 5.66), is based on photographs of jet debris dispersed on the ground. Made in pure gold, charred remains turn into precious objects. "The images imprinted in these brooches bear witness to our current reality," Bar-Amotz (2008, n.p.) writes. "It is a reality that we see in the mirror every day. The jet planes and bombs in these pieces reflect man's ability to create advanced technology yet use it for patently immoral purposes, striking at mankind and upsetting the order of the universe."

5.65 Top: Shirly Bar-Amotz, brooches from the series "A Minor Bump on the Wing", 2008, sterling silver, hot enamel, oxide, dimensions variable

5.66 Bottom: Shirly Bar-Amotz, brooch from the series "A Minor Bump on the Wing", 2008, 24-ct gold, 2.0 × 6.0 × 0.03 cm

5.67 Einat Leader, *Green Inside*, neckpiece from the series "Order Has Not Been Restored", 2009, copper thread, diam. 28.0 cm

Einat Leader, too, bears witness to Israeli wrongdoing, whose roots predate the establishment of the State of Israel. Her 2009 series "Order Has Not Been Restored" (exhibited in a show curated by Sari Paran at Periscope Gallery, Tel Aviv, 2009) comprises six pure silver brooches whose form outlines in three-dimensional form the maps of six Arab villages in the Tel Aviv area before the 1948 war: Summayl, Sheikh Muwannis, Salama, Manshiyyah, Jamasin and Abu Kabir (figs. 5.68, 5.69). These villages were destroyed in favour of Jewish development in the area. The names of the villages still appear on some street signs, some were changed into Hebrew names, but all have disappeared from the current map of Tel Aviv. To make these brooches, Leader used the Nakba map prepared by the Zochrot (Remembering) organisation.[29] The brooches are attached to the wearer's clothes, in a way reminiscent of pins worn by school children on Memorial Day or Independence Day, by symbolically sticking a pin through the village land. In the same exhibition Leader showed necklaces made of thin metal threads which she made by undoing a metal fabric and crushing the threads between her fingers. The threads depict an abstracted outline of the same villages (fig. 5.67). These necklaces are a continuation of her series "Orientation Jewellery" (2008), exhibited in the group exhibition "Amnesia", curated

29_ According to the Zochrot website, "Nakba is an Arabic word that means 'catastrophe'. The Nakba was the destruction, expulsion, looting … of the Palestinian inhabitants of this country. It was keeping refugees out by force at the end of the war, in order to establish the Jewish state. … Zochrot (Remembering) seeks to raise public awareness of the Palestinian Nakba, especially among Jews in Israel, who bear a special responsibility to remember and amend the legacy of 1948." Available at <http://zochrot.org>, accessed 28 January 2013.

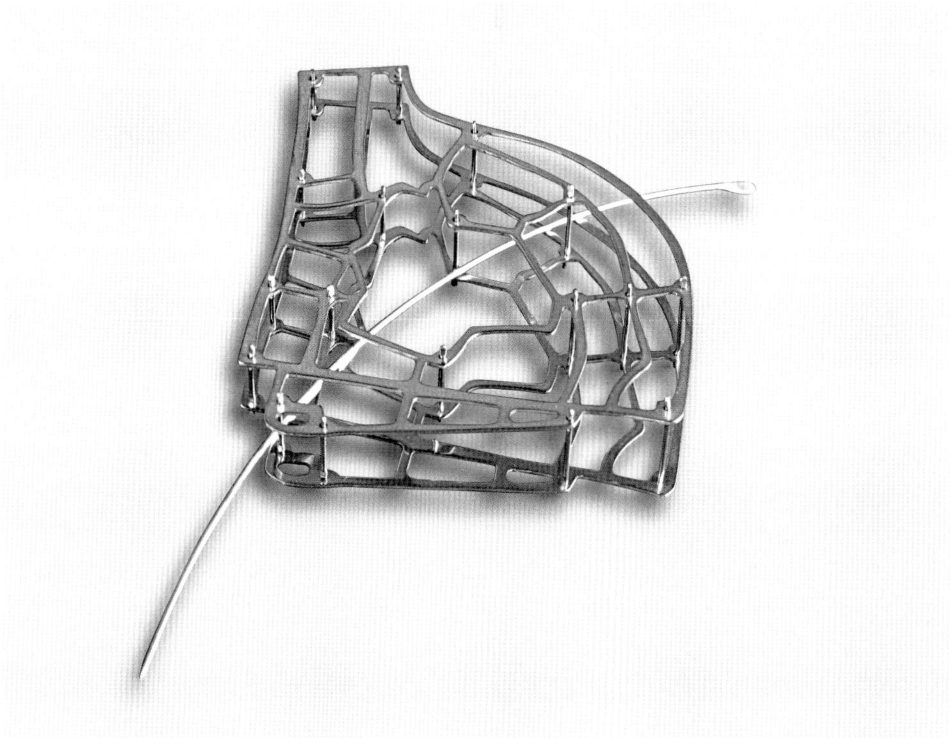

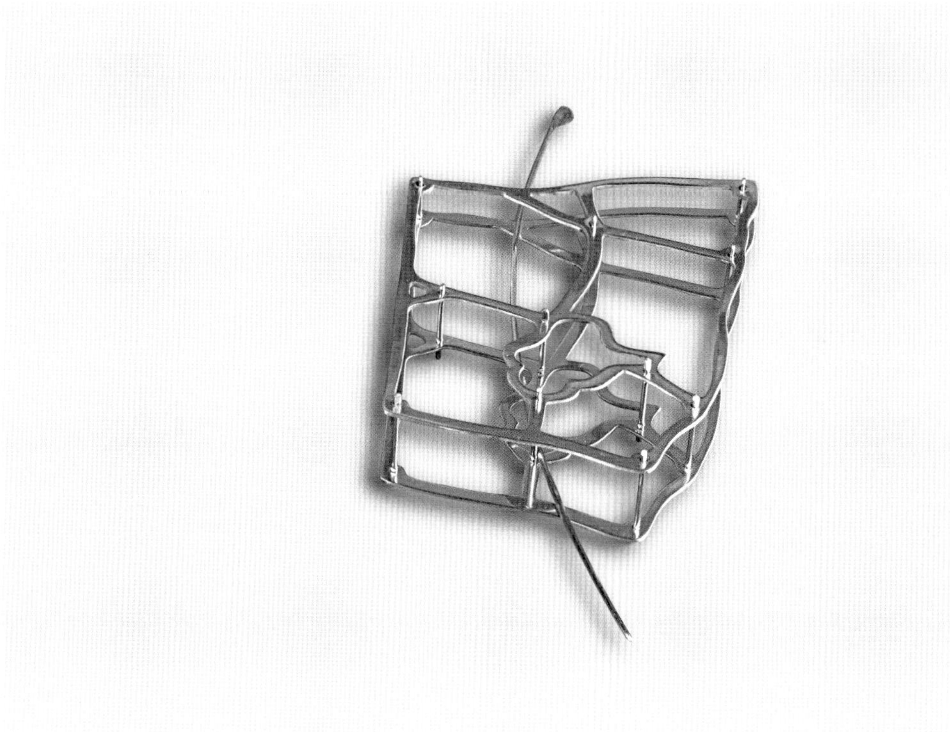

5.68 Top: Einat Leader, *Salama*, brooch from the series “Order Has Not Been Restored”, 2009, fine silver, 2.3 × 7.0 × 8.5 cm

5.69 Bottom: Einat Leader, *Abu Kabir*, brooch from the series “Order Has Not Been Restored”, 2009, fine silver, 2.0 × 5.3 × 6.9 cm

by Shlomit Bauman at Zochrot Gallery in Tel Aviv. In the exhibition at Periscope Gallery, mentioned above, Leader also exhibited spiral stainless-steel forms that function as a dividing wall of sorts on the wearer's body (Bar-Amotz 2009).

Deganit Stern Schocken's political series "Kalandia Checkpoint", protesting the way Palestinians are treated at military checkpoints, has already been addressed in detail in the previous chapter. So have her other politically motivated series, such as "Figure of Speech", which points out the basic humanity of the "neighbours' children" (see figs. 4.77 and 4.78 in Chapter 4 above).

Attai Chen, who often deals with cycles of growth and decay in nature (see this chapter above), has also created works that relate to the conflict in which his country is steeped. In 2008 he made a wooden pendant carved in arabesque forms – a typical Arab ornamental form – which, on taking a closer look, was revealed to be composed of multiple Kalashnikov rifles (fig. 5.70) (Chen 2012c, p. 36). To my mind, the work is a visual manifestation of the biblical prophecy "And they shall beat their swords into plowshares, and their spears into pruninghooks" (Isaiah 2:4). Often, however, Chen does not wish to make a firm stand but rather to "put issues on the table for discussion," as he puts it.[30] Since conscription to the Israeli army is mandatory, most Israelis serve. Chen, too, was among their numbers and like all soldiers had to wear a dog tag with his military identity number and blood type. In 2010 he put this military identity in question when he created a pendant made of a dog tag which he covered in blood and called *A Negative* (Chen 2012c, p. 38).

In 2013 Chen showed his work *Predictions of a Well-Wisher* (fig. 5.71) in the group exhibition "The Lunatic Swing" at Galerie Kunstarkaden in Munich. The work consisted of five hundred pins made of small dried anchovies, each with its own individual form, covered in gold leaf. He installed them in lines, like a school of fish swimming in perfect synchronisation – or like soldiers on parade. Eva Tolkovsky (2013, p. 19) describes this collective form of existence: "In this timeless, unified and gilded condition of being, one will gladly die, because the pleasure of such experience surpasses anything that the individual self can ever achieve in its effort to survive and feed. We are born to be addicts of the toxic nature of our life form, the secret and sacred principle of bonding."

Art jewellery in Israel today

As we have seen in this chapter, Israeli jewellery artists give expression to the entire range of issues with which Israeli society at large is concerned. They use their artistic production to convey their ideas and feelings on matters ranging from the memory of the Holocaust to the Israeli-Palestinian conflict, from their ethnic, cultural heritage to the cycle of nature and ecological preservation.

Having examined the themes that preoccupy contemporary jewellers from Israel, it is interesting to note the artistic language with which they tell their stories. For jewellery is a language of materials, techniques, forms, colours and styles. There is no uniformity of style in the corpus of works discussed in this chapter. However, there appear to be some common characteristics. As pointed out already at the beginning of this survey, the materials used are usually relatively inexpensive, ranging from silver to recycled paper. Gold is hardly used and stones are scarce. In addition to silver, some base metals are used, as well as synthetic materials and found objects. The subdued colour scheme reflects the Israeli landscape and perhaps also a severe underlying mood. Other pieces, however, make use of bright colours that resonate with Israeli street culture. Global trends such as the return to ornamentation are also evident in jewellery made in Israel. These include the use of the arabesque (inspired by the neighbouring culture) as well as ornamental motifs – ranging from flowers and weeds to tanks. Together, all these formal and thematic characteristics constitute a novel aesthetic in which an avoidance of lustre, combined with material restraint, often result in a striking poetic aura.

30_ Attai Chen in an e-mail exchange with the author, January 2012.

5.70 Attai Chen, *Kalashnikov*, pendant, 2008, wood, nylon, 9.0 × 9.0 × 0.5 cm

Following pages:
5.71 Attai Chen, *Predictions of a Well-Wisher*, pin brooches, 2013, approx. 500 dried anchovies, fine gold leaf, brass, stainless steel

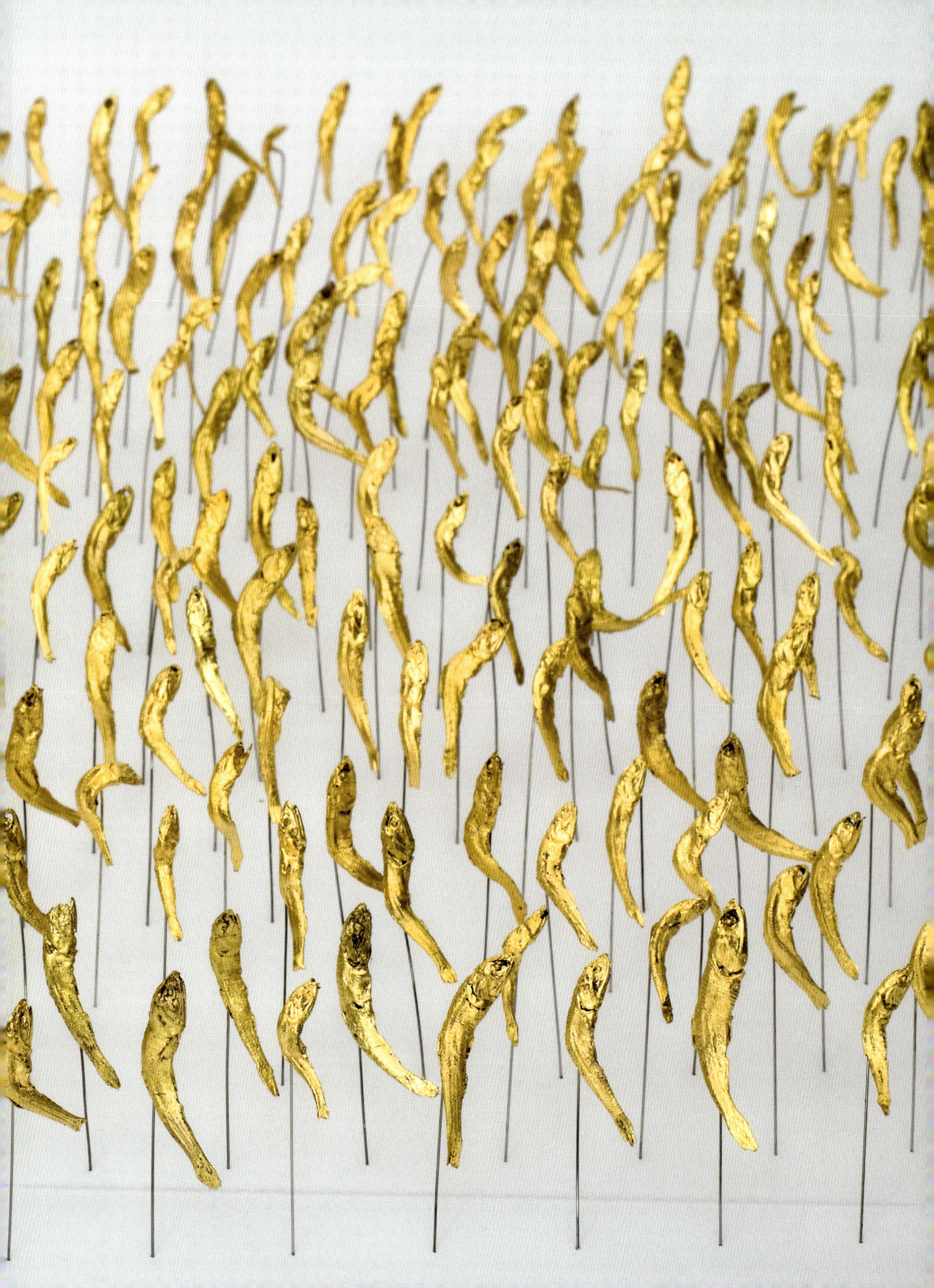

Reference List

Abdar, C., ed. (2008). *Ma'ase Rokem: Dress and Jewellery in the Tradition of the Jews of Yemen* (Hebrew). Tel Aviv: Amutat E'ele Betamar.

Aboucaya Grozovski, A. (2012). Artist Statement. In: Eickhoff, J., ed. (2012). *Transit: Contemporary Jewellery from Israel* (German and English). Exhibition catalogue. Translated into German by Constanze Kirmse. Munich: Galerie Spektrum, p. 51.

Ami, S. (2008). The Story of a Comb. *Ha'Yahalom* (Hebrew), 193, September, pp. 32–38, 159–161 (English).

Anon. (1954). Israele alla Triennale. *Domus* (Italian with English summary), 299, October, pp. 13–16.

Anon. (1963). A Meeting of Jewellers. *LaMerhav* (Hebrew), 22 December, p. 3.

Anon. (1964). Silver Jewellery – Made by Female Jewellers: An Exhibition of Eight Jewellers Opens at Bat-Sheva in Tel Aviv. *Haaretz* (Hebrew), 21 December, p. 14.

Anon. (1967). 42 Objet d'Art Artists Compete for Prizes. *Ma'ariv* (Hebrew), 24 December, p. 8.

Anon. (1967). Brooch and Earrings Set Is the Subject of Jewellery Competition. *Haaretz* (Hebrew), 31 December, p. 11.

Anon. (1968). Schmuck aus Israel auf der Frankfurter Frühjahrsmesse 68 (Jewellery from Israel at the 1968 Frankfurt Fair). *Kunst+Handwerk* (German), January, pp. 25–29.

Anon. (1971). An "Oscar" Prize for Israeli Jewellery Design. *Letzte Naies* (Yiddish), 8 October, p. 12.

Anon. (1971). "Oscar" for Israeli Jewelry Design. *Zionist Record & S.A. Jewish Chronicle*, 15 October, p. 7.

Anon. (1971). Prize-Winning Comb. *The Jerusalem Post*, 1 October, p. 17.

Anon. (1971). The Jewellery That Won the Great Prize. *Yedioth Ahronoth, 7 Days* supplement (Hebrew), 15 October, p. 29.

Anon. (1971). Untitled review. *Ma'ariv* (Hebrew), 6 October, p. 16.

Anon. (1999). *Yemini* (Hebrew). A publication in honour of Yaacov Yemini's 70th birthday. Jerusalem: Yemini family self-publication.

Ardon-Bronstein, M. (early 1940s). *Craft and Art* (radio play). Jerusalem City Archive, container 218, file 63.

Babai, V. (n.d.). *Vered Babai: Intermediate Hues*. Self-publication, p. 38.

Bar-Amotz, S. (2008). *A Minor Bump on the Wing* (Hebrew). Unpublished manuscript.

Bar-Amotz, S. (2009). "Order Has Not Been Restored." In: Paran, S., ed. (2009). *Einat Leader: "Order Has Not Been Restored"* (Hebrew, Arabic and English). Exhibition catalogue. Tel Aviv: Periscope Contemporary Design Gallery.

Bar-Amotz, S. (2012). Artist Statement. In: Eickhoff, J., ed. (2012). *Transit: Contemporary Jewellery from Israel* (German and English). Exhibition catalogue. Translated into German by Constanze Kirmse. Munich: Galerie Spektrum, p. 27.

Barkai, S. (2010). Marked for Life. In: Barkai, S., and Saggee, G., eds. (2010). *Sequences, Identities: Israeli Jewellery 5* (Hebrew and English). Translated into English by Daria Kassovsky. Tel Aviv: Eretz-Israel Museum.

Bar-On Shaish, M. (2012). Artist Statement. In: Eickhoff, J., ed. (2012). *Transit: Contemporary Jewellery from Israel* (German and English). Exhibition catalogue. Translated into German by Constanze Kirmse. Munich: Galerie Spektrum, p. 147.

Bat-Ya'ar, N. (1979). Blue-and-White Jewellery. *Yedioth Ahronoth, 7 Days* supplement (Hebrew), 27 April, pp. 32–33.

Behroozi, N. (2002). *The Hand of Fortune: Khamsas from the Gross Family Collection and the Eretz-Israel Museum Collection* (Hebrew and English). Exhibition catalogue. Tel Aviv: Eretz-Israel Museum.

Ben-Arieh, Y. (1979). The Jewish Population in Jerusalem and in Eretz Israel in the 19th Century. In: Fischer, Y., ed. (1979). *Art and Craft in Eretz Israel in the 19th Century* (Hebrew). Jerusalem: The Israel Museum, pp. 9–12.

Benjamin, C. (2003). Zeyde Schulmann (1890–1981): The Life and Travels of the Collector. *North African Lights; Hanukkah Lamps from the Zeyde Schulmann Collection in the Israel Museum, Jerusalem*. Exhibition catalogue. Translated into English by Gabriel Sivan and Dani Barkai. Jerusalem: The Israel Museum, pp. 12–25.

Benjamin, C. (2008). *Early Israeli Arts and Crafts: Bezalel Treasures from the Alan B. Slifka Collection in the Israel Museum*. Translated into English by Annie Lopez. Jerusalem: The Israel Museum.

Breitberg-Semel, S. (1995). Stepdaughter: Sarah Breitberg-Semel in Conversation with Bianca Eshel Gershuni. *Studio* (Hebrew), 66, November–December, pp. 15–20.

Brosh, N. (1987). *Islamic Jewelry*. Jerusalem: The Israel Museum.

Chen, A. (2012a). Forgotten Things. *Attai Chen Contemporary Jewellery* (website). Available at <http://www.attaichen.com/jewellery/index.php?/work/forgotten-things/> [Accessed 22 June 2013].

Chen, A. (2012b). Compounding Fractions. In: Betz, D., and Chen, A. (2012). *Doris Betz, Attai Chen* (German and English). Exhibition catalogue. Munich: Galerie Spektrum, n.p.

Chen, A. (2012c). Artist Statement. In: Eickhoff, J., ed. (2012). *Transit: Contemporary Jewellery from Israel* (German and English). Exhibition catalogue. Translated into German by Constanze Kirmse. Munich: Galerie Spektrum, p. 35.

Chinski, S. (2002). Eyes Wide Shut: The Acquired Albino Syndrome of the Israeli Art Field. *Theory and Criticism* (Hebrew), 20, Spring, pp. 57–86.

Cohn, S. (2012). *Unexpected Pleasures: The Art and Design of Contemporary Jewellery*. New York: Rizzoli International Publications.

D., L. (1976). Künstler-Porträt … Hanna Bachar-Paneth [*sic*] (Portrait of an Artist … Hanna Bachar-Paneth [*sic*]). *Schweizerische Uhrmacher und Goldschmiede Zeitung* (Swiss Watchmaker and Goldsmith Magazine) (German and French), 6, June, pp. 70–71.

Dallal, D. (2004). Collectio Judaica: The Exhibition. In: Dallal, D., and Soloviev-Friedman, D. (2004). *Collectio Judaica: Zoya Cherkassky* (Hebrew and English). Translated into English by Daria Kassovsky. Tel Aviv: Rosenfeld Gallery, pp. 114–119.

David, M. (2008). Show Me Thy Face: The Dress, Jewellery and Body Care of Jewish Women in Beihan. In: Abdar, C., ed. (2008). *Ma'ase Rokem: Dress and Jewellery in the Tradition of the Jews of Yemen* (Hebrew). Tel Aviv: Amutat E'ele Betamar, pp. 247–269.

Dayan, R., and Dudman, H. (1973). *And Perhaps ... The Story of Ruth Dayan.* New York: Harcourt Brace Jovanovich.

Dayan, R., and Feinberg, W. (1974). *Crafts of Israel.* New York: Macmillan Publishing Co.; London: Collier Macmillan Publishers.

Den Besten, L. (2011). The Mind in the Hand. *On Jewellery: A Compendium on International Contemporary Art Jewellery.* Stuttgart: Arnoldsche Art Publishers, pp. 102–103.

Den Besten, L. (1994). Esther Knobel: Sketches in Raw Material. In: Knobel, E. (1994). *Esther Knobel.* Exhibition catalogue. Amsterdam: Ra Gallery and the Françoise van den Bosch Foundation, n.p.

Derrez, P. (1994). Foreword. In: Knobel, E. (1994). *Esther Knobel.* Exhibition catalogue. Amsterdam: Ra Gallery and the Françoise van den Bosch Foundation, n.p.

Derrez, P. (2012). Introductory essay to Vered Kaminski's exhibition "Cycles of Mishap" at Ra Gallery, Amsterdam. Available at <http://www.galerie-ra.nl/vered-kaminski?lang=en&vsig50_0=0> [Accessed 30 March 2013].

Donner, B. (2003). A Conversation with Ruth Dayan. In: Donner, B., ed. (2003). *Maskit: A Local Fabric* (Hebrew and English). Translated into English by Daria Kassovsky and Mike Rogoff. Tel Aviv: Eretz-Israel Museum, pp. 4–10.

Dormer, P., and Turner, R. (1985). *The New Jewelry: Trends & Traditions.* London: Thames and Hudson.

Drutt English, H. W., and Steiner, W. (1998). *Brooching It Diplomatically: A Tribute to Madeleine K. Albright.* Exhibition catalogue. Philadelphia, Pennsylvania: Helen Drutt Gallery.

Falk, F. (1978). *Bezalel Academy Jerusalem: Jewellery and Silversmithing Department.* Exhibition catalogue. Pforzheim: Schmuckmuseum; Hanau: Deutsches Goldschmiedehaus; Antwerp: Provinciaal Diamantmuseum; London: Electrum Gallery.

Fisch, A. (1975). *Textile Techniques in Metal for Jewelers, Textile Artists & Sculptors.* New York: Van Nostrand Reinhold.

Fischer, Y. (1963). *Today's Form: Young Israeli Artists* (Hebrew). Exhibition catalogue. Jerusalem: Bezalel National Museum.

Fischer, Y. (1966). Bianca Eshel: Jewellery and Statuettes. *Kav* (Hebrew), 6, October, pp. 28–37.

Fischer, Y. (1973). Raffi Lavie: Paintings, 1962–1972. *Hamidrasha* (Hebrew), 2 (*Regarding Raffi* issue), May 1992.

Fischer, Y. (1977). *Bianka* [*sic*] *Eshel Gershuni: Jewelry* (Hebrew and English). Translated into English by Susan Eisenstat. Exhibition catalogue. Jerusalem: The Israel Museum.

Fischer, Y., ed. (1979). *Art and Craft in Eretz Israel in the 19th Century* (Hebrew). Jerusalem: The Israel Museum.

Fischer, Y., and Manor-Friedman, T. (2008). Conversations. *The Birth of Now: Art in Israel in the 1960s* (Hebrew and English). Translated into English by Anat Schultz. Ashdod: Ashdod Art Museum, pp. 7–14.

Fishof, I. (2010a). *Inyanim Group: No Problem(?).* Montclair, New Jersey: Gallery Loupe for Contemporary Art Jewelry.

Fishof, I. (2010b). Deganit Stern Schocken. *Inyanim Group: No Problem(?).* Montclair, New Jersey: Gallery Loupe for Contemporary Art Jewelry, pp. 40–43.

Fishof, I. (2010c). Facing Israel's Jewellery Today. *Inyanim Group: No Problem(?).* Montclair, New Jersey: Gallery Loupe for Contemporary Art Jewelry, pp. 6–10.

Fishof, I. (2012a). In Search of a Lost Identity. *Shirly Bar-Amotz: Happy Days* (Hebrew and English). Translated into English by Einat Adi. Tel Aviv: Tel Aviv Museum of Art, pp. 94–112.

Fishof, I. (2012b). Is There Contemporary Israeli Jewellery? In: Eickhoff, J., ed. (2012). *Transit: Contemporary Jewellery from Israel* (German and English). Exhibition catalogue. Translated into German by Constanze Kirmse. Munich: Galerie Spektrum, pp. 6–15.

Fishof, I., and Bar'am-Ben Yossef, N. (1996). *Souvenirs aus dem heiligen Land für Pilgrim im 19. und 20. Jahrhundert* (Souvenirs from the Holy Land for Pilgrims in the 19th and 20th Centuries) (German and French). Translated into French by Muriel Namrovski and Michelle Mazel. Translated into German by Vered Gumpel and Hanna Porat. Jerusalem: The Israel Museum.

Fishof, I., and Zalmona, Y. (1992). *In a Single Statement: Works by Zelig Segal.* Jerusalem: The Israel Museum.

Gaon, I. (1988). Design: 1988 Model. *Omanuyot* (The Arts) (Hebrew), 1, July, pp. 4–7.

Gaon, I. (1991). *Special Exhibit: Palevsky Design Pavilion, the Israel Museum.* Jerusalem: The Israel Museum. Reprinted in: Kaminski, V. (2004). *Vered Kaminski.* Raanana: The Studio, College of Art Studies, Artist-book series.

Geldman, M. (2007). *In The Silver Mirror: Bianca Eshel Gershuni* (Hebrew with English introduction). Tel Aviv: HaKibbutz HaMeuchad Publishing.

Gerstein, D. (1989). Jewellery as an Event. *Omanuyot* (The Arts) (Hebrew). Translated into English by Lea Aharonov. English version available at <http://www.deganitschocken.com/texts/jewelry-event> [Accessed 28 January 2013].

Guilat, Y. (2009). *Yemeni Jewish Silver Craft in the Israeli "Melting Pot": Yemeni Jewish Crafts within the Emerging National Visual Culture in Israel, 1882–1967* (Hebrew). Beersheba: The Ben-Gurion Research Institute, Ben-Gurion University of the Negev.

Gumbel, D. H. (1941). Form Is Attained by Four Means: Feel, Purpose, Material Perception and Execution. In: Ardon-Bronstein, M., ed. (1941). *The New Bezalel: Publications on Matters Pertaining to Artistic Design* (Hebrew). Jerusalem: The New Bezalel School of Arts and Crafts, p. 12.

Hakim, D. (2012). Artist Statement. In: Eickhoff, J., ed. (2012). *Transit: Contemporary Jewellery from Israel* (German and English). Exhibition catalogue. Translated into German by Constanze Kirmse. Munich: Galerie Spektrum, p. 67.

Halpert, M. (1970). Women Jewellers in Old Jaffa Show. *The Jerusalem Post Magazine*, 17 April, p. 20.

Hill, R. (1992). A Knobel Manufacture. *Crafts*, 119, November–December. Reprinted in: Gaon, I., ed. (1995). *Esther Knobel: Jewellery*. Jerusalem: The Israel Museum, n.p.

Kaminski, V., and Tamir, T. (2002). Chain Reaction: Reflections on the Israeli Jewel 2002. In: Kaminski, V., ed. (2002). *Chain Reaction: Israeli Jewellery 2* (Hebrew and English). Exhibition catalogue. Translated into English by Yael Shapira. Tel Aviv: Eretz-Israel Museum, pp. 5–8.

Karpel, D. (2004). Zoya Cherkassky's Festival of Sacrifice. *Haaretz Online* (Hebrew). 5 April. Available at <http://www.haaretz.co.il/misc/1.957902> [Accessed 18 June 2013].

Kenaan-Kedar, N. (2008). *The Art of Goldsmithing: Jacobi Jewelry in the Early Years of Israel's Statehood* (Hebrew and English). Translated into English by Gail Aricha. Tel Aviv: Eretz-Israel Museum; Jerusalem: Yad Ben-Zvi.

Knobel, E., and Eshel Gershuni, B. (1998). *Studs of Silver: Israeli Jewelry* (Hebrew and English). Exhibition catalogue. Translated into English by Joseph Shadur. Tel Aviv: Eretz-Israel Museum, p. 12e, no. 32, fig. 31.

Kolb, E. (1955). Introduction. *Village Craft Exhibition: Maskit, Israel Village Craft Ltd.* Exhibition catalogue. Tel Aviv: Tel Aviv Museum, n.p.

Larin, G. (2012). Artist Statement. In: Eickhoff, J., ed. (2012). *Transit: Contemporary Jewellery from Israel* (German and English). Exhibition catalogue. Translated into German by Constanze Kirmse. Munich: Galerie Spektrum, p. 99.

Leader, E. (2010). Hi-Craft: Academic Metalwork – From Handicraft to Valued Craft. *History and Theory: The Protocols* (e-journal), 16, April. Available at <http://bezalel.secured.co.il/zope/home/en/1270136285/1270160371> [Accessed 28 January 2013].

Levi Hyndman, T. (2012). Artist Statement. In: Eickhoff, J., ed. (2012). *Transit: Contemporary Jewellery from Israel* (German and English). Exhibition catalogue. Translated into German by Constanze Kirmse. Munich: Galerie Spektrum, p. 83.

Levine, S. (1971). First Ever Israeli Award for Jewellery. *The Jewish Chronicle, London*, 22 October, p. 24.

Lukić, B., and Katz, B. M. (2011). *Nonobject*. Cambridge, Massachusetts: MIT Press.

Manor-Friedman, T. (2008). Esther Knobel in Conversation with Tamar Manor-Friedman. In: Knobel, E. (2008). *Esther Knobel: The Mind in the Hand* (English and Hebrew). Translated into English by Dani Barkai. Jerusalem: Carmel Publishing House, pp. I–XXVI.

Miron, U. (2003). Deganit Stern Schocken: How Many Is One. *Studio* (Hebrew), 148, November, pp. 72–73. English translation available at <http://www.deganitschocken.com/texts/how-many-one-3> [Accessed 28 January 2013].

Miron, U. (2013). Findings. *Deganit Stern Schocken*, an artist book published in conjunction with the exhibition "In the Air" at Gallery Loupe for Contemporary Art Jewelry, Montclair, New Jersey. Self-publication.

Muchawsky-Schnapper, E. (1999). *The Yemenites: Two Thousand Years of Jewish Culture*. Jerusalem: The Israel Museum.

Nelson, N., ed. (2012). *I Am an Other: Israeli Jewellery 6* (Hebrew and English). Exhibition catalogue. Translated into English by Eppie Bat-Ilan. Tel Aviv: Eretz-Israel Museum.

Nevo, R. (1964). Eight Jewellers Exhibiting at Bat-Sheva. *Davar* (Hebrew), 22 December, p. 6.

No Author (1984). *Contemporary Jewellery: The Americas, Australia, Europe and Japan* (Japanese with foreword in English). Exhibition catalogue. Kyoto: Kyoto National Museum of Modern Art.

Noy, I. (2012). Artist Statement. In: Eickhoff, J., ed. (2012). *Transit: Contemporary Jewellery from Israel* (German and English). Exhibition catalogue. Translated into German by Constanze Kirmse. Munich: Galerie Spektrum, p. 115.

Ofir, A., and Bury, C. (1978). *Bezalel Akademie: Ergebnisse eines Experiments* (Bezalel Academy: Results of an Experiment). *Goldschmiede Zeitung* (Goldsmith Magazine) (German), December, pp. 31–38.

Ofrat, G. (1978). Longing for the Good Forest: On Bianca Eshel Gershuni's Jewellery. *Tsi'ur VePisul* (Painting and Sculpture) (Hebrew), 17, pp. 28–30.

Ofrat, G. (1984). Bezalel and Bauhaus. *Ariel*, 57, pp. 80–102.

Ofrat, G. (1987). *The New Bezalel 1935–1955* (Hebrew with English synopsis). Jerusalem: Bezalel Academy of Arts and Design.

Ofrat, G. (1989). *Yemini* (Hebrew). Jerusalem: Yemini Silversmiths.

Ofrat, G. (2006). The Ideological Background of the New Bezalel. In: Tartakover, D., and Ofrat, G. (2006). *Bezalel 100* (Hebrew). Jerusalem: Bezalel Academy of Arts and Design, vol. 2, pp. 71–123.

Ofrat, G. (2006a). *Zahara Schatz 1916–1999* (Hebrew with English summary). Exhibition catalogue. Jerusalem: The Artists' House.

Oren, M. (2012). Artist Statement. In: Eickhoff, J., ed. (2012). *Transit: Contemporary Jewellery from Israel* (German and English). Exhibition catalogue. Translated into German by Constanze Kirmse. Munich: Galerie Spektrum, p. 123.

Pariser, R. (1993). *Rachel Pariser: Works 1962–1993* (Hebrew and English). Jerusalem: Self-publication.

Polak-Sahm, V. (2009). *The House of Secrets: The Hidden World of the Mikveh* (Hebrew). Translated into English by Anne Harstein Pace. Boston: Beacon Press.

Pundik, H. (1964). *Sølvsmedene fra Jemen* (Silversmiths of Yemen). *Dansk Kunsthåndværk* (Danish Crafts) (Danish), 1 (37), pp. 7–15.

Pundik, H. (1966). The Jewish Silversmiths from Yemen. *Ariel: A Quarterly Review of the Arts and Sciences in Israel*, 15, pp. 21–26.

Raz, A. (1996). *Changing of Styles* (Hebrew). Tel Aviv: Yedioth Ahronoth.

Ron, Z. (1990). Brooches: Bianca Eshel Gershuni. *Omanuyot* (The Arts) (Hebrew), 7, May, pp. 12–13.

Ronnen, M. (1964). Bezalel Students' Skills. *The Jerusalem Post*, 27 March, p. VI.

Schepers, W., and Scholten, L. (1991). *Arsenale: Aggression im Schmuck* (Arsenale: Aggression in Jewellery) (German). Cologne: Forum für Schmuck und Design.

Schollmayer, K. (1974). *Neuer Schmuck: Ornamentum Humanum* (New Jewellery: *Ornamentum Humanum*) (German). Tübingen: Verlag Wasmuth.

Schon, M. (2001). The Wearable Art Movement, Part I: Modern Jewelry under Fifty Dollars. Available at <http://www.modernsilver.com/Walkerarticle.htm> [Accessed 28 January 2013].

Schwarz, A. (2001). Between Figuration & Abstraction. *Love at First Sight: The Vera, Silvia, and Arturo Schwarz Collection of Israeli Art.* Exhibition catalogue. Jerusalem: The Israel Museum.

Shachar, I. (Hebrew edn. 1971; English edn. 1981). *Jewish Tradition in Art: The Feuchtwanger Collection of Judaica.* Translated into English by R. Grafman. Jerusalem: The Israel Museum.

Sorger, M. (1977). *Gold, Silber, Hanf und Edelstein, komponiert von Hana Bechar-Paneth* [*sic*] (Gold, Silver, Hemp, Gems, Composed by Hana Bechar-Paneth [*sic*]). *Die Vitrine* (The Showcase) (German), 44, May, pp. 24–25.

Stern Schocken, D. (2000). *Body and Sign: Urban Jewellery.* Unpublished manuscript.

Stern Schocken, D. (2010). Inyanim Group Presents: No Problem(?). In: Fishof, I. (2010). *Inyanim Group: No Problem(?).* Montclair, New Jersey: Gallery Loupe for Contemporary Art Jewelry, pp. 4–5.

Strauss, C. (2007). *Ornament as Art: Avant-Garde Jewelry from the Helen Williams Drutt Collection, The Museum of Fine Arts, Houston.* Stuttgart: Arnoldsche Art Publishers; Houston: Museum of Fine Arts.

Sukman, R. (1995). An Architecture of Little Things. In: Sukman, R., ed. (1995). *Deganit Stern Schocken.* Exhibition catalogue. Translated into English by Richard Flantz. Tel Aviv: Office in Tel Aviv.

Tamir, T. (2007). Branchings. Leaflet accompanying Vered Kaminski's exhibition "Branchings". Jerusalem: Ziggurat Gallery of Contemporary Jewelry.

Tamir, T. (2010). Branchings: Works by Vered Kaminski. *History and Theory: The Protocols* (e-journal), 16, April 2010. Available at <http://bezalel.secured.co.il/zope/home/1270136285/1270961759_en?curr_issue=1270136285> [Accessed 28 January 2013].

Taragin, D. S. (2012). Vered Kaminski: Enigma, *Metalsmith*, 32 (1), p. 55.

Taragin, D. S., Ward, A., and Drutt English, H. W. (2006). *Women's Tales: Four Leading Israeli Jewelers.* Jerusalem: The Israel Museum; Racine: Racine Art Museum; New York and Manchester: Hudson Hills Press.

Tartakover, D., ed. (1996). *Finy Leitersdorf: Israeli Fashion Designer.* 2nd edn. Exhibition catalogue. Tel Aviv: Tel Aviv Museum of Art.

The Israel Export Institute (n.d.). *Israel's Jewelry.* Tel Aviv: Israel Export Institute.

The Israel Export Institute (n.d.). *The Israel Arts and Crafts Center.* Tel Aviv: The Israel Export Institute.

Tolkovsky, E. (2013). Untitled text. In: Maurer Zilioli, E., Künzli, O., and Tolkovsky, E. (2013). *The Lunatic Swing – Attai Chen: Compounding Fractions* (German and English). Translated into English by Jeremy Gaines. Exhibition catalogue. Munich: Kunstarkaden.

Untracht, O. (1982). *Jewelry: Concepts and Technology.* New York: Doubleday & Company.

Vardimon Gudnason, E. (2012). Artist Statement. In: Eickhoff, J., ed. (2012). *Transit: Contemporary Jewellery from Israel* (German and English). Exhibition catalogue. Translated into German by Constanze Kirmse. Munich: Galerie Spektrum, p. 59.

Vardimon, Y., ed. (2007). *Heaven and Earth: Israeli Jewellery 4* (Hebrew and English). Exhibition catalogue. Translated into English by Yael Shapira. Tel Aviv: Eretz-Israel Museum.

Wang, B. (2010). Unpublished manuscript.

Ward, A. (2006). Vered Kaminski. In: Taragin, D. S., Ward, A., and Drutt English, H. W. (2006). *Women's Tales: Four Leading Israeli Jewelers.* Jerusalem: The Israel Museum; Racine: Racine Art Museum; New York and Manchester: Hudson Hills Press, pp. 54–77.

Weinstock, T. (1963). Amos from Denmark Teaches the Yemenis. *Ma'ariv* (Hebrew), 21 July, p. 13.

Weiser-Ferguson, S. (2012). *Forging Ahead: Wolpert and Gumbel, Israeli Silversmiths for the Modern Age.* Jerusalem: The Israel Museum.

Wolf, E. (2012). Artist Statement. In: Eickhoff, J., ed. (2012). *Transit: Contemporary Jewellery from Israel* (German and English). Exhibition catalogue. Translated into German by Constanze Kirmse. Munich: Galerie Spektrum, p. 163.

Wolpert, L. Y. (1941). Letters in Ceremonial Objects. In: Ardon-Bronstein, M., ed. (1941). *The New Bezalel: Publications on Matters Pertaining to Artistic Design* (Hebrew). Jerusalem: The New Bezalel School of Arts and Crafts, p. 10.

Yagid-Haimovici, M. (2003). *How Many Is One: Deganit Stern Schocken* (Hebrew and English). Exhibition catalogue. Translated into English by Einat Adi. Tel Aviv: Tel Aviv Museum of Art.

Yagid-Haimovici, M. (2008). A Fragmented Continuum. In: Yagid-Haimovici, M., ed. (2008). *Esther Knobel: Long Distance Runner* (Hebrew and English). Translated into English by Beatrice Smedley. Tel Aviv: Tel Aviv Museum of Art.

Zalmona, Y. (2010). *100 Years of Israeli Art* (Hebrew). Jerusalem: The Israel Museum.

Zalmona, Y., and Nelson, N. (1998). *Good Kids, Bad Kids: "Childliness" in Israeli Art* (Hebrew). Jerusalem: The Israel Museum.

Zalmona, Y., and Shilo-Cohen, N. (1983). The Style and Iconography of Bezalel Objects. In: Shilo-Cohen, N., ed. (1983). *Bezalel 1906–1929.* English edition. Jerusalem: The Israel Museum, pp. 213–245.

Index